TALKING THE TALK

For Fran + Jonathan
with love.
April 2011

Talking the Talk

The Fall of King David for Today

A dramatic exposition of
2 Samuel 5.11 to 1 Kings 2.11

Pete Wilcox

The Lutterworth Press

The Lutterworth Press
P.O. Box 60
Cambridge
CB1 2NT
United Kingdom

www.lutterworth.com
publishing@lutterworth.com

ISBN: 978 0 7188 9234 0

British Library Cataloguing in Publication Data
A record is available from the British Library

Contents

The Spirit of the Lord speaks through me,
His word is upon my tongue.

2 Samuel 23.2

Introduction

Take the traditional taboos of dinner party conversation (sex, religion and politics) out of the David story and not much remains – except bloodshed, on the battlefield and off it. The story of David is a story about power: about the use and abuse of power in his relations with women (sex), with God (religion) and with officials, vassals or rivals (politics).

The story of David is lengthy. He is a prominent character in the Bible: his name occurs over 800 times in the Old Testament and over 50 times in the New. He is introduced for the first time in 1 Samuel 16 and dominates not just the following 15 chapters of that book, but the whole of 2 Samuel (another 24 chapters), and even the first 2 chapters of the first book of Kings. The story thus spans 42 chapters of Scripture in all.

Apart from Jesus himself, there is no figure in the Christian Scriptures to whom as much narrative space is devoted. The Jesus material may be more than twice as long, but it is one story, told four times. The story of David is one continuous narrative, which falls into two halves. 'The rise of King David' runs from 1 Samuel 16.1 to 2 Samuel 5.10: from his anointing by Samuel to the moment he achieves kingship over all Israel. I have attempted a 'dramatic exposition' of that text in *Walking the Walk: the Rise of King David for Today* (2009). 'The fall of King David' then runs from 2 Samuel 5.11 to 1 Kings 2.11. It is this part of Scripture that is the subject of this book.

The Story of King David's Fall: *Talking the Talk*?

In *Walking the Walk*, I argued that the distinctive characteristic of David's behaviour in his rise to power is his restraint. It is in what he refuses to do, as much as in what he does, that David shows himself to be 'a man after God's own heart' (the phrase is used of David in the Acts of the Apostles 13.22, alluding to 1 Samuel 13.14). He refuses to raise his hand against Saul, 'the Lord's anointed', or to grasp at the throne to which he knows God has called him.

This book argues that as king David casts restraint aside and becomes as grasping as any ruler. This is the first reason for the title of this sequel. In popular parlance 'to walk the walk' is to be authentic and to offer 'the real thing'. By contrast merely 'to talk the talk' is to fake something you do not truly possess. The title of this book reflects the fact that David's career as king fails to live up to his impressive early faithfulness to God.

Notoriously it is as king that David sins. True, there are moments when his flaws surface even in the story of his rise to power, but all the most outrageous examples of his frailty occur after he has become king. His adultery with Bathsheba is no isolated incident. Rather it is representative of the whole story of his fall. First, exercising his power inappropriately, David sins; then, confronted with his sin, he repents wholeheartedly. This is the second reason for the title of this book: in the simplicity of his contrition, his *words* of confession, David remains a model of faithfulness to God. 'Talking the talk' in this sense has more positive connotations.

Thirdly, the title draws attention to a significant feature of the biblical text. Relative to the first half of David's story, the second is especially rich in dialogue. This dialogue has an important dramatic (and therefore theological) function. It is mostly through dialogue that the personalities of the bible characters are fleshed out; and this is often how the narrative discloses the will of God. It is a rare thing in any biblical story-telling for God to speak or act directly. Usually the purpose of God is not explicit. It has to be inferred, and it is often the sections of dialogue which make this inference possible. It is as the characters speak of the Lord (or fail to speak of him) that some sense is conveyed of what the providence of God might be.

The Story of King David's Fall: Private Citizen or Public Servant?

It has become something of a given in contemporary western countries that the conduct of a person's private life has no bearing on their fitness for public office (at least in politics). It is thought to be self-evident that a man is not necessarily an untrustworthy custodian of the nation's purse, for example, just because he has cheated on his wife.

The Bible has a different take on this question. It looks for a greater degree of coherence in a person and assumes that a common set of values will shape both public and private behaviour. It is not always in the public interest for the domestic details of public servants to be made known and the life of David illustrates the extent to which a person in office needs privacy. But the Bible does suggest it is a healthy thing when a person achieves a measure of integration between their public and private roles. It may be helpful to distinguish the two, but they are not to be separated. In fact they cannot be easily disentangled.

The issue goes to the heart of what this part of the Bible is about. Is it only a morality tale with lessons for individuals engaged in a spiritual quest, and especially for Christian believers in their quest of discipleship; or is it just a piece of dynastic propaganda, designed to legitimise a claim to the throne of Israel by one house over another? Is this a story about personal peccadilloes or about political principles, about a private citizen or a public servant?

The answer of course is that it is both. More than that: part of the point of this story is precisely the interplay between these two apparent alternatives. This is undeniably a story about David as a king: establishing his reign, facing rebellion, finding allies, dealing with opponents, struggling to secure the succession. But equally it is about David as a man: establishing a family, facing bereavement, finding friendship, dealing with conflict, struggling to secure a good death. But it is especially a story about the extent to which his life as a husband and father impacted on his role as a king; about the extent to which his life as a king impacted on his role as a husband and a father; and about how his relationship with God impacted (and failed to impact) on both roles.

In this book the story of David's fall is divided into four Acts. Act One (2 Samuel 5.11-8.18) tells how David prospered in the early part of his reign. Act Two (2 Samuel 9-20) is often called 'the Succession Narrative', as if it dealt only with the question of who would sit on David's throne after him. But these chapters are as much about the private citizen as they are about the public servant: indeed, it is an oddity about this part of the story, that so little attention is given to David's military prowess, to his tactical genius in war or international diplomacy. The narrative is much more interested in his personal issues. His adultery with Bathsheba occurs in this section; and in the account of the rebellion of Absalom, the focus of the text is as much on the difficulties this creates for David the father as it is on the difficulties it creates for him as a king. His grief for his sons when they die is a key element in this section, as is his failure to discipline them while they are alive. Act Three (2 Samuel 21-24) consists of a carefully structured appendix to the narrative proper. Act Four (1 Kings 1.1 to 2.11) brings down the curtain on the drama as a whole with an account of David's demise and death. References in the text which are simply to chapter and verse (e.g., 19.12) are always to the second book of Samuel (e.g., 2 Samuel 19.12).

If there is a single question which the story sets out to answer, it is not, as it was once fashionable to argue, 'Who will succeed David on his death?'. This fails to account for great swathes of material. A more adequate way of framing the central question is, 'How are the purposes of God for Israel worked out through the humanity of the king?'; or 'What has the example of David to teach the person who aspires to serve God – particularly the person who is called to public office?'. In either case, the focus in the narrative on David's contrition is a significant part of the answer.

The Story of King David's Fall: 'A Dramatic Exposition'

The story of David is sometimes described as 'the David cycle'. There are similar cycles of stories in the Bible, for example about Joseph (in Genesis 37-50) and about Elijah (in 1 Kings 17-2 Kings 2). A 'cycle' is a series of connected and continuous narratives about a central figure, in which the component parts nevertheless have their own coherence and integrity – like episodes in a TV drama series (or individual plays in a 'cycle' of 'Medieval Mysteries').

This is how the David story is approached in the chapters that follow. Each 'episode' is treated as a drama in its own right, made up often of several distinct 'scenes'; but with attention to its place in the unfolding of the narrative as a whole. The narrative sequence and chronology are respected – and interrogated for meaning. (In a similar vein, see my exposition of Genesis 37-50 in *Living the Dream: Joseph for Today* (2007).)

Generally speaking, a chapter in this book corresponds to a chapter of the biblical text. In each chapter special effort has been made to follow the contours of the Bible passage, attending carefully to its shape and structure. The text has been read realistically, marking its literary details. Like a novel, this text has to be taken at face value if its meaning is to be distilled. There has been a certain amount of reading between the lines of the text, but always with the aim of enabling the narrative to have its full impact.

To assist in this task, the biblical text is printed together with the commentary. The translation is the 'anglicized' *New Revised Standard Version* – chosen for the balance it achieves between a closeness to the Hebrew text and a fluency of contemporary English.

But what is offered here is also a Christian theological exposition. This does not mean that in the following chapters every opportunity has been taken to draw parallels between David and Jesus. There is a long tradition of this kind of 'typology' in the church. Instead, this book asks what the Word of the Lord might be through this story today, and attempts to answer the question 'in the light of Christ'. What do we learn from this text, in other words, given the nature of God as he has made himself known in Jesus Christ? In the concluding paragraphs of each chapter I have tried to indicate – with the interests of preachers particularly in mind – the lines along which each episode might be applied today.

There is little here in the way of interaction with other interpreters of the text (there are no footnotes) or with current academic scholarship. During the last two hundred years or more, much has been written about the development of this text as part of the biblical canon. It is clear that the text has a history: it took shape over time, almost certainly at first in an oral culture as a spoken tale. It wasn't written in a single sitting by a single author. But the form it now has, it has had for at least two thousand years, and what is offered here is a reading of the text in this form. Readers wishing to pursue questions of source criticism should turn to the standard commentaries. In particular where this book comments on the Hebrew text, its observations are derived from the insights of others.

In my own reading of the story I have been especially helped by the interpretations of Robert Alter, Walter Brueggemann, John Goldingay and Ralph Davis – and readers who know their work will doubtless discern my indebtedness, which I am glad to acknowledge. I would also like to reiterate my heartfelt thanks to Cathy, Jonathan and Tom. More than anyone else, they influence the way in which I read the Bible.

This book is dedicated with gratitude and all my love to my parents, David and Pam Wilcox. They have modeled for me, and for many others over the years, the way of restraint and contrition.

Pete Wilcox
Lichfield Cathedral
Easter 2011

ACT ONE

The Rule of David Established

2 Samuel 5.11–8.18

Chapter One
2 Samuel 5.11–25

David Established as King

Introduction

'Pride goes before a fall' (Proverbs 16.18). In fact there is no particular stress in the text on any arrogance or complacency on David's part as he becomes king. He is not obviously smug or haughty, conceited or self-important. Yet many ordinary Christians have found, as David was about to do, that when life is going swimmingly, it is all too easy to lose one's spiritual bearings, one's sense of vocation and of direction under God, so that a fall frequently follows.

The story of David's *rise* ends triumphantly: 'David became greater and greater, because the Lord, the God of Hosts was with him'(5.10). The story of David's *fall* opens in a series of scenes which consolidate the impression of David as a man with the Midas touch: politically, domestically and militarily everything he touches turns to gold. Politically (in scene one), a neighbouring kingdom seeks an alliance with him; domestically (in scene two), he acquires wives and concubines and produces sons in abundance; and militarily (in scenes four and five) his old foes the Philistines are routed – not once, but twice.

Nor is there any very obvious cloud on the horizon. For the attentive reader, however, there are subtle hints of what is to come – just the first indications that with power come new challenges, to which even the great David might not be equal.

Scene One (verses 11–12): David's kingship is established

11 King Hiram of Tyre sent messengers to David, along with cedar trees, and carpenters and masons who built David a house. 12 David then perceived that the Lord had established him king over Israel, and that he had exalted his kingdom for the sake of his people Israel.

David's accession to the throne of Judah in 2.4 seems not to have precipitated much response among neighbouring kingdoms. When he assumes the throne of Israel, however, everything changes. Now he is a player on the international stage. As king of Judah, his role was of interest only to his rival, ruling over the northern tribes. As king of all Israel, David's position attracts the interest of both potential allies and traditional enemies.

First, a new alliance is established. King Hiram of Tyre, David's neighbour to the north, takes the initiative. His gifts are an overture, intended to indicate support for the new regime and to secure peace and co-operation for the future. But the gifts are also powerfully symbolic. He sends the resources to assist David in building a palace fit for a king – both the raw materials and the technical expertise.

The gift reflects a predictably worldly view of kingship on Hiram's part. 'Come', he seems to be saying to David, 'this is how we do sovereignty around here. You'll be needing a glorious palace. I'll help you'. Hiram's message expresses solidarity with David: 'Welcome to the club: we are colleagues and peers and our collaboration will be of mutual benefit'. The gifts hint not just at a wealth, but also at a potential for trade and prosperity beyond the wildest dreams of a shepherd boy.

And while David accepts the gifts, the reader is doubly heartened by David's response. In the generosity of Hiram, David perceives both that the Lord has graciously established him as king, and (in addition) that the Lord has done so and has exalted David's kingdom, 'for the sake of his people Israel'.

The story thus begins with a note about the purpose of kingship within the will of God. There will be a similar note towards the end of the story, in David's 'last words' (23.3-4). A godly king is to reign on behalf of his people, in their interests and for their welfare. David is only 'over Israel' for Israel. This is the way the Scriptures understand all leadership: those in authority are always called to exercise power for the common good and for the benefit of others. The principle is as hard to implement as it is easy to state. Experienced leaders will be all too aware how often their actions and priorities are shaped by their own needs (for approval from the 'right' people perhaps, or for success) rather than by the needs of their community.

There is a warning implied here. David's privilege carries responsibility. More than that, the transition from verse 11 to verse 12 may be subversive, inviting the reader to perceive with David that it is the Lord, not Hiram, who has established him as king and that it is on the Lord, and not Hiram, that David's continued security and prosperity depend. There may be an allusion here to Deuteronomy 17.14-20 – a 'role specification' for Israel's king, and a recognition of the corrupting effects of power and wealth: those who have silver and gold in abundance, and cedar trees, risk trusting in these things. It has inevitably always been those most bereft of worldly resources who have found it most easy to trust in the Lord, and it has inevitably always been the wealthy who have found it most difficult to do so. How hard it is for the rich to enter the kingdom of heaven! (Matthew 19.23 and parallels).

Scene Two (verses 13-14): David's dynasty is established

13 In Jerusalem, after he came from Hebron, David took more concubines and wives; and more sons and daughters were born to David. 14 These are the names of those who were born to him in Jerusalem: Shammua, Shobab, Nathan, Solomon, 15 Ibhar, Elishua, Nepheg, Japhia, 16 Elishama, Eliada, and Eliphelet.

On the face of it, this second pair of verses further consolidates David's power and authority. Perhaps the Psalmist had David in mind when he wrote, 'sons are indeed a heritage from the Lord… like arrows in the hand of a warrior are the sons of one's youth; happy [blessed] is the man who has his quiver full of them' (Psalm 127.3-5). In his personal life, as well as in public office (although for a king in Israel the two are difficult to distinguish), David is prospering.

This list corresponds to the brief account in 3.2-5, where a list was provided of the six sons who were born to David of six wives during the seven years he was king of Judah in Hebron. They include Amnon, Absalom and Adonijah, who will play such prominent roles in this story.

Here another eleven sons are named. The list is a summary, and includes offspring whose births lie in the future. Only one of these, Solomon, will reappear in the story. It is worth noting that, assuming the sons are listed in birth order, Solomon was only the tenth born son of his father. For all the prestige associated in the Bible with 'the firstborn', it is remarkable how often a family line by-passes this conventional route: neither Isaac nor Jacob, Joseph nor David himself were the oldest among their brothers. Divine blessing is always sheer gift in Scripture. It tends to confound human assumptions and expectations. In this story, the Hebron sons will prove ill-fated.

If there was an allusion to Deuteronomy 17 in the previous scene, it is less veiled here: Israel's king is expressly forbidden there to 'acquire many wives for himself, or else his heart will be turned away' (Deuteronomy 17.17). But David conforms to the conventional categories of kingship. He will have not just a palace fit for a king, but a harem fit for one also. As king of Judah, he acquired only wives. Now he has concubines too. Again, a faint alarm bell rings in the mind of the reader.

Scene Three (verses 17-21): David defeats the Philistines at Baal-perazim

17 When the Philistines heard that David had been anointed king over Israel, all the Philistines went up in search of David; but David heard about it and went down to the stronghold. 18 Now the Philistines had come and spread out in the valley of Rephaim. 19 David inquired of the Lord, 'Shall I go up against the Philistines? Will you give them into my hand?' The Lord said to David, 'Go up; for I will certainly give the Philistines into your hand.' 20 So David came to Baal-perazim, and David defeated them there. He said, 'The Lord has burst forth against my enemies before me, like a bursting flood.' Therefore that place is called Baal-perazim. 21 The Philistines abandoned their idols there, and David and his men carried them away.

When Hiram heard that David was king in Jerusalem, he sent messengers with peaceful intent, armed with gifts. When the Philistines heard it, they sent out a search party with hostile intent. When David hears of it, he takes refuge in 'the stronghold'. That he 'went down' suggests that the stronghold in question was not Jerusalem. But the valley of Rephaim is not far from David's new capital, so he didn't go a long way.

The passage is full of echoes of an earlier stage in David's life. These associations are all positive and contribute to the gathering impression of him as being at the pinnacle of his career. The narrative suggests it is many years since David has had contact with the Philistines (and certainly since he fought them). It is the first time since the death of Saul that they have attacked Israel. The renewed hostility may imply that David's erstwhile ally Achish (whom David had not met since he was forced to leave the camp at Aphek on the eve of the battle on Mount Gilboa, 1 Samuel 29, 31) is dead, and there is a new king in Gath. It is likewise many years since David sought refuge in strongholds (1

Samuel 22.4; 23.14, 19, 29; 24.22); and it is many years since David is recorded as having enquired of the Lord (1 Samuel 22.10; 30.8; 2 Samuel 2.1; and especially 1 Samuel 23.2-4). As in those earlier instances, the reader is invited to note how readily David seeks the Lord's guidance and how readily the Lord gives it. As king-in-waiting, this was David's consistent pattern. The narrative stresses that nothing has changed in this respect now that he has become king. His hand is now mightier than ever, but David takes nothing for granted. He understands that if the Philistines are to be delivered into his hand, it will be because the Lord delivers them. So he acts only as he is authorised to act.

Sure enough, David defeats the Philistines. Something about the encounter (such as a sudden breaching of the enemy lines) presumably resembled an eruption or water-burst, because it gave the place the name Baal-perazim (which means something like, 'the Lord has burst forth'). The word *perez* (bursting) occurs four times in verse 20 (compare Isaiah 28.21).

The Philistines fled, leaving their idols behind. When David and his men captured these and carried them off it was like the settling of an ancient score: a full generation previously, in the final days of the prophet Samuel, the Philistines had defeated Israel in battle and had carried off the ark (1 Samuel 4.11). Here the tables are turned.

Scene Four (verses 22-25): David defeats the Philistines at Rephaim

22 Once again the Philistines came up, and were spread out in the valley of Rephaim. 23 When David inquired of the Lord, he said, 'You shall not go up; go round to their rear, and come upon them opposite the balsam trees. 24 When you hear the sound of marching in the tops of the balsam trees, then be on the alert; for then the Lord has gone out before you to strike down the army of the Philistines.' 25 David did just as the Lord had commanded him; and he struck down the Philistines from Geba all the way to Gezer.

There is considerable repetition in this final scene of what has just taken place. Again, the Philistines 'were spread out in the valley of Rephaim'. Again, David is quick to 'inquire of the Lord'; and again, the Lord is quick to respond. Again, David sensed the presence of the Lord in the decisive moment of the battle and again he won a great victory, 'from Geba all the way to Gezer'.

But a detail is different. In the earlier conflict, David had asked 'Shall I go up?' and was told, 'Yes: go up'. Here he evidently asks the same question, but is told, 'No: don't go up – go round and attack them from behind'. There is a theological point at stake here. With the Living God, nothing is ever entirely predictable or routine. David's reliance on the will of God does not lapse into presumption on the basis of past experience. Inquiring of the Lord is always new and must always be freshly attentive. Yesterday's answer is not sufficient for today's question. It is necessary to listen again for the Word of the Lord.

David is instructed first to circle around and to approach his enemies from the rear – opposite the balsam trees. He is then told to wait for a definite signal: 'when you hear the sound of marching in the tops of the balsam trees, then be on the alert'. Presumably 'the sound of marching' in the treetops is a reference to the wind. The noise it makes in the balsam trees provides David with cover for an attack so that their advance is not heard. The sense of waiting for the Spirit of God, alert to the opportunities of the moment, is thoroughly familiar to most believers.

Conclusion

When the episode concludes 'David did just as the Lord com-manded him', the comment seems appropriate not just to the final scene, but to all David's early work as king of all Israel. He is cast here as the faithful and obedient servant of the Lord. He is so much in tune with his God that the text can state in one verse (verse 24) that 'the Lord has gone out before [him] to strike down the army of the Philistines' and in the next (verse 25) that 'David struck down the Philistines'. God and David are in absolute concert.

This is the ideal to which Christians aspire: to discern so accurately what God is doing, and to join in so effectively, that our work is God's work, and God's work is ours. This is presumably what Jesus meant when he spoke of his ministry in these terms: 'My Father is working and I also am working'. At this point in his life, David might justifiably claim something similar.

Chapter Two
2 Samuel 6.1–23

David and the Ark

Introduction

In the previous episode – the first in the story of David's fall – he is presented as a man with the Midas touch. If there are shadows in the sunshine they are few and faint.

But in this second episode, there is a shift. For the first time since his coronation, David is thwarted. He experiences failure and frustration. For the first time in the whole narrative about him, David encounters the anger of the Lord; and for the first time it is stated explicitly that David himself is angry. Previously, Eliab (1 Samuel 17.28), Saul (1 Samuel 18.8, 20.30), Jonathan (1 Samuel 20.34), the Philistine commanders (1 Samuel 29.4) and Abner (3.8) have been described as angry, but not David. It will not be the last time, however. He will be angry again over the incident which defines his 'fall': first (perhaps) at the news of the death of Uriah in 11.20, and then (definitely) at Nathan's account of an injustice done to a poor man in 12.5.

The text is troubling. There is an unambiguous brutality about the incident at its heart: God strikes a man dead for what seems to a modern Christian reader to be a relatively trivial offence, or even an innocent, well-meaning act. God smites him. There is no attempt to explain or justify this judgment in the text.

There are, however, hints that not all the culpability rests with Uzzah. It is possible that in the first two scenes (verses 1 to 11) the real villain is David himself; there is little doubt that in the latter two scenes (verses 12 to 23) it is Michal.

In the first two scenes, David sets out to bring the ark of God up from Baale-judah to Jerusalem. He fails and in the process Uzzah dies. The action is both backward and forward looking. It looks back to the time when the Philistines took the ark captive and removed it from Israelite soil (1 Samuel 5-6). It looks forward to the time when the temple would be built in Jerusalem, a permanent symbol of the covenant presence of God with his people (1 Kings 6-8). The action is one Saul could never have contemplated. He never enjoyed sufficient respite from, never mind dominance over, his Philistine neighbours. The action presupposes the defeats of the Philistines described in the previous episode.

In the latter two scenes, David achieves his goal. The ark comes into the city of David. But in the process, Michal – the daughter of Saul – takes offence and is irrevocably estranged from her husband.

Scene One (verses 1-5): David attempts to bring up the ark of God, dancing before the Lord

> *David again gathered all the chosen men of Israel, thirty thousand. 2 David and all the people with him set out and went from Baale-judah, to bring up from there the ark of God, which is called by the name of the Lord of hosts who is enthroned on the cherubim. 3 They carried the ark of God on a new cart, and brought it out of the house of Abinadab, which was on the hill. Uzzah and Ahio, the sons of Abinadab, were driving the new cart 4 with the ark of God; and Ahio went in front of the ark. 5 David and all the house of Israel were dancing before the Lord with all their might, with songs and lyres and harps and tambourines and castanets and cymbals.*

Fresh from his victory over the Philistines and his capture of their idols, David is confident to attempt what had awaited the right moment for decades: the rehabilitation of the ark of the Lord. It had been captured by the Philistines in the days of the prophet Samuel (1 Samuel 4). And although it had been evicted by the Philistines and returned to Israelite territory, it had languished ever since in Kearith-jearim (1 Samuel 7.1, compare Joshua 15.9), about nine miles northwest of Jerusalem. In this passage, the place is called 'Baale-judah'. It is hard to imagine that a place name which includes the title 'Baal' could ever be a suitable resting place for the ark of the Lord.

When it is said that David assembled 30,000 men of Israel (even if the Hebrew word *'elep* is taken to mean 30 divisions or battalions of men, rather than 30 'thousands' as such), to bring up the ark of the God 'which is called by the name of the Lord of hosts, who is enthroned on the cherubim', there is no hint that disaster lurks just around the corner. It sounds like a natural continuation of the previous episode.

David's star is still rising. If 'the Lord, the God of hosts, is with him' (5.10), what is more fitting than that he should bring back into use the ark 'which is called by the name of the Lord of hosts'? Indeed, 30,000 is precisely the number of Israelites slain when the Philistines captured the ark in 1 Samuel 4.10, to which this story plainly harks back.

All seems well. It is twice stressed that the ark is placed on 'a new cart'. This appears to be a mark of honour. The procession leaves the house of Abinadab, led by his two sons Uzzah and Ahio, whose family have been custodians of the ark for more than forty years. The procession is accompanied by exuberant worship – and a lack of inhibition which is rare in the western world today.

Scene Two (verses 6-11): David and the anger of the Lord

> 6 *When they came to the threshing-floor of Nacon, Uzzah reached out his hand to the ark of God and took hold of it, for the oxen shook it. 7 The anger of the Lord was kindled against Uzzah; and God struck him there because he reached out his hand to the ark; and he died there beside the ark of God. 8 David was angry because the Lord had burst forth with an outburst upon Uzzah; so that place is called Perez-uzzah to this day. 9 David was afraid of the Lord that day; he said, 'How can the ark of the Lord come into my care?' 10 So David was unwilling to take the ark of the Lord into his care in the city of David; instead David took it to the house of Obed-edom the Gittite. 11 The ark of the Lord remained in the house of Obed-edom the Gittite for three months; and the Lord blessed Obed-edom and all his household.*

But all is not well. At a certain point, Uzzah stretched out his hand impulsively (apparently to steady the ark at a moment when the cart shook), and 'the anger of the Lord was kindled against Uzzah; and God struck him there... and he died there beside the ark of God'.

What is the reader to make of this text? In terms of the biblical narrative, Uzzah's action is perhaps doubly negligent. For one thing, the ark was meant to be handled by Levites alone, and it is not absolutely clear that Uzzah belonged to the tribe of Levi. The evidence (in 1 Samuel 7.1, 1 Chronicles 15.13) is inconclusive. Moreover, even a new cart is not appropriate as transportation for the ark of God. The biblical text is specific about this. Exodus 25.14 states that it is to be carried on poles, threaded through rings on the sides of the ark.

Carried like that, there would have been no cart or oxen to shake it and no need for Uzzah to reach out and steady it. To put the ark on a cart was a Philistine invention (1 Samuel 6.11), and for that reason hardly to be emulated.

Certainly verse 13 suggests that when the attempt to bring the ark to Jerusalem was renewed, a lesson had been learnt: the text refers not to any cart, but to 'those who bore the ark'. The account in 1 Chronicles 15.11-15 is as follows: 'Because you did not carry it the first time, the Lord our God burst out against us, because we did not give it the proper care. So the priests and the Levites sanctified themselves to bring up the ark of the Lord the God of Israel. And the Levites carried the ark of God on their shoulders with the poles, as Moses had commanded according to the word of the Lord'.

The point is that Uzzah was as much a victim as a villain. He died not because his act was one of fleeting individual overfamiliarity, but because it was one of chronic corporate neglect of proper ceremonial reverence.

The result is that the Lord breaks out again. Just as, in the previous episode, he had 'burst out' on the Philistines at Baal-perazim, now he bursts out against his own people at Perez-uzzah (*perez* occurs three times in verse 8). The holiness and majesty of God is not something to be trifled with or presumed upon: it is as potentially dangerous to his own people as it is to their enemies.

But there is a further point to be made. In verse 8, it is said that this incident provoked David's anger. First, in verse 7, the anger of the Lord was kindled. Then, in verse 8, David was angry. The juxtaposition is suggestive.

It is worth stopping to consider where the ark is being taken from and to – and why? In terms of the story of David, a lot of chapters (and upwards of forty years) have passed since the captured ark was returned by the Philistines to Israelite territory in 1 Samuel 7. Since then, Samuel had ruled Israel as judge (1 Samuel 7-9) and Saul as king (that's 1 Samuel 10-31). In all that time, the ark has not been mentioned once.

Now David rules. And one of his very first acts as king of all Israel is this attempt to restore the ark to a place of community worship. But on what authority is David making this attempt? Unlike the previous episode, where he twice 'inquires of the Lord', there is no such consultation here. Rather, David seems to be acting very much on his own initiative.

In worldly terms, it might be considered an inspired piece of political opportunism. Having moved his centre of power from Hebron to Zion, how better to consolidate its reputation than by locating the ark there? What could be better than to make the city of David, the city of God. It is brilliant – except that it lacks any divine authorisation.

The reader may be confronted here with an archetypal moment. As the servant of God, David is called to align himself with the will and purpose of God. But here he may be making the fundamental, but all too common, error of aligning the will and purpose of God with himself. The crucial question (which is not capable of a final answer) is whether this is an act of faith or an act of hubris on David's part? Is he genuinely facilitating the worship of Yahweh, or is he seeking to manipulate the worship of Yahweh for his own ends? Is David using God for his own political advantage?

On this reading, the real crime in this episode is not Uzzah's at all. It is David's. And it is not David's arrogance exactly, but his characteristic chutzpah – his opportunism and ambition. After an interval of forty years, the ark is being pressed into the service of David (rather than the service of God) to shore up his claim to the throne of Israel.

In this context, David's anger in verse 8 may be illuminating. With whom is David angry? With Uzzah for his rashness? With God for 'breaking out' against his own people and thus spoiling David's celebratory day? Or is David angry with himself for presuming on God? Verses 9-10 certainly imply that the outcome of the incident was a fresh chastening for David, and a fresh reverence for the power of God in his midst.

Part of the point of this incident is surely that the presence of God is something volcanic and unpredictable (it 'bursts out', verse 8). It is not something cosy and cuddly. The Philistines had already discovered this much earlier in the story. If nothing else, this incident is a testimony to the consistency of God. The Israelites are just as vulnerable before the holiness of God as the other nations. This is a solemn lesson, in an age where an assumed familiarity with God is more of a danger for the church than an undue awe and fear of him.

The text warns the reader against presuming on the power of God; and it is not Uzzah with whom the reader is invited to identify, but David. Uzzah is a minor character in the story: a pawn one might almost say. The tragedy has a salutary effect: David is freshly afraid of God. He is the greater sinner. The text invites the reader to consider that when God is no longer held in awe by the leaders of his people, they place at risk not only themselves but the community they lead.

In his fear, David abandons his quest to bring the ark into Jerusalem – the city of David. He leaves it, instead, in the care of Obed-edom, a Gittite.

Scene Three (verses 12-19): David again brings up the ark of God, dancing before the Lord

> *12 It was told King David, 'The Lord has blessed the household of Obed-edom and all that belongs to him, because of the ark of God.' So David went and brought up the ark of God from the house of Obed-edom to the city of David with rejoicing; 13 and when those who bore the ark of the Lord had gone six paces, he sacrificed an ox and a fatling. 14 David danced before the Lord with all his might; David was girded with a linen ephod. 15 So David and all the house of Israel brought up the ark of the Lord with shouting, and with the sound of the trumpet.*

> *16 As the ark of the Lord came into the city of David, Michal daughter of Saul looked out of the window, and saw King David leaping and dancing before the Lord; and she despised him in her heart.*

> *17 They brought in the ark of the Lord, and set it in its place, inside the tent that David had pitched for it; and David offered burnt-offerings and offerings of well-being before the Lord. 18 When David had finished offering the burnt-offerings and the offerings of well-being, he blessed the people in the name of the Lord of hosts, 19 and distributed food among all the people, the whole multitude of Israel, both men and women, to each a cake of bread, a portion of meat, and a cake of raisins. Then all the people went back to their homes.*

In Scripture anger never has the last word; that always belongs to the loving purpose of God. So here the story ends in blessing. Within three months, the ark is again associated with life, not death. As so often in the Bible, the object of God's blessing is not an Israelite. Obed-edom is a Gittite (likely from Gath, and possibly a retainer recruited by David during his sojourn with king Achish (1 Samuel 27, 29)). The blessing of God was presumably manifest in the fertility Obed-edom experienced in the home (in the birth of healthy children) and in the field (in abundant harvests, flocks and herds).

The evidence was sufficient to persuade David to make a fresh attempt to accomplish his goal. The procession of the ark resumes as it had been abruptly left off at the point of Uzzah's death: with David 'dancing before the Lord with all his might' (compare verse 5).

This time no liberties are taken with the holiness of God: the ark is carried by human bearers. Moreover, after the procession has moved forward a mere six paces, a sacrifice is offered. There was no such ritual carefulness the first time around.

The image of David dancing 'with all his might' is arresting. This was no gentle swaying or rhythmic step. It was an energetic leaping and whirling, with shouting and the sound of the trumpet. It will have left David (clad only in a linen ephod) breathless and sweating as well as half-naked. Such energy in worship is almost unheard of in the western Church today, even in Pentecostal and charismatic circles – to be so caught up in a sense of the presence of God that the worshipper expresses it not in contemplative stillness, but frenzied movement.

But not all are impressed with David's exhibition of devotion to the Lord. As the procession arrives in the city of David, Michal (her attention perhaps drawn by its noise) saw her husband from a window, leaping and dancing, 'and despised him in her heart'.

The note is an aside, to be developed in the next scene. The emphasis in this scene is on the arrival of the ark. Verse 17 marks an important moment: Jerusalem, the administrative and political capital of David's kingdom, is now its centre of worship also. David has pitched a tent for the ark, and once he has set up the ark in its place, he exercises a priestly ministry: first (presumably still clad in the priestly ephod) he offers sacrifices to the Lord, and then he blesses the people 'in the name of the Lord of hosts'. If David was usurping here an office that did not rightly belong to him, there is no hint of disapproval in the text. Perhaps the king's office was deemed to carry priestly responsibilities with it. Certainly, his sons will soon afterwards be listed as priests (8.18) – which implies that they exercised on a regular basis what David is here only glimpsed doing.

The scene closes with David, as father of the nation, distributing cakes (party food!) 'to the whole house of Israel, men and women'. Mission accomplished, the people returned to their homes – and David to his.

Scene Four (verses 20-23): David's confrontation with Michal

20 David returned to bless his household. But Michal the daughter of Saul came out to meet David, and said, 'How the king of Israel honoured himself today, uncovering himself today before the eyes of his servants' maids, as any vulgar fellow might shamelessly uncover himself!' 21 David said to

> *Michal, 'It was before the Lord, who chose me in place of*
> *your father and all his household, to appoint me as prince*
> *over Israel, the people of the Lord, that I have danced before*
> *the Lord. 22 I will make myself yet more contemptible than*
> *this, and I will be abased in my own eyes; but by the maids*
> *of whom you have spoken, by them I shall be held in honour.'*
> *23 And Michal the daughter of Saul had no child to the day*
> *of her death.*

Having blessed the people, David returns home to bless his own household. But Michal is in no mood to accept her husband's blessing.

What follows is, surprisingly, the first recorded conversation between David and Michal in the whole story. She has featured in several previous episodes (1 Samuel 18.20-29, 19.11-17, 25.44; 2 Samuel 3.12-16). Her voice has even been heard (1 Samuel 19.17). But this is the first time that either David or Michal is reported as speaking to the other.

Decades have passed since Michal was said to love David (1 Samuel 18.20). She was his first wife, but they were separated for many years during David's wilderness exile. During that time, she was given in marriage to another man, who wept bitterly at losing her when she and David were re-united (3.16); and during the same interval, David acquired numerous additional wives. It is not clear at what point Michal's love for David soured – but the loathing she felt for David when she saw him dancing before the Lord (verse 16) cannot have come out of the blue. There is something hardened about the contempt with which in verse 20 she refers to him, to his face, in the third person. A lover may be embarrassed, even mortified, by the behaviour of her beloved; but the usual response is to mitigate, or at least to attempt to understand. To despise another person, love must be entirely absent. This is the first time in the story that David has been called 'the king of Israel' – and the sarcasm is hard to miss. It is a long time since David harvested 200 Philistine foreskins to win Michal's hand in marriage.

Michal is appalled at what David has done. It is not his religious devotion that she criticises so severely, but the way that, in his dancing, he forgot his modesty and exposed himself for all to see. It may be that she speaks as a wife, shocked that her husband could allow his nakedness to be seen by others. Her reference to 'the servant girls' suggests rather that she speaks as a princess, shocked that a king could demean his office in such a way. David's response certainly indicates that, whatever the presented subject of the argument, what was really at issue between them was David's relationship to Saul. Is he a worthy successor to Michal's father, or is he not?

David is stung by Michal's words and replies with stinging words of his own. Three things about his reply are worth noting. The first is the gushing incoherence in his references to the Lord: 'it was before the Lord… that I have danced before the Lord'. David feels unfairly criticised. He knows that his dancing was a sincere expression of worship, fit for the Lord – and that it was an offering intended for the Lord's eyes and not for those of the servant girls. Even in worship however, there comes a point when a lack of awareness of the impact our actions are having on those around us amounts to a kind of self-indulgence. On the other hand, there is a proper disregard for the reactions of other people when worship is offered. All too often worshippers are more conscious of what those around them will make of their devotion, than of what the Lord will make of it.

The second noteworthy thing is David's reference to Saul. This is the first time in the story that David has allowed his scrupulous loyalty to Saul to lapse. His words may have been spoken in the heat of the moment – but for the first time it is clear that David understood Saul to be rejected by God, and himself to be selected in his stead: 'the Lord chose me in place of your father and all his household, to appoint me prince over Israel, the people of the Lord'.

Finally, David counters Michal's charge that his behaviour had made him (and his royal office) a laughing stock. There is a careful reversal in verse 22 of the sequence Michal used in verse 20. Where she spoke of honour, maids and shame, David now refers to shame, maids and honour. David is convinced that those who had witnessed his actions would respect him more for it, and not less; and that he would do the same again – and more – in the same circumstances. David is convinced that ordinary people recognise sincere worship when they see it, and value it especially in leaders and holders of public office.

The scene closes with what sounds like a statement of the judgment of God upon Michal, and a vindication of David's worship: 'Michal, the daughter of Saul, had no child to the day of her death'. In fact it might mean no more than that David and Michal never again resumed a sexual relationship. It is hard to imagine this breakdown in trust and mutual respect was ever fully healed. But just as the figure of Saul was lurking just beneath the surface of the dialogue in verses 20-22, it may be that he lurks just below the surface of this conclusion also. From a political point of view, it might once have seemed that the offspring of the union between David and Michal would be capable of uniting the houses of Saul and David, bringing stability to the kingdom still presumably recovering from the ravages of seven years of civil war. Now it is clear that there is no such prospect. The Lord's rejection of Saul is final: no descendant of his will sit on the throne of Israel. The only question now is which member of David's own house will succeed him?

Conclusion

This episode closes with David apparently vindicated and Michal utterly humiliated. David has again achieved what he set out to do: the ark is in Jerusalem. But at what cost? Did David stop to reflect on what had happened and to ask himself whether there were alternative paths he might have taken? Did he not ponder the impact of his behaviour even in retrospect (which is when most leaders find it easiest to recognise their mistakes).

Thus the reader is left with a measure of unease. The death of Uzzah in the first two scenes and the challenge of Michal in the latter two raise a question mark against David's triumphant progress. In the following episode, the king's ambitions will be checked not by the disastrous death of a member of his retinue, or the unconcealed contempt of a member of his family, but by the Lord himself.

Each of the first two episodes has also contributed to the development of Jerusalem: in the first episode, the city of David was adorned with his royal palace. It is now also the holy place, where the ark of the Lord dwells. There are other cities in David's kingdom which had existing reputations as holy sites, such as Shiloh, Gilgal and Bethel. But Jerusalem is now established as foremost among them – a step towards the building of a temple, to which David's mind now turns.

Chapter Three
2 Samuel 7.1–29

David and his House

Introduction

There is a case for dividing the David story between his rise on the one hand and his fall on the other at 6.23 rather than at 5.10. Now, not only is David's throne established so that he has rest from his enemies (verse 1), but the ark (the symbol of the presence of God) and David's palace are settled in Jerusalem. David and his court prophet Nathan are now at ease reflecting on a good job well done.

This is the first time Nathan has appeared. There is no attempt in the text to explain his origins, or how he came to a position of such prominence. But he will be David's principal prophet to the end of his life (compare 1 Kings 1-2; although in the interim he appears only in 2 Samuel 12).

The episode is essentially composed of two long speeches. In the first, it is Nathan who speaks in response to David's proposal to build the Lord a house. He prophesies what God in grace will do for David. He will make David a great name. In the second, it is David who speaks, in grateful response for what the Lord has promised. He praises the greatness of God. Grace and gratitude are two key hallmarks of biblical faith. There is an inevitable thankfulness which characterises the lives of those who know themselves to have been blessed by God beyond what is deserved. A sense of God's grace invariably tends to drive out meanness and competitiveness, and replace them with generosity. Every believer knows from heartfelt experience that a generosity of spirit is the only proper response to the bounty of God. Where that generosity is absent, it is an open question whether the grace of God has been truly known.

However, there is a further indication here of the perils to which David is prone. When Saul was king, the Lord's prophet Samuel was based at Shiloh. Now David's prophet is based with him in Jerusalem – bolstering the reputation of 'the city of David'. This is just one mark among many of the policy of centralisation the king has adopted.

Having brought the ark of God into his own city, it is predictable that David's mind will turn to its proper accommodation. If a
tabernacled ark symbolises the mobility (and hence the transcendent
freedom of God), a templed ark represents his stability (and hence the
reliable immanence of God). But there is a fine line to be drawn here:
is David's ambition for the glory of God or for his own greater glory?
Is he here aligning himself with the symbols of God's presence, or is
he once more aligning them with himself? It is obviously in David's
political interests for the presence of God to inhabit a more permanent
structure. If there is a temple, is God not tied to it?

The word of the Lord which comes to David via Nathan in scene
one is undeniably a rebuke: the king's ambitions are checked. Yet, in
his response in scene two, David re-establishes himself as a model of
faithful trust in God.

Scene One (verses 1-17): The Lord promises to make David a great name

*Now when the king was settled in his house, and the Lord
had given him rest from all his enemies around him, 2 the
king said to the prophet Nathan, 'See now, I am living in a
house of cedar, but the ark of God stays in a tent.' 3 Nathan
said to the king, 'Go, do all that you have in mind; for the
Lord is with you.'*

*4 But that same night the word of the Lord came to Nathan:
5 Go and tell my servant David: Thus says the Lord: Are
you the one to build me a house to live in? 6 I have not
lived in a house since the day I brought up the people of
Israel from Egypt to this day, but I have been moving about
in a tent and a tabernacle. 7 Wherever I have moved about
among all the people of Israel, did I ever speak a word with
any of the tribal leaders of Israel, whom I commanded to
shepherd my people Israel, saying, 'Why have you not built
me a house of cedar?' 8 Now therefore thus you shall say to
my servant David: Thus says the Lord of hosts: I took you
from the pasture, from following the sheep to be prince over
my people Israel; 9 and I have been with you wherever you
went, and have cut off all your enemies from before you; and
I will make for you a great name, like the name of the great
ones of the earth. 10 And I will appoint a place for my people*

Israel and will plant them, so that they may live in their own place, and be disturbed no more; and evildoers shall afflict them no more, as formerly, 11 from the time that I appointed judges over my people Israel; and I will give you rest from all your enemies. Moreover, the Lord declares to you that the Lord will make you a house. 12 When your days are fulfilled and you lie down with your ancestors, I will raise up your offspring after you, who shall come forth from your body, and I will establish his kingdom. 13 He shall build a house for my name, and I will establish the throne of his kingdom for ever. 14 I will be a father to him, and he shall be a son to me. When he commits iniquity, I will punish him with a rod such as mortals use, with blows inflicted by human beings. 15 But I will not take my steadfast love from him, as I took it from Saul, whom I put away from before you. 16 Your house and your kingdom shall be made sure for ever before me; your throne shall be established for ever. 17 In accordance with all these words and with all this vision, Nathan spoke to David.

Much is implied in the opening words, 'the king was settled in his house'. It means more than that David was settled in his palace. It means he is settled in his city, his kingdom. It means he and his people are at peace. His throne is established and secure. And this is God's doing: the Lord has 'given him rest from all his enemies' (compare Deuteronomy 12.10).

Now David is free to contemplate new projects. He notes that (thanks to King Hiram of Tyre) he himself lives in a house of cedar, while the ark of God is in a tent (6.17). His proposal is so obvious, there is no need to state it. His court chaplain intuits at once what the king has in mind: to build a proper house for the ark of the Lord. And why not? What could possibly be wrong with such a plan to honour the presence of God?

Nathan hardly has to give the matter a second thought. He doesn't even wait for the king to finish what he is apparently wanting to say. 'Yes!', he says. 'Just do it! The Lord is with you!'.

But Nathan's instinct has let him down. He is not the first prophet of God in this narrative to be wrong in supposing what the will of the Lord might be (1 Samuel 16.6-7). But a night's sleep puts him right. The word of the Lord comes to him unambiguously and he faithfully relays the message to David. The word of the Lord is not 'Just do it!'. It's 'Just let me do it!'. There are plenty of examples in the literature of the ancient Near East of a king building a temple for his god. Often it expresses thanks for benefits in the past; sometimes it seems calculated to secure benefits in the future. There is no parallel for such a word of the Lord as this in which the offer to build a house is rejected, but the promise of future blessing nevertheless affirmed.

Nathan is instructed by the Lord to go and address 'my servant' David (verse 4). The phrase is a relatively rare one in the Bible. It is used of Abraham just once (Genesis 26.24), perhaps surprisingly of Caleb just once (Numbers 14.24) and of Moses three times (Numbers 12.7-8, Joshua 1.2, 2 Kings 21.8). But of David, the phrase is used more than twice as often as all these occurrences put together – twelve times in all (in addition to this reference, at 2 Samuel 3.18; 7.8; 1 Kings 11.13, 32, 34, 36, 38; 14.8; 2 Kings 19.34; 20.6 and 1 Chronicles 17.4). The phrase implies both a title of great honour (the servant *of the Lord);* and a position of humble ministry (*the servant* of the Lord). Martin Luther purportedly caught the paradox of this vocation, which in fact belongs to every Christian, when he described a disciple of Christ as 'a perfectly free lord, subject to none; and a perfectly dutiful servant, subject to all'.

The word of the Lord to David via Nathan poses a question: 'Are you the one to build me a house?'. It is some time since David was subject to enquiry (3.24). In recent years, he has mostly done the asking (3.33, 3.38, 4.11, 5.19, 6.9). The question implies a negative answer. Contrary to the king's expectations and those of his prophet, God is not pleased with David's proposal. The Lord accepts that a house will indeed be built; but David will not be the one to build it.

There follows in verses 5-7 a theologically loaded review of Israel's history, and especially of Israel's pre-conquest history, in which the Lord asserts his divine freedom. The point is this: not only has the Lord not invited David to build him a house, he never asked any of Israel's tribal leaders who were commanded to shepherd the people of Israel (a nice allusion to David's own history) to build him a permanent home. Rather the Lord chose (and for the time being still chooses) to move about 'in a tent and a tabernacle'. He is the pilgrim God of a pilgrim people and his sovereign freedom is essential to his being: God is essentially and infinitely dynamic. Mobility befits him. He will not be tied down. While a house of cedar is a thing of beauty and delight to a human king, to God it implies a limitation. If God is to sponsor David, it will be on his own terms not David's. God can never be constrained by human constructions or categories: he can never be boxed or domesticated. God is by definition free. If God has never commanded any of David's predecessors to build him a house, why would he do so now?

In verse 8 there is a shift of focus: from the Lord's relationship with his pilgrim people to the Lord's relationship with David. This relationship is defined in the first sentence. The Lord states, 'I took you'. Again there is an allusion to David's shepherd origins (compare 5.2). The emphasis is not on anything David has done or will go on to do in future, but on what the Lord has done and now promises to do: he has taken David from being a shepherd and has made him a prince; he has accompanied David wherever he has been and has cut off all his enemies from before him; but more than that, he will now make of him a great name. The future will be as much gift – the work of grace – as the past. If, in seeking to build the Lord a house, David's aim has been to seek legitimation, there is no need. David's validation is in his election: the Lord has chosen him and has established him and will continue to bless him.

There is a further shift of focus in verse 10: from the Lord's relationship with David to the Lord's relationship with his people once again. The Lord promises that he will indeed provide a place for his chosen ones, where they will be settled and secure. The work that the Lord began when he appointed judges over his people, he will bring to completion. The tenses are odd here however: what the Lord promises he will do, the narrative suggests the Lord has already done. The Lord says that he will plant his people; but did this not happen at the conquest in the days of Joshua? The Lord promises to give his people rest from their enemies; but is not the whole premise of this episode precisely the fact that the Lord has now already done this (compare verse 1)?

Half way through verse 11, the focus promptly shifts once more from the people back onto David and remains there right through to verse 17. At heart, Nathan's prophecy is not about the people of Israel. Primarily it is about David in person. The key phrase is the pun in the middle of verse 11 when the Lord tells Nathan that it is not David who will build the Lord a house; on the contrary – the Lord will build David a house. David planned to build the Lord a temple; the Lord here promises to build David a dynasty.

At the heart of the prophecy, absolutely at the climax of Nathan's speech in verse 11, the Lord who has been speaking in the first person is suddenly spoken of in the third. But this happens, as any prophet can testify: especially at key moments it is easy to slip from one mode of discourse to another, and particularly to lapse out of 'role' into 'reality'. Ironically, while it might be supposed that generally a prophet gains credibility for a prophecy by speaking the words in the first person singular, following the formula 'Thus says the Lord' apparently in the voice of God himself, here Nathan gives this particular sentence due emphasis precisely by lapsing into third person. This is without doubt the sentence Nathan would most wish David to hear and take to heart.

At a stroke a new principle is established for the Israelite monarchy: the king will be succeeded by a son. But this does not necessarily imply the law of primogeniture. The promise is vague: it is not said that David's oldest son will succeed him; only that his successor 'shall come forth from [his] own body'. When a similarly vague promise was made to Abraham (in Genesis 15.4), it turned out to refer to his second-born, rather than his first-born son. As a general rule in the story of Israel to this point, the eldest son has seldom proved to be the chosen one. In the event, four sons will make a bid for David's throne; and the youngest of these will inherit it.

An even more startling theological development comes in verses 13-16. Three times over the Lord promises that David's throne (or his son's kingdom) will be established 'for ever'. The language of eternity is not entirely new. It is a natural to move from speaking of an eternal God, to speak of the work of God as lasting for ever. Earlier in the story Jonathan declared that the Lord would not just come between David and himself, but between David's descendants and his own 'for ever' (1 Samuel 20.42). And yet the language seems especially loaded from the mouth of God himself, and these verses have an essentially Messianic flavour to them as a result. Interestingly, David picks up on exactly this aspect of the promise in his response (in verses 25-29). He may not understand their full implication, but he does recognise that these words have particular significance. He also returns to this theme in his 'last words' recorded in 23.5: 'is not my house like this with God? For he has made with me an everlasting covenant, ordered in all things and secure'. In fact the word covenant is not used in this passage, although it is in other apparent references to this episode in David's story, in Psalms 89 (verses 3, 28 and 34) and 132 (verse 12). As Abigail had intuited in 1 Samuel 25.28, God will make David's house 'sure'.

It is not only the references to eternity which have made these verses such fertile territory for Christian theology, but also the emphasis on the divine gift. David's kingdom is secured not by his own effort or deserving, but by the unmerited favour of God. Here too Christians discern a foreshadowing of the pattern of salvation in the kingdom of Christ.

A third new principle is introduced in verse 14. The 'son' who will eventually inherit David's throne will not only be his son but God's – and God will be his father. As a result the son's iniquity will not prove fatal to the kingdom. If death will not bring this covenant to an end nor will sin. When (not 'if'!) he commits iniquity, there will be consequences of course: 'I will punish him with a rod'. But there will not be rejection: 'I will not take my steadfast love from him as I took it from Saul'. The Lord doesn't say so, but the succeeding chapters show that David too will enjoy this privilege. No explanation is offered for this distinction between Saul and his successor – this too is an expression of God's sovereign freedom. Grace and mystery are closely related theologically.

As a matter of historical fact of course the throne of David did not last for ever – but these verses preclude the most obvious theological explanation of the fact: namely that the Lord cut off the kingdom of David on account of the iniquity of its kings. This too has fuelled a Messianic reading of this passage among both Jews and Christians, by introducing a note of unfulfilled hope. If the promise of the Lord is 'for ever' but the throne of David has lapsed, what future fulfillment of it yet remains? It is hardly surprising that Christian readers have found seeds of the incarnation sown here.

Scene Two (verses 18-29): David acknowledges the greatness of God

18 Then King David went in and sat before the Lord, and said, 'Who am I, O Lord God, and what is my house, that you have brought me thus far? 19 And yet this was a small thing in your eyes, O Lord God; you have spoken also of your servant's house for a great while to come. May this be instruction for the people, O Lord God! 20 And what more can David say to you? For you know your servant, O Lord God! 21 Because of your promise, and according to your own heart, you have wrought all this greatness, so that your servant may know it. 22 Therefore you are great, O Lord God; for there is no one like you, and there is no God besides you, according to all that we have heard with our ears.

23 Who is like your people, like Israel? Is there another nation on earth whose God went to redeem it as a people, and to make a name for himself, doing great and awesome things for them, by driving out before his people nations and their gods? 24 And you established your people Israel for yourself to be your people for ever; and you, O Lord, became their God.

25 And now, O Lord God, as for the word that you have spoken concerning your servant and concerning his house, confirm it for ever; do as you have promised. 26 Thus your name will be magnified for ever in the saying, "The Lord of hosts is God over Israel"; and the house of your servant David will be established before you. 27 For you, O Lord of hosts, the God of Israel, have made this revelation to your servant, saying, "I will build you a house"; therefore your servant has found courage to pray this prayer to you. 28 And now, O Lord God, you are God, and your words are true, and you have promised this good thing to your servant; 29 now therefore may it please you to bless the house of your servant, so that it may continue for ever before you; for you, O Lord God, have spoken, and with your blessing shall the house of your servant be blessed for ever.'

David's response is to go in and sit before the Lord. Given that there is no temple at this point, the king is presumably to be pictured making his way to the tabernacle and sitting there before the ark. When it comes to hearing the word of the Lord, David needs a prophet as intermediary. When it comes to a response, he speaks to God directly.

It is a mark of David's capacity to receive correction in all humility, so characteristic of him in this story of his 'fall', that in his response to Nathan's prophecy he doesn't refer at all to his original intention to build a temple. He is able to let that plan go and to move on. When he now speaks of a house, it is in the sense in which God used the word. The idea of a building project has been driven from his mind by the dynasty God has promised to give him.

David's response develops in three stages. First in verses 18-22 ('Who am I?') he expresses his awe and wonder at what God has done for him, personally. Then in verses 23-24 ('Who is like your people?') he goes on to celebrate what God has done for his people Israel. Finally, in verses 25-29 ('And now, O Lord God'; repeated in verse 28 with a further 'now' in verse 29) he closes his prayer with a plea that God will indeed fulfil what he has promised. It is a common experience of those who pray to find that praise precedes petition.

The whole prayer is an outpouring of humble gratitude and praise. The first and last sections are linked by the repetition of three features. First, picking on the title repeatedly assigned to him in verses 4-17, David speaks of himself as 'your servant' three times in the opening section and seven in the last. Second, he uses the invocation 'O Lord God' five times in the opening section and three in the last. Third, in each section he refers to himself by name (verses 20, 26). None of these features occurs in the middle section.

The prayer is at its most personal in the opening section. The Lord had reminded David through Nathan of all that he had done for him, and had spoken of further blessings still to come. Here David acknowledges both. All the benefits he has already experienced are 'a small thing' in comparison with what has been promised. David begins by pondering his own nature and identity, but ends this section pondering the nature and identity of God: 'therefore you are great, O Lord God'. The final verse (22) contains what is for this part of the Hebrew Scriptures an unusually explicit statement of monotheism: 'there is no God besides you' (though compare 1 Samuel 2.2). David, the man 'after God's own heart' (see 1 Samuel 13.14; compare Acts 13.22) acknowledges that what God has done, God has done 'according to [his] own heart' (verse 21).

The prayer also includes a textual difficulty. Translators are baffled by verse 19. A literal translation would be 'this is the torah of Adam'. But it is hard to see what David's words have to do with either the law of God or Adam. The NRSV opts for 'this is instruction for the people': that is, perhaps, 'may the way you have treated me be recognised as typical of your grace and goodness'. An alternative (though it perhaps amounts to much the same thing) might be, 'this is the destiny of the human race' (namely, to be called into relationship by God and to be the recipient of his promise and blessing).

In the central section of his prayer, David's focus moves from wonder at God's dealings with him personally to wonder at God's dealings with his people Israel. He acknowledges in verse 23 the story of redemption reviewed in verses 6-11. Where God spoke four times in those verses of 'my people Israel', David here speaks twice of 'your people [Israel]'. This central section is significant for the way in which two key phrases picked up from Nathan's prophecy (where they refer narrowly to either David himself or to his house) are applied to Israel. For example, in Nathan's prophecy the Lord promises that he will establish the kingdom of David's offspring (verses 12, 13 and 16). Sure enough, in the final section of his prayer David echoes this terminology precisely: in verse 26 he looks forward to the fact that God will establish 'the house of your servant'. But in this central section in verse 24, he uses the same terminology differently, declaring that God has already established Israel as his people. Similarly, in Nathan's prophecy the phrase 'for ever' is used specifically in reference to God's purpose for David's house. Sure enough, in the final section of his prayer David again echoes this terminology precisely: first in verse 25 and then twice in verse 29, he prays that God will indeed bless his house 'for ever'. But in this central section, in verse 24, he declares that Israel will be the Lord's own people 'for ever'. There is something exceptionally attractive about David's prayer at this point: he might easily have become entirely absorbed in pondering the personal benefits of the promises made to him in Nathan's prophecy. But here he shows a breadth of perspective which ought to be characteristic of the Christian community, and of Christian leaders in particular. He understands that the promises made to him are not intended for his own benefit, but for the benefit of the people he serves. He holds the office of king, and his dynasty will do so, not for his own gain but for the sake of all Israel.

The climactic nature of the final section is emphasised by the repetition of the grand title, 'O Lord of Hosts' in verses 26 and 27. Having poured out his heart in praise and adoration in the first two parts of his prayer, David makes a bold petition in the closing section. He means to hold God to his promise: 'As for the word you have spoken, confirm it... do as you have promised' (verse 25). His boldness is not based on himself or his own merits, however. His courage to pray is based only on the revelation he has been granted (verse 27). His confidence that his house will be blessed is based only on the promise of God.

Conclusion

Towards the end of the previous episode, David was the one doing the blessing. He blessed his people (6.18) and he blessed his household (6.20). It reflects the crucial transformation which takes place in the course of this episode that in its climactic final verse David is the one seeking the blessing of God: 'bless the house of your servant... with your blessing shall the house of your servant be blessed for ever'.

Nathan's prophecy turns David's experience on its head. In the opening few verses of the chapter, he is very much the subject. He has a plan. He proposes to act. He intends to build a house for God. David is the subject and the temple of God is his object. But by definition God himself is never an object. He is always and everywhere the Eternal and Infinite Subject. He is the Great Builder. Nathan's speech is effectively a list of verbs of which God, not David, is subject. David is thus renewed in his sense of being the object – but the object of God's good plan and purpose, of God's loving kindness and grace.

But once this principle is established – the universal and essential priority of God – then the initiative of David is in fact accepted. At the heart of Nathan's prophecy is a concession. A temple for God there will be (verse 13); only David's offspring, not David himself, will build it. Why? Because created things associated with God (arks and temples, sacraments and Scriptures) can never be safely reduced to mere objects by the people who handle them. In his goodness and grace, God is ready to grant what David desires: that there should be a permanent symbol of God's presence in Jerusalem. But for this symbol to be effective, it must bear the mark of God's fundamental freedom and power.

Chapter Four

2 Samuel 8.1–18

David and his Enemies

Introduction

This episode strikes a jarring note. The transition from the lofty
theological vision of the previous chapter to the brutal political realities
of the present one is abrupt. The high rhetoric of Nathan's prophecy
(and indeed of David's response) seems a long way from the military
pragmatism of this episode. In addition, the actions attributed to David
seem at odds, somehow, with the promises of steadfast love so recently
received from God.

This chapter falls into three parts. The first fourteen verses (two
scenes) are concerned with a territorial expansion of David's kingdom.
The following four verses (the third and final scene) are concerned with
a corresponding administrative expansion. In the first two scenes, the
Hebrew word *nakah* (to smite or strike down) is prominent. It is used
seven times in the opening fourteen verses (in verses 1, 2, 3, 5, 9, 10,
13), and creates a dynamic, if violent (even cruel), impression of the
king. Until this point, David has generally led the armies of Israel into
defensive battles (compare 5.17, 22). Now he attacks. Moreover, he
attacks not just the Philistines in the southwest, but also the Edomites
to the south, the Moabites to the southeast, the Ammonites to the east,
the Arameans and the Zobahites to the northeast. What jars in the first
two scenes is not so much the fact that David consistently inflicts defeat
on his enemies, as the fact that he occasionally inflicts humiliation on
them too. In the final scene, the portrait of David is more positive
– what jars there is the fact that in his emerging administration he
appoints his own sons to be priests.

But Scripture generally depicts its heroes warts and all. Human
frailty is allowed to underline the grace of God.

The present chapter thus further heightens a growing tension. On the
one hand, it is clear that the Lord still identifies utterly with David and
with his success. It is the Lord who gave David victory 'wherever he

went' (verses 6, 14). On the other hand, the outcome of these victories is emphatically not what David himself had anticipated in the previous episode: that is, 'that [the name of the Lord] will be magnified for ever' (7.26). Nor is the outcome a straightforward fulfillment of what the Lord had promised: that he would make for David 'a great name, like the name of the great ones of the earth' (7.9). There is presumably a pejorative implication when instead the text states in 8.13 that David won a name *for himself.*

Scene One (verses 1-8): The Lord gives victory to David wherever he goes

Three vignettes make up this scene: David is victorious against the Philistines, the Moabites and King Hadadezer. Increasing attention is given to each in turn.

Some time afterwards, David attacked the Philistines and subdued them; David took Metheg-ammah out of the hand of the Philistines.

2 He also defeated the Moabites and, making them lie down on the ground, measured them off with a cord; he measured two lengths of cord for those who were to be put to death, and one length for those who were to be spared. And the Moabites became servants to David and brought tribute.

3 David also struck down King Hadadezer son of Rehob of Zobah, as he went to restore his monument at the river Euphrates. 4 David took from him one thousand seven hundred horsemen, and twenty thousand foot-soldiers. David hamstrung all the chariot horses, but left enough for a hundred chariots. 5 When the Arameans of Damascus came to help King Hadadezer of Zobah, David killed twenty-two thousand men of the Arameans. 6 Then David put garrisons among the Arameans of Damascus; and the Arameans became servants to David and brought tribute. The Lord gave victory to David wherever he went. 7 David took the gold shields that were carried by the servants of Hadadezer, and brought them to Jerusalem. 8 From Betah and from Berothai, towns of Hadadezer, King David took a great amount of bronze.

This is not the very first time that David has taken the initiative in launching an attack against the Philistines. He had done so as early as 1 Samuel 19.8. However, as a general rule, before David became king it was the Philistines who were on the attack and David who took up arms to defend Israel (compare 1 Samuel 17.1, 18.30, 23.1; also 1 Samuel 28.1, 31.1). Immediately after he became king, the situation was unchanged: when David defeated the Philistines, it was because they attacked him and not vice versa (5.17). Those days however are gone. The Philistines will never pick a fight with David again. Now it is David who attacks them and seizes their territory. Apart from some summary reports of incidents featuring Israelite warriors performing deeds of heroism in 2 Samuel 23, this is the very last report in David's story of conflict between Israel and the Philistines, who are now effectively eliminated as a threat.

But as soon as the Philistines are fully and finally subdued it emerges that there are other foes to fight. Previously David has only led his people into battle against the Philistines (his raid against the Amalekites in 1 Samuel 30 was hardly a national conflict involving the armies of all Israel). Now he leads them into battle on all fronts.

It is something of a surprise to find David fighting the Moabites. Earlier in the narrative Moab was a place of refuge to which David turned (in 1 Samuel 22.3) when he entrusted his parents to its king. According to one biblical tradition David's own line was traced from here via Ruth (Ruth 4.17). Evidently times have changed.

Exactly what is meant in verse 2 is unclear. The text seems to suggest that David made his prisoners of war lie on the ground, before consigning some to death and sparing others, using a length of cord to effect his judgment. Were two Moabites killed for every one who was spared? It is an unappealing image of the king – apparently dispensing life and death in public, and in arbitrary fashion.

It is just about possible to read this as an exercise in mercy. Some act of betrayal now lost to us may have turned Moab from an ally into a legitimate enemy. If so, as the conquering king David might have been expected simply to slaughter every prisoner. Perhaps it was in acknowledgement of past favours that David chose to liberate one Moabite in three. But there is at least a hint of subjugation into forced labour when it is said that the Moabites 'became servants to David'.

Thirdly David attacks an enemy to the north: 'King Hadadezer son of Rehob of Zobah, as he went to restore his monument' (verse 3; on which compare the action of Saul in 1 Samuel 15.12, and of Absalom in 2 Samuel 18.18). Capturing horsemen presents David with a dilemma for Israel made no military use of cavalry at this time. From a martial point of view David has no use for horses. So he follows the example of Joshua (Joshua 11.6, 9: perhaps David also understood himself to be engaged in holy war?). Chariots were a feature not of Israel's army, but of the armies of the Egyptians (Exodus 14.7-29) and later of the Philistines (2 Samuel 1.6). It may be a mark of their notoriety that in both cases, David's sons made use of chariots in the lead up to their rebellions (Absalom in 2 Samuel 15.1, and Adonijah in 1 Kings 1.5). It may have been these very horses of which they subsequently made use.

In the closing verses of this scene two further points are made. The first is that these military victories brought David not only political but also economic benefits. Especially in his victories over Hadadezer and the Arameans, David acquired great tribute: treasures of gold and bronze. Perhaps more importantly the point is made that these victories were not David's own: it was the Lord who gave him victory wherever he went (verse 6b).

Scene Two (verses 9-14): The Lord again gives victory to David wherever he goes

9 When King Toi of Hamath heard that David had defeated the whole army of Hadadezer, 10 Toi sent his son Joram to King David, to greet him and to congratulate him because he had fought against Hadadezer and defeated him. Now Hadadezer had often been at war with Toi. Joram brought with him articles of silver, gold, and bronze; 11 these also King David dedicated to the Lord, together with the silver and gold that he dedicated from all the nations he subdued, 12 from Edom, Moab, the Ammonites, the Philistines, Amalek, and from the spoil of King Hadadezer son of Rehob of Zobah.

13 David won a name for himself. When he returned, he killed eighteen thousand Edomites in the Valley of Salt. 14 He put garrisons in Edom; throughout all Edom he put garrisons, and all the Edomites became David's servants. And the Lord gave victory to David wherever he went.

The second scene (comprising two vignettes) reiterates and develops the first, most obviously in the second vignette, where a further military victory is recorded against the Edomites, and above all in the phrase 'the Lord gave victory to David wherever he went'. But in verses 5-6 and 13-14, the reiteration extends beyond this phrase. In both cases an exact number is given of enemies killed by David – the only two such cases in this episode. Furthermore in both cases the text goes on to state first that David 'put garrisons' in the territory of his opponents and then that they 'became servants to David'.

But there is development in this scene as well as repetition, particularly in the first vignette. This is the only incident in these first two scenes which is not a military encounter. No neighbouring king seeks an alliance with David in the first scene as king Toi of Hamath does in verse 10, when he sends his son Joram 'to greet [David] and to congratulate him' on the defeat of Toi's longstanding foe Hadadezer. It is not just territory and spoil (as in verses 1 and 7-8) that David is acquiring through these victories or even just spoil (as in verses 7-8): he is acquiring allies or even vassals.

The effect of this second scene, both in its reiteration and in its development, is to bring David's military victories more closely into relation with the Lord. Thus when Joram (whose name may reflect Hamath's vassal status: it appears to be a Hebraised name meaning 'the Lord is exalted') brings with him 'articles of silver, gold and bronze', the text is careful to state that David dedicated these to the Lord, 'together with the silver and gold that he dedicated from all the other nations that he subdued'. In the first scene, it had only been stated that the spoil had been taken 'to Jerusalem' (verse 7). Presumably the spoil is being collected there in readiness for the day when David's offspring will build a house for the Lord.

A list of 'all the nations [David] subdued' then follows in verse 12. Significantly, it replicates (in almost the same order) the list of nations over which it is recorded that Saul was victorious in 1 Samuel 14.47-48: Moab, Ammon, Edom, Zobah, Philistia and Amalek. But Saul's victories are not brought into relation with the Lord. Of Saul it is simply stated that 'he fought against his enemies on every side... wherever he turned he routed them'. With David it is different. His victories are not attributed to his own valour. Rather, 'the Lord gave him victory wherever he went'.

Scene Three (verses 15-18): David administers justice and equity

15 So David reigned over all Israel; and David administered justice and equity to all his people. 16 Joab son of Zeruiah was over the army; Jehoshaphat son of Ahilud was recorder;

> *17 Zadok son of Ahitub and Ahimelech son of Abiathar were priests; Seraiah was secretary; 18 Benaiah son of Jehoiada was over the Cherethites and the Pelethites; and David's sons were priests.*

Scene three comprises a further summary – not of nations David conquered beyond the borders of Israel, but of officers he appointed within them.

These verses mark the moment when David's power was at its height. The earlier two scenes demonstrate that in terms of foreign policy, everything is peace and security. The reader now discovers that in terms of domestic policy everything is 'justice and equity'. What more could any ruler be expected to deliver for his people? It is precisely to dispense 'justice and equity' that the prophets repeatedly call kings in Israel (*mishpat* and *tzedakah:* see for example Isaiah 9.7; Jeremiah 22.15; Amos 5.7; Psalms 72.2, 99.4; Proverbs 1.3, 2.9).

David cannot rule his kingdom single-handed however. He delegates. There are apparently three 'portfolios' or cabinet departments. Over the army he has appointed Joab, leader of the sons of Zeruiah (on whom see 2.13 and following chapters). Over the civil service is Jehoshaphat, son of Ahilud (to whom there is reference only here and in the closely parallel passage in 20.23-26). And over the priesthood he has appointed Zadok son of Ahitub (2 Samuel 15.24-29, 1 Kings 1.32-48, 2.35; compare also 1 Samuel 14.3 for the priest Ahitub) and Ahimelech son of Abiathar (but the reference in 15.24-29 suggests that this is in fact Abiathar son of Ahimelech, on whom see also 1 Samuel 22.20 and his ultimate betrayal of David's cause in 1 Kings 1.7, 2.26-27. If Abiathar is son of Ahimelech, then – as Ahimelech is son of Ahitub, 1 Samuel 22.9 – it is likely that Zadok and Abiathar are uncle and nephew).

Assisting Joab is Benaiah, son of Jehoiada, who has particular responsibility for the Cherethites and the Pelethites. Benaiah is not an insignificant figure in this narrative. His valour is celebrated in 23.20-23, and he will eventually be both Joab's undoing and his successor (1 Kings 2.28-35). The Cherethites and Pelethites are almost always referred to in tandem (see, for example, 15.18, 20.7; 1 Kings 1.38, 44; but the Cherethites are singled out in 1 Sam 30.14). The two tribes are believed to have been Cretan in origin. Perhaps David, following the example of King Achish of Gath in his use of David himself (1 Samuel 28.2), is employing a foreign legion as his own personal body guard.

In the light of verses 17 and 18, the force of verse 16 may be that David did not delegate his judicial responsibility, but like Samuel before him ruled over Israel as judge (see 1 Samuel 7.15).

Conclusion

This is the high point of David's reign. He is powerful and wealthy, and yet is doing what a king is called to do; he governs not just over the people but for the people. He is king not just 'of Israel' or 'over Israel' but for Israel. Act One ends on an apparently triumphant high.

And yet. The discordant notes in this chapter, like those in earlier episodes, pose a question to the reader: is the expansion of David's kingdom his own achievement or the gift of God? Does it redound to the glory of God, or does it merely enhance David's own reputation? Is his success a blessing or a curse? As so often in human experience, there is a significant ambiguity here.

ACT TWO

The Rule of David Threatened

2 Samuel 9.1–20.26

Chapter Five
2 Samuel 9.1–13

David and Mephibosheth

Introduction

After the oracular character of 2 Samuel 7 and the summary character of 2 Samuel 8, the narrative proper resumes in this episode. These verses contain one of the few chronological clues in the story. In 4.4 (shortly before David became king over all Israel), Mephibosheth (Jonathan's son) was 5 years old. In this episode, he is an adult with (verse 12 reports) a young son of his own. An interval of at least a decade is implied, or more likely 15 or 20 years.

Traditionally, this chapter has been regarded at the start of a 'story within the story' occupying 2 Samuel 9-20 that is usually called 'the succession narrative'. In this exposition it marks the start of 'Act Two', in which the king's relationship is clarified in regard to both his predecessor (or the members of Saul's house) and his successor (or the members of his own house). In turn both of David's two oldest sons (Amnon and Absalom) assert themselves. Both die as a result. (In 1 Kings 1 their next oldest sibling, Adonijah, will similarly attempt a coup and fail.) An important characteristic of 'the succession narrative' is the absence of God. That is to say, God speaks less often in these chapters than elsewhere in the narrative and acts less directly – as if to imply that his blessing is withheld in all these intrigues. None of these pretenders is the one spoken of by Nathan in chapter 7 as chosen by God to succeed David.

A key word in this episode is one of the great words of the Hebrew Scriptures: *hesed*. It is such a significant word in the Bible that English translators struggle to do it justice. It means something like 'love'. But it is a word that implies covenant loyalty, and is sometimes translated as 'steadfast love' or 'loving kindness'. It is one of the words most often used to describe not just God's dealings with Israel, but his very nature as it is revealed to humankind. When, for example, God declares his name to Moses in Exodus 34.6, this word is used: 'The Lord, the Lord, a God merciful and gracious, slow to anger and abounding in [*hesed*] steadfast love and faithfulness'. Thus, for a person to show *hesed* is to show a God-like loving kindness.

The word *hesed* occurs three times (in verses 1, 3 and 7) in this episode. Each time it is spoken by David, who wishes to keep the covenant promise he made to Jonathan (see 1 Samuel 20.14-16) by showing loving kindness to the house of Saul. Indeed, in verse 3, David calls it 'the kindness of God'. The picture of David could hardly be more positive: he has power, but is using it kindly. In practising *hesed*, he is exercising kingship in a way that honours and reflects the kingship of God. If only such kindness always epitomised Christian leadership.

The episode has a neat literary structure. It divides into three symmetrical scenes, in each of which there is a dialogue between two characters: the first scene (verses 1 to 4) features king David and a servant of king Saul called Ziba; the second (verses 5 to 8) features king David and Mephibosheth; and the third (verses 9 to 13) again features David and Ziba. Scholars have detected an overarching 'chiastic' (symmetrical) structure to the episode, pivoting around the climactic verse 7. Either side of the central moment, when David promises to show kindness to Mephibosheth for Jonathan's sake, Mephibosheth bows down (verses 6 and 8). Either side of that act of obeisance come David's two conversations with Ziba (verses 2-5 and 9-11). Either side of those dialogues come the introduction and conclusion to the story: it opens with the announcement of David's intention to fulfil his promise to Jonathan and closes with the announcement that the promise is duly fulfilled.

Scene One (verses 1-4): David speaks to Ziba about Mephibosheth

> *David asked, 'Is there still anyone left of the house of Saul to whom I may show kindness for Jonathan's sake?' 2 Now there was a servant of the house of Saul whose name was Ziba, and he was summoned to David. The king said to him, 'Are you Ziba?' And he said, 'At your service!' 3 The king said, 'Is there anyone remaining of the house of Saul to whom I may show the kindness of God?' Ziba said to the king, 'There remains a son of Jonathan; he is crippled in his feet.' 4 The king said to him, 'Where is he?' Ziba said to the king, 'He is in the house of Machir son of Ammiel, at Lo-debar.'*

Perhaps the recent promise David has received from God (7.28) about his own house reminds him of the promise he himself had made about the house of his friend Jonathan, which he now determines to fulfil.

But is there anyone still left of the house of Saul? The question makes especially good sense if, as most scholars suppose, the story recorded in 2 Samuel 21 (where David gives up to their death at the hands of the Gibeonites seven 'sons of Saul') took place before this current episode (though compare 21.7). That episode is part of a series in 2 Samuel 21-24 which constitute something of an appendix to David's story and is clearly out of chronological sequence, so the suggestion has merit. At any rate there is sufficient doubt about the answer to David's question for it to be necessary to summon someone qualified to give a definitive answer. Three of Saul's sons died with him on the battlefield (1 Samuel 31.6), and Ishbosheth subsequently also died a violent death (4.7). It may well be that other members of the household suffered a similarly bloody fate during the period of civil war.

So a former servant of Saul is summoned. His response ('There remains a son of Jonathan') really does create the impression that Mephibosheth is the last surviving member of the household. Moreover, it is stressed that Mephibosheth is severely disabled. Perhaps Ziba was unsure whether he could take David's words about showing kindness to Saul's house at face value (any more than, centuries later, the Magi could trust Herod's words about wanting to worship the new-born king of the Jews). It may be that he stressed Mephibosheth's disability in order to impress on David that (if he were contemplating an execution for example) Jonathan's son posed no threat.

In fact in this first scene Mephibosheth is not named. He is just 'a son of Jonathan'. The one name we are given is of the man who has been sheltering Mephibosheth: Machir son of Ammiel. This man will one day show loyalty and hospitality to David too (see 17.27).

Scene Two (verses 5-8): David speaks to Mephibosheth

5 Then King David sent and brought him from the house of Machir son of Ammiel, at Lo-debar. 6 Mephibosheth son of Jonathan son of Saul came to David, and fell on his face and did obeisance. David said, 'Mephibosheth!' He answered, 'I am your servant.' 7 David said to him, 'Do not be afraid, for I will show you kindness for the sake of your father Jonathan; I will restore to you all the land of your grandfather Saul,

> *and you yourself shall eat at my table always.' 8 He did*
> *obeisance and said, 'What is your servant, that you should*
> *look upon a dead dog such as I am?'*

Machir, son of Ammiel, at Lo-debar is solemnly mentioned again. But then for the first time in this episode Mephibosheth is called by name: Mephibosheth son of Jonathan son of Saul. The naming coincides with his arrival before David and announces his presence. At once he fell on his face and did obeisance. This kind of prostration (and, one imagines, still more the act of getting back on one's feet again) is difficult for someone 'crippled in his feet'.

David greets Mephibosheth by name and seeks to reassure him. Mephibosheth's is not an auspicious name. It means 'from the mouth of shame' and is almost certainly a religiously motivated change from an original 'Meribbaal' (compare 1 Chronicles 9.40). Perhaps Mephibosheth grew up stigmatised not only by his disability, but also by a shameful name? But there is nothing derogatory in David's invocation. David then continues, 'Do not be afraid'. It is easy to imagine how fearful Mephibosheth might be, suddenly and unexpectedly summoned from the security of his life in Lo-debar into the king's presence in Jerusalem, especially if among Saul's servants David has a reputation as a killer (compare 16.5-8). But David's intentions are sincere: for the sake of Jonathan, he truly will show Mephibosheth kindness. He will even take the politically risky step of restoring to him Saul's lands, as well as providing a place for Mephibosheth at his own table.

Again Mephibosheth bows down. He only speaks twice in this episode, but both times he calls himself David's servant. When he refers to himself as 'a dead dog', one wonders if David remembered using the same phrase about himself, while he was on the run from Saul (1 Samuel 24.14).

Scene Three (verses 9-13): David again speaks to Ziba about Mephibosheth

> *9 Then the king summoned Saul's servant Ziba, and said to*
> *him, 'All that belonged to Saul and to all his house I have*
> *given to your master's grandson. 10 You and your sons and*
> *your servants shall till the land for him, and shall bring*
> *in the produce, so that your master's grandson may have*
> *food to eat; but your master's grandson Mephibosheth shall*

always eat at my table.' Now Ziba had fifteen sons and twenty servants. 11 Then Ziba said to the king, 'According to all that my lord the king commands his servant, so your servant will do.' Mephibosheth ate at David's table, like one of the king's sons. 12 Mephibosheth had a young son whose name was Mica. And all who lived in Ziba's house became Mephibosheth's servants. 13 Mephibosheth lived in Jerusalem, for he always ate at the king's table. Now he was lame in both his feet.

David at once effects what he has just told Mephibosheth he will do. It is not clear what the impact of this change was on Ziba. The sequels in 16.1-4 and 19.24-30 may suggest that this intervention by David was unwelcome to him. Perhaps he had assumed control of Saul's lands for himself. He describe himself as David's servant in verse 11, but verse 10 makes it clear that he is a man of substantial wealth with a large household including servants of his own. There is surely a loss of face for Ziba (and the sowing of the seeds of future trouble) when it says 'all who lived in Ziba's house became Mephibosheth's servants'.

Two repetitions at the end of the chapter are striking. One is the reference to the king's table. As early as verse 7 David had told Mephibosheth 'you shall always eat at my table'. Then in verse 10, he tells Ziba 'Mephibosheth shall always eat at my table'. The narrator then reports in verse 11 that Mephibosheth ate at David's table 'like one of the king's sons'. So it seems like a labouring of the point when the narrator again states in the final verse of the episode that Mephibosheth 'always ate at the king's table'. It has sometimes been suggested that the repetition is a cryptic way of saying that Mephibosheth was effectively put under house arrest by David – that David's motive in bringing this last representative of Saul's house to Jerusalem and into his palace was political, not personal: he wanted Mephibosheth (and indeed his son Mica) where he could see him. But while it may be true that Mephibosheth had little choice but to comply with David's proposal, there is no evidence that David was anxious about a threat from Saul's house in general, let alone from Mephibosheth in particular. Moreover David would later find in the case of his son Absalom that bringing a potential rival into Jerusalem was likely to increase rather than reduce the risk of rebellion.

In any case the second repetition in the very last few words of the closing verse seriously undermines the view that David was acting punitively towards Mephibosheth rather than generously: 'Now he was lame in both his feet'. These are odd words with which to conclude, unless they are intended to emphasise how little threat Mephibosheth was to David. After all, the essential information about Mephibosheth's disability was included when he was introduced at the start of this episode in verse 3, as well as earlier in the narrative in 4.4. In the light of this stress on Mephibosheth's lameness (and so harmlessness), it makes better sense to understand the repetition of his place at David's table simply as an underlining of the fact that David had truly fulfilled his promise to show kindness to Jonathan's house.

Conclusion

Of all the episodes in the story of David after he becomes king, this is perhaps the one in which he comes over best. It is always a good sign in a leader when he is able to exercise power with kindness and with consideration for the vulnerable. Similarly, it is always a good sign in a leader when promises are kept. This is the nature of *hesed*. These two things (the exercise of power with kindness, and the keeping of promises) are key indicators of Christian leadership wherever it is exercised today.

Chapter Six
2 Samuel 10.1–19

David and the Arameans

Introduction

The focus of attention in these opening episodes of the story has basically alternated between 'home affairs' and 'foreign affairs': David was fighting foreign armies in chapter 5, but not in chapters 6 or 7; he was fighting again in chapter 8, but not in chapter 9; now for the last time before the narrative turns decisively onto domestic issues, David is engaged in battle once more.

This episode is linked to the previous one by the recurrence of the word *hesed*. It is not only in relation to domestic policy that David intends to act with loyalty and loving kindness. He approaches foreign policy in the same spirit. Where a nation has proved faithful to him, his instinct is to respond in kind. Just as in the previous episode David showed *hesed* to Mephibosheth, so he now extends *hesed* to Hanun, son of Nahash, king of the Ammonites – in acknowledgement of the loyalty Nahash himself had shown David.

This episode unfolds in three scenes. In the first, David's intention to honour Hanun is thwarted by the latter's misjudgment; in the second, Joab leads Israel into battle against the Ammonites and their allies; in the final scene, David routs the Arameans who had come to the aid of the Ammonites.

The middle scene gives the reader pause for thought, however. David is absent from it. This might be an example of good and appropriate delegation: he had after all entrusted the leadership of the army to Joab in 8.16. But in retrospect it seems sinister that it is only in this scene, from which David is entirely absent, that there is reference to the Lord.

Scene One (verses 1-5): The king of the Ammonites spurns David's kindness

> *Some time afterwards the king of the Ammonites died, and his son Hanun succeeded him. 2 David said, 'I will deal loyally*

with Hanun son of Nahash, just as his father dealt loyally with me.' So David sent envoys to console him concerning his father. When David's envoys came into the land of the Ammonites, 3 the princes of the Ammonites said to their lord Hanun, 'Do you really think that David is honouring your father just because he has sent messengers with condolences to you? Has not David sent his envoys to you to search the city, to spy it out, and to overthrow it?' 4 So Hanun seized David's envoys, shaved off half the beard of each, cut off their garments in the middle at their hips, and sent them away. 5 When David was told, he sent to meet them, for the men were greatly ashamed. The king said, 'Remain at Jericho until your beards have grown, and then return.'

The chronology ('some time afterwards') is once again vague. But this episode is only credible at an early point in David's kingship, when his full stature is not yet clear. Later the new king of the Ammonites would surely have known better than to incur David's wrath.

King Nahash of the Ammonites is dead. He and David had been allies. No trace of this survives in the narrative. The only previous reference to Nahash comes in 1 Samuel 11, where he is defeated in battle by Saul. Perhaps Nahash and David became partners while David was fleeing from Saul. At any rate, to honour the relationship he and Nahash had enjoyed, David sends envoys to extend his good wishes to Hanun, Nahash's son.

But kings are not always well advised (compare 1 Kings 12.6-11). The princes of the Ammonites persuade Hanun that David is not acting in good faith at all, but is spying out the land with a view to invading it. Presumably in line with their advice, Hanun treats the envoys badly: he humiliates them by shaving off half their beards and cutting off half their cloaks and sending them away. To this day it is a shaming thing in Middle Eastern cultures for a man to be unable to grow a beard, or to be clean shaven. It speaks well of David's pastoral care (compare 1 Samuel 30.23-24) that he offers the envoys a period of seclusion in Jericho in which to allow their beards to grow back. Jericho would be an appropriate stopping place for an envoy returning to Jerusalem from Ammon.

Scene Two (verses 6-14): Joab leads Israel into battle against the Ammonites and the Arameans

6 When the Ammonites saw that they had become odious to David, the Ammonites sent and hired the Arameans of Beth-rehob and the Arameans of Zobah, twenty thousand foot-

*soldiers, as well as the king of Maacah, one thousand men,
and the men of Tob, twelve thousand men. 7 When David
heard of it, he sent Joab and all the army with the warriors.
8 The Ammonites came out and drew up in battle array at
the entrance of the gate; but the Arameans of Zobah and of
Rehob, and the men of Tob and Maacah, were by themselves
in the open country.*

*9 When Joab saw that the battle was set against him both
in front and in the rear, he chose some of the picked men
of Israel, and arrayed them against the Arameans; 10 the
rest of his men he put in charge of his brother Abishai, and
he arrayed them against the Ammonites. 11 He said, 'If the
Arameans are too strong for me, then you shall help me; but
if the Ammonites are too strong for you, then I will come
and help you. 12 Be strong, and let us be courageous for
the sake of our people, and for the cities of our God; and
may the Lord do what seems good to him.' 13 So Joab and
the people who were with him moved forward into battle
against the Arameans; and they fled before him. 14 When
the Ammonites saw that the Arameans fled, they likewise fled
before Abishai, and entered the city. Then Joab returned from
fighting against the Ammonites, and came to Jerusalem.*

Meanwhile, as the envoys wait in Jericho, it dawns on the Ammonites
that they can expect a hostile response from David. So they galvanise
support among others of David's natural enemies, including some of
those (the Arameans of Zobah) recently defeated by David (compare
8.3-8), but also the men of Tob and Maacah. Thirty-three thousand
mercenaries are recruited for the inevitable forthcoming battle.

David is no longer always leading his troops into battle himself.
More and more he delegates that responsibility to Joab and his brother.
Abishai was another of David's trusty warriors (compare for example
1 Samuel 26.6-9, 2 Samuel 2.18-28). On the battlefield, finding himself
under attack on two fronts, Joab divides his forces. One part, under his
own command, is to confront the Arameans in the open country. The
rest are to attack the Ammonites who have drawn up at the entrance to
the gate of their city (Rabbah in Ammon, on which see 11.1, is modern
day Amman in Jordan). This is, then, a rare scene: one in which David
himself is not centre stage.

On the eve of battle, Joab speaks to his brother. This is the only
moment in the entire David story when Joab is cast as a faithful

servant of the Lord. His words are reminiscent of those of the Lord to Joshua, on the eve of the conquest of the Promised Land (Joshua 1.2-9). He exhorts Abishai to be strong and courageous and to trust in the providence of God. It is important to do the right thing for the sake of 'our people' (the people of God) and of 'the cities of our God'. But Joab acknowledges that there are no guarantees as to the outcome of the enterprise: 'may the Lord do what seems good to him'.

The contemporary church generally demands much more than this. Christian leaders are expected to succeed. But there is no such presumption in Scripture and the history of the church testifies that often it is faithfulness in adversity, rather than success, which is the hallmark of true leadership among the people of God. It is necessary to do the right thing, and to keep on doing the right thing, even when there is no immediate victory, trusting in the good will and purpose of God. It is necessary to do so in the assurance that this in itself is pleasing to God (as well as in the greater assurance that the kingdom belongs to God) but without any explicit assurance that our own work will be fruitful or successful.

When Joab says, 'May the Lord do what seems good to him', this is not an expression of fatalism but of trust. He does not mean 'It's in the lap of the gods' – as if the outcome were a matter of chance. He means that he understands the outcome to be utterly in the hands of a particular God, whose nature he knows and whose faithfulness and loving kindness he relies upon. To the will of this God, he is prepared to commit himself, knowing full well that this will may not – in the short-term – coincide with his own. Ultimately, since what he seeks is the kingdom and glory of this God, he is able to affirm that all will be well. But he understands and accepts that the route to this destination may from his personal point of view be harsh and difficult. It is a noble and neglected tradition not to assume that God's glory and one's own coincide.

On this occasion, however, Joab need not have worried. The Arameans in the open country flee before him and the Ammonites, seeing what has happened to their allies, at once retreat before Abishai into their city. At this point Joab returns to Jerusalem.

Scene Three (verses 15-19): David leads Israel into battle against the Arameans

*15 But when the Arameans saw that they had been defeated
by Israel, they gathered themselves together. 16 Hadadezer*

sent and brought out the Arameans who were beyond the Euphrates; and they came to Helam, with Shobach the commander of the army of Hadadezer at their head. 17 When it was told to David, he gathered all Israel together, and crossed the Jordan, and came to Helam. The Arameans arrayed themselves against David and fought with him. 18 The Arameans fled before Israel; and David killed of the Arameans seven hundred chariot teams and forty thousand horsemen, and wounded Shobach the commander of their army, so that he died there. 19 When all the kings who were servants of Hadadezer saw that they had been defeated by Israel, they made peace with Israel, and became subject to them. So the Arameans were afraid to help the Ammonites any more.

The Ammonites were Israel's principal enemy in this conflict. It was they who had abused David's emissaries and caused such offence. Their withdrawal into the city is not the end of the matter. Hostilities will be resumed in due course. But the focus of the narrative shifts briefly off them and onto Israel's battle against the Arameans, whose retreat turns out to have been merely tactical.

King Hadadezer was not mentioned by name in verse 6, but is still apparently king of Zobah (see 8.3-12). He sends for reinforcements from beyond the Euphrates and the news of their coming prompts David to enter the fray himself. He mobilises all Israel and crosses the Jordan. Battle is joined at Helam. The outcome is decisive. Hadadezer's army is routed and the victory is attributed to Israel's king in person: 'David killed of the Arameans seven hundred chariot teams and forty thousand horsemen'. He wounded Hadadezer's general, Shobach, who died; and all the kings allied to Hadadezer became subject to David. There would be no further help for Ammon from that quarter.

Conclusion

The story of the rise of king David (1 Samuel 16.1 to 2 Samuel 5.10) ends with the climactic declaration that 'David became greater and greater because the Lord the God of Hosts was with him'. The opening chapters of the story of the fall of king David illustrate the point. He enjoys success at every turn. He brings the ark to Jerusalem. He is promised a dynasty. He finally defeats the Philistines and establishes his authority over other neighbouring kingdoms. He dispenses justice with equity. He is faithful to his promises and generous to Saul's house. He leads his armies into battle and achieves a heroic victory, as a result of which all the kings who had formerly been vassals of Hadadezer transfer their allegiance to David. The sun is shining and there is not a cloud in the sky. What could possibly go wrong? But his arrival back in Jerusalem was perhaps the last moment when it was possible for David to survey his kingdom, his family and indeed his own soul with contentment.

The more onerous a leader's responsibilities, the more necessary effective delegation becomes. The art of delegation is an important one for senior leaders to acquire. However, wise leaders recognise that there is a fine line between a constructive delegation of responsibility on the one hand, and a destructive dereliction of duty on the other. Somewhere between the end of this episode and the start of the next one, David crosses that line.

David and Bathsheba

Introduction

If the story of David and Goliath exemplifies the story of David's rise, then this is the equivalent episode in the story of his fall: the story of David and Bathsheba. The two stories are to some extent opposites: in the first, David refuses to be taken in by appearances; in the second, he is seduced by them. In the first, he resorts in the face of testing to God in prayer; in the second he conspicuously fails to do so.

The episode is a real turning point. Whenever the story of David's rise reached its climax (when he became king of all Israel, or received the prophecy of his dynasty; when he subdued the surrounding nations and established justice and equity in his own kingdom), that point is now behind him. In this episode, the decline of David's fortunes has undeniably begun. What had been a story of personal and political success becomes one of failure. A life which had been marked by blessing now seems cursed.

The episode is universally known as 'the story of David and Bathsheba'. It is arguably better entitled 'the story of David and Uriah'. It is told in five scenes: the introduction features David and Joab; the second begins the drama proper and features David and Bathsheba; the third and fourth (which occupy about three quarters of the length of the whole chapter) feature David and Uriah. It is thus David's dealings with Uriah rather than with Bathsheba which constitute the heart of the story. The act of David's adultery is told sparingly; the same is not true of his repeated attempts to deceive Uriah. The fifth, brief, scene again features David and Bathsheba ('the wife of Uriah') and concludes with one of the most damning indictments in all Scripture. The man after God's own heart displeased the Lord.

The whole episode is a case study in the abuse of power. One indication of this is the repetition of the word-group 'send-sent-sending' (*shalach* in Hebrew). The word occurs twelve times in this episode (in verses 1, 3, 4, 5, 6 [three times], 12, 14, 18, 22 and 27), at least once in each of the five scenes. Only a person of power can send, or send for, things or people. It's a term that implies getting others to do your will. Thus in the course of the episode David frequently does the sending; he is never sent for. Joab and Bathsheba both send and are sent for. Uriah is sent for, but never sends. In the first verse of 2 Samuel 12, it is the Lord himself, displeased with David, who does the sending.

Scene One (verse 1): David sends Joab to war

> *In the spring of the year, the time when kings go out to battle, David sent Joab with his officers and all Israel with him; they ravaged the Ammonites, and besieged Rabbah. But David remained at Jerusalem.*

The previous battle season had concluded with David's emphatic victory over the Arameans. But the conflict against the Ammonites, begun in 10.6-14, remains unresolved. Now it is springtime and hostilities can be resumed. (Even in western Europe, the month of March is associated with Mars, the god of war.) So, as in 10.7, David sends Joab to complete the unfinished business, with his officers and 'all Israel' with him.

The outcome of the campaign is positive from Israel's point of view: they ravage the Ammonites and besiege Rabbah (a city only 70 miles east of Jerusalem, across the river Jordan). Yet the focus of the narrative is not with Joab on the battlefield, but with David in his palace. A criticism of the king may well be implied in the simple sentence 'David remained at Jerusalem'. Certainly for Uriah later in the episode, Jerusalem is a place of inappropriate leisure when the armies of Israel are in the field.

Scene Two (verses 2-5): David sends for Bathsheba

> *2 It happened, late one afternoon, when David rose from his couch and was walking about on the roof of the king's house, that he saw from the roof a woman bathing; the woman was very beautiful. 3 David sent someone to inquire about the woman. It was reported, 'This is Bathsheba daughter of Eliam, the wife of Uriah the Hittite.' 4 So David sent messengers to fetch her, and she came to him, and he lay with her. (Now she was purifying herself after her period.)*

Then she returned to her house. 5 The woman conceived;
and she sent and told David, 'I am pregnant.'

Youths are impatient with the notion of a siesta. It is a mark of
David's mature adulthood that he is resting in the heat of the day. Rising
from his couch late one afternoon, he strolls (rested but restless) on the
palace roof – the house built for him by Hiram, king of Tyre (see 5.11),
the house in which he was settled when he first had thoughts of building
the Lord a temple (7.1). Palace roofs were spacious (Judges 3.20). From
there David sees a beautiful woman bathing. If she knew herself capable
of being seen, or even set out to be seen, there is no hint of it in the
text. No element of entrapment is implied and no blame in what follows
attaches to Bathsheba as far as the narrator is concerned.

The spaces between the verses in this first scene are not empty. The
silences speak volumes. There are steps of terrible magnitude between
verses 2 and 3, and verses 3 and 4. Having seen the woman, David has
choices. It is not inevitable that he should pursue his interest. It is not
necessary for him to discover who she is. But he chooses to find out
more about her. He is told not only her name, Bathsheba, but her key
relationships: she is the daughter of Eliam and crucially the wife of
Uriah the Hittite. This is the only time in the story that Bathsheba is
named and her name is pointedly linked to her status. This information
is surely an invitation to David to draw back from any further interest
in her. The fact that Bathsheba's father's name is given at all, and
particularly that it is given first, may mean that Eliam was someone
David knew well (or at least, knew even better than Uriah). But he
must surely have recognised Uriah's name too. The story later lists
him (in 23.39) among the Thirty (see page 184), the band of the king's
most senior and valiant warriors. He must have been aware of Uriah's
loyalty to him and of the debt of loyalty that he in turn owed to this
foreigner. Although he has a thoroughly Hebrew forename (meaning,
'the Lord is my Light'), there is consistent emphasis throughout the
episode on Uriah's Hittite origins (verses 6, 17, 21, 24; rather as in
the book of Ruth, she is consistently 'the Moabite'). It is as if the
narrator wishes to emphasise that while David behaves as a godless
pagan, Uriah plays the part of the devout Israelite. Sometimes it takes
an outsider to model the kind of behaviour which befits the people of
God.

Having discovered her identity, it is not inevitable that David should
pursue his interest. It is not necessary for him to send for Uriah's wife.
But he does so. It is possible that the whole process from the stroll on
the roof to Bathsheba's arrival in his palace took days. But it is more

likely that it took only hours and was all accomplished within the one evening. The narrative creates the impression that matters unfolded with speed.

Events in verse 4 could hardly be told any more succinctly. To an extent that is highly unusual in Hebrew story-telling there is no dialogue, no detail, no delay. The bare facts are reported, clinically and impersonally. David sends and fetches Bathsheba. Samuel had warned the people of Israel when they first asked for a king (1 Samuel 8.11-18) that it is in the nature of kings to grab and to take. Until this moment David has resisted the temptation to snatch at things. Now he fetches a woman. Then he lies with her. The brevity of the description of this act at this point simply emphasises its callousness. Whether Bathsheba was consenting or even enthusiastic in the encounter, whether she was hesitant or even reluctant does not concern the narrator, whose perspective is focused on David's adultery.

The fact that she was purifying herself after her period explains both why she was bathing on the roof and why it was not possible for her to be pregnant by Uriah. But there is an extreme irony here: Bathsheba's carefulness with regard to ritual cleanliness is in vain – the act of adultery leaves her morally unclean, and no amount of bathing will remove the stain. Bathsheba returns to her own home.

Where only a brief passage of time may be implied between verses 2 and 3, and again between verses 3 and 4, a far longer interval is implied between verses 4 and 5. It must be at least three weeks later, and perhaps seven, before Bathsheba sends her fateful message to David, 'I am pregnant'. These are the only words attributed to Bathsheba in the entire episode (her message consists of only one word in Hebrew). But what a dramatic message this is. In almost every circumstance, these words are either the most welcome or the least welcome of all. Her message includes no bitter threat or desperate plea. Again the narrative gives just the essential information.

At the end of the episode Bathsheba is still 'the woman'. As with the absence of dialogue, this impersonal reference emphasises that a sexual relationship has been established by David, but no intimacy. Steadfast love has been a major theme of both the last two episodes; but this is a story about lust.

Scene Three (verses 6-13): David sends for Uriah

6 So David sent word to Joab, 'Send me Uriah the Hittite.'
And Joab sent Uriah to David. 7 When Uriah came to him,

David asked how Joab and the people fared, and how the war was going. 8 Then David said to Uriah, 'Go down to your house, and wash your feet.' Uriah went out of the king's house, and there followed him a present from the king. 9 But Uriah slept at the entrance of the king's house with all the servants of his lord, and did not go down to his house. 10 When they told David, 'Uriah did not go down to his house', David said to Uriah, 'You have just come from a journey. Why did you not go down to your house?' 11 Uriah said to David, 'The ark and Israel and Judah remain in booths; and my lord Joab and the servants of my lord are camping in the open field; shall I then go to my house, to eat and to drink, and to lie with my wife? As you live, and as your soul lives, I will not do such a thing.' 12 Then David said to Uriah, 'Remain here today also, and tomorrow I will send you back.' So Uriah remained in Jerusalem that day. On the next day, 13 David invited him to eat and drink in his presence and made him drunk; and in the evening he went out to lie on his couch with the servants of his lord, but he did not go down to his house.

Again David is immediately decisive. Again he sends. He issues an instruction to Joab, who at once complies by sending Uriah to David. David gets what he demands. He appears to be in control; but he is not. He is on the point of discovering that far from controlling events or the future, he can't even control Uriah.

In verse 7, the text includes the word *shalom* three times. *Shalom* is one of the richest words in the Hebrew Scriptures. It means peace and prosperity, safety and security, wholeness and healing, fullness and completion. 'Is it *shalom* with Joab?', David asks, 'and *shalom* with the people and *shalom* with the war?'. These questions too are superficial; but they stress that David has not even any pretended interest in Uriah's *shalom*.

He tells Uriah to go down to his house and to 'wash [his] feet'. The reference to 'feet' probably carries a sexual connotation. Of course after a long journey Uriah would need quite literally to wash his feet. But there are many examples in the Hebrew Bible where 'feet' is a euphemism for the genitals (for example, 1 Samuel 24.3, Isaiah 7.20, Isaiah 6.2 and possibly Ruth 3.4) and Uriah's eventual protest in verse 11 that this would be an inappropriate time for him to lie with his wife suggests that he caught the innuendo in David's words. This is unquestionably David's goal: he wants Uriah to have sex with his wife. That way no-one except Bathsheba and himself need ever know that her pregnancy is the result of their encounter.

But Uriah does not go down to his house. (The phrase 'go down to your/his house' is a recurring one in verses 8, 9, 10, 10, 13). Instead on his first night back in Jerusalem, he sleeps in the king's palace among the king's servants. The group presumably included the very person(s) who, days or weeks before, had been asked to identify Bathsheba (verse 3) and then had been sent to fetch her (verse 4). Who knows what gossip Uriah overheard that night? In any case, Uriah is no fool. Presumably he wasn't summoned home by the king every week; he must have been curious to discover why he had been singled out at this moment and why. What was it the king wanted which Uriah and no-one else could provide? Was there some promotion in the offing? Some special commission? And if not that, what?

When in verse 10 his servants tell David that Uriah did not go down to his house, it implies that they knew what was going on. They knew why David was so keen that Uriah should go home and what the implications were when he did not go.

David again summons Uriah. But there is apparently no great business of state to discuss. David has only one important issue to address. He challenges Uriah, 'Why did you not go down to your house?' Uriah's reply merits closer attention. First he reminds David that the ark and the armies of Israel and Judah, led by Joab, are in the open country. His reference to the ark (which has presumably accompanied the armies of Israel into battle) is as near as either man gets to speaking of God in this episode. Neither the ark nor the Lord are at the front of David's mind at this stage. There are hints in the Old Testament that it was customary for soldiers to fast from food and sexual relations on the eve of battle (compare Joshua 3.5, 1 Samuel 14.24, 21.5). It may be that Uriah feels bound by this custom. Uriah's reference to the ark certainly suggests that his refusal to return home is motivated by a sense of what is holy, not just what is reasonable or even respectable.

His words also imply a much stronger sense of solidarity with his troops than David seems to have. 'Given the hardships my colleagues are currently enduring, how could I possibly savour home comforts – and especially the comfort of my wife's embrace?'. Where David has put pleasure before duty, Uriah here puts duty before pleasure. More than that, where David has put illicit pleasure before duty, Uriah puts here duty before legitimate pleasure. It is possible that Uriah's response is a thoroughly knowing one and that his final words, 'As you live, and as your soul lives, *I* will not do such a thing', are more an expression of defiance than of loyalty.

David realises that Uriah is not going to change his mind, so he plays for time. 'Stay here a second night', he says, 'and tomorrow I will send you back to Joab'. But the following day he does no such thing. Instead he invites Uriah to dinner and deliberately gets him drunk. Yet still Uriah opts to sleep with the king's servants rather than to return home. His stubbornness makes complete sense if he suspects what is at stake. Even a drunk Uriah provides a better example of faithfulness and loyalty than a sober David (though it is more than likely that David got himself drunk in the process too!).

The scene closes with nightfall. It is the third night Uriah has spent in Jerusalem. The sun has set on David's 'Plan A'. His preferred outcome at this point would have been for Uriah and Bathsheba to remain together. He might want her (and when Uriah is gone he wastes no time in sending for her); but more than he wants her, he wants a cover-up for her pregnancy. Yet while there are some things David can control, he has discovered there are others he cannot: he can get Uriah to Jerusalem, he can get him drunk; but he cannot get him to go to his house and he cannot get him to sleep with his wife.

Scene Four (verses 14-25): David sends Uriah back to war

14 In the morning David wrote a letter to Joab, and sent it by the hand of Uriah. 15 In the letter he wrote, 'Set Uriah in the forefront of the hardest fighting, and then draw back from him, so that he may be struck down and die.' 16 As Joab was besieging the city, he assigned Uriah to the place where he knew there were valiant warriors. 17 The men of the city came out and fought with Joab; and some of the servants of David among the people fell. Uriah the Hittite was killed as well.

18 Then Joab sent and told David all the news about the fighting; 19 and he instructed the messenger, 'When you have finished telling the king all the news about the fighting, 20 then, if the king's anger rises, and if he says to you, "Why did you go so near the city to fight? Did you not know that they would shoot from the wall? 21 Who killed Abimelech son of Jerubbaal? Did not a woman throw an upper millstone on him from the wall, so that he died at Thebez? Why did you go so near the wall?" then you shall say, "Your servant Uriah the Hittite is dead too." '

22 So the messenger went, and came and told David all that Joab had sent him to tell. 23 The messenger said to David, 'The men gained an advantage over us, and came out against us in the field; but we drove them back to the entrance of the gate. 24 Then the archers shot at your servants from the wall; some of the king's servants are dead; and your servant Uriah the Hittite is dead also.' 25 David said to the messenger, 'Thus you shall say to Joab, "Do not let this matter trouble you, for the sword devours now one and now another; press your attack on the city, and overthrow it." And encourage him.'

The new scene opens the following morning. David resorts to 'Plan B'. If 'Plan A' was to cover up for one gross lapse of judgment, 'Plan B' is to commit another.

David writes a letter to Joab and entrusts it to Uriah. Perhaps Uriah had not suspected David's real purpose at all and hurried away from Jerusalem under the impression that the letter he was now bearing was the whole reason he had been summoned to the king in the first place. Or perhaps he wondered how urgent a message could be which it had taken the king four days to get around to writing. The letter is in fact Uriah's death warrant. It is an act of extreme cynicism on David's part to ask Uriah to deliver it himself. The letter instructs Joab in detail: he is to set Uriah not just on the front line, but where the fighting is fiercest. Then he is to withdraw, so that it is inevitable Uriah will be struck down and will die. The text does not record what Joab thought about this letter – what he felt about the morality of its contents or what conclusions he drew about the king's motives. Instead it moves on directly to describe what he did. Joab did as he was told. He put David's instructions into effect at once. 'Plan B' is quickly successful: Uriah is killed.

Presumably with Uriah dead, the pregnancy can be attributed to him with impunity. Any child born in these circumstances will be regarded as having been conceived on the father's final home visit, before his untimely and tragic death. Even at this point, in other words, it may be not so much Bathsheba that David wants as escape from blame and public shame.

David's plan was flawed, however. In battle it is not possible neatly to engineer the death of one particular man. There is always a risk of collateral damage. In order to guarantee Uriah's death, Joab had deployed his troops in ways that from a strictly military point of view were reckless. He had ordered them close to the city wall and there had been significant casualties which now have to be reported to David. Joab anticipates that David will be angry. He is well aware of the awful precedent for what has happened in Israel's history; and he rightly anticipates that David will refer to it. How could any military leader order his men close to a city wall, knowing that king Abimelech effectively died at the hands of a woman when he besieged the city of Thebez, drew too close to its wall and was hit on the head by a millstone dropped from a tower (Judges 9.52-53)? Joab fears that David will be outraged by the news of these losses. But he knows that he will be mollified by the news of Uriah's death. So he carefully instructs the messenger what he is to say. It may have puzzled the messenger to find Uriah's death treated here as good news to offset the bad, rather than as worse news to compound it.

In the event, the messenger's words in verses 23-24 go beyond anything described in verses 16-17 and even beyond what he was instructed to say in verses 18-21. He doesn't wait for the king's initial reaction before introducing the fact of Uriah's death – which was due, it is now for the first time related, to archers. Messengers delivering news of violent death have not fared well in the story of David until now (compare 1.15 and 4.12). This is the first time such a messenger has lived to tell the tale.

If it was cynical of David to entrust the letter for Joab into Uriah's keeping, it is still more cynical of him to behave as if Uriah's death was just the sort of unfortunate but unavoidable incident that happens in battle. Perhaps he is trying to persuade himself this is so. He certainly won't persuade Joab, who may still hold David's letter. It can be safely assumed that this mutual conspiring changed the dynamics of the relationship between the king and his general. David has already complained of his inability to control these men of violence (see 3.39). He has hardly improved his ability to do so through this incident.

He urges Joab to intensify the assault on Rabbah – the fall of which will follow in the next episode (see 12.26).

Scene Five (verses 26-27): David again sends for Bathsheba

26 When the wife of Uriah heard that her husband was dead, she made lamentation for him. 27 When the mourning was over, David sent and brought her to his house, and she became his wife, and bore him a son. But the thing that David had done displeased the Lord.

Meanwhile Bathsheba somehow learns of her husband's death and formally mourns for him. David apparently respects her privacy during this time; but as soon as it is over he sends for her again, just as he had done in scene two (verse 4).

This is the first time Bathsheba has featured in the story since she sent word to David in verse 5 that she was pregnant (apart that is from her role as the wife off-stage to whom Uriah refused to return in verse 11). Here she is not named. She is still 'the wife of Uriah'.

The story passes in silence over her feelings – although when David sends for her once again, the impression is that she went with a spring in her step, rather than grieving inconsolably. Presumably she was complicit with David in keeping from her husband the news of her pregnancy and the identity of the father. It would surely have been possible for her to take the initiative and to explain to Uriah what had transpired. But perhaps she felt herself trapped, a powerless pawn in a game played by a powerful man. This time, however, David is at least embarking on a relationship and not just an impersonal sexual encounter: he brings the woman to his house and she becomes his wife.

The closing words of the episode are not just a rare value judgment in this story, they are an unprecedentedly negative judgment on David. The phrase at the end of verse 27 is a play on verse 25: 'the thing that David had done was evil in the Lord's eyes'. David had earlier urged the messenger to tell Joab, 'Don't let the matter seem evil in your eyes'. The parallel is exact in Hebrew.

This final clause leaves the reader in no doubt that David has not 'got away with it'. He may feel that he has. Uriah is dead. But the Lord knows the truth; and not only the Lord. It goes without saying that Bathsheba knows. So does Joab. Possibly, David's household servants know too. And perhaps the prophet Nathan also has suspicions.

Conclusion

In the English translation, as in the Hebrew, the very last word of this episode is 'the Lord'. This is the only reference to God in this chapter and it comes right at the end. The reader knows what this means: the Lord not only is the last word, he has the last word.

'The thing that David had done displeased the Lord'. The only question is, 'What thing?'. Is it David's idleness on the couch at the time when kings go to war? Is it his lust on the roof top, or his pursuit of the woman he saw? Is it the essential act of adultery or David's attempt to deceive Uriah into believing himself to be the father of the child? Is it his cynical ploy to get Uriah drunk, or still more cynical decision to send his death warrant by Uriah's own hand? Is it the death of Uriah or the other Israelites who died with him? Is it the fact that he enlisted Joab in his malice and the messenger too? Or is it the sum total of these many steps?

Ultimately the transgression at the heart of this story is one of violence rather than of sex. While it probably is the whole sequence of events as they unfolded which displeased the Lord, the development which most stands out is David's capacity for violence against an ally. Although he has previously shown himself capable both of personally perpetrating violence (for example against Goliath in 1 Samuel 17.51) and of ordering violence to be done (for example in 1.15 and 4.12), he has shied away from shedding innocent blood. Previously David has been the model of restraint. His restraint was perhaps his defining characteristic in the story of his rise. Where he sensed a moral constraint, he refused to act violently, and would not countenance the violence of others. But that was then – in the days when his power was limited. Now he is king and those days are gone.

Chapter Eight
2 Samuel 12.1–31

David and Solomon

Introduction

Life can be difficult. Circumstances can be distressing. Facts can be uncomfortable. It is a measure of a person's spiritual maturity if they are able to confront the painful truth, especially if it is the painful truth about themselves. Denial can be a tempting strategy, but it is seldom a healthy one in the long run.

David is assailed in this episode on two fronts. First he is faced with his own sinfulness. Then he is faced with a tragic bereavement. Much to his credit, David is able to accept the reality confronting him in both respects.

There had been much sending of messages and messengers in the previous episode. Now it is the Lord's turn to send a message to David via Nathan. In fact the Lord does so twice. He does so at the start of the chapter and again in the middle. In scene one the message is lengthy and condemnatory; in scene three, it is brief and consoling. In scene two, David's response to the Lord's judgment in the sickness and death of his son puzzles his servants. In the final scene the account of Israel's battle against the Ammonites – interrupted by David's adultery and its aftermath – is resumed and brought to a conclusion. In the course of it, normal routines are re-established: Joab sends messengers to David with news from the battlefield.

The first scene is the key not just to this episode but to the whole story of David's fall, for he is forced to live with the consequences until his death.

Scene One (verses 1-15a): The Lord sends a message to David via Nathan

and the Lord sent Nathan to David. He came to him, and said to him, 'There were two men in a certain city, one rich and the other poor. 2 The rich man had very many flocks and herds; 3 but the poor man had nothing but one little ewe lamb, which he had bought. He brought it up, and it grew up with him and with his children; it used to eat of his meagre fare, and drink from his cup, and lie in his bosom, and it was like a daughter to him. 4 Now there came a traveller to the rich man, and he was loath to take one of his own flock or herd to prepare for the wayfarer who had come to him, but he took the poor man's lamb, and prepared that for the guest who had come to him.'

5 Then David's anger was greatly kindled against the man. He said to Nathan, 'As the Lord lives, the man who has done this deserves to die; 6 he shall restore the lamb fourfold, because he did this thing, and because he had no pity.'

7 Nathan said to David, 'You are the man! Thus says the Lord, the God of Israel: I anointed you king over Israel, and I rescued you from the hand of Saul; 8 I gave you your master's house, and your master's wives into your bosom, and gave you the house of Israel and of Judah; and if that had been too little, I would have added as much more. 9 Why have you despised the word of the Lord, to do what is evil in his sight? You have struck down Uriah the Hittite with the sword, and have taken his wife to be your wife, and have killed him with the sword of the Ammonites. 10 Now therefore the sword shall never depart from your house, for you have despised me, and have taken the wife of Uriah the Hittite to be your wife. 11 Thus says the Lord: I will raise up trouble against you from within your own house; and I will take your wives before your eyes, and give them to your neighbour, and he shall lie with your wives in the sight of this very sun. 12 For you did it secretly; but I will do this thing before all Israel, and before the sun.'

13 David said to Nathan, 'I have sinned against the Lord.' Nathan said to David, 'Now the Lord has put away your sin; you shall not die. 14 Nevertheless, because by this deed you have utterly scorned the Lord, the child that is born to you shall die.' 15 Then Nathan went to his house.

The previous episode concludes with the report that Bathsheba bore David a son. It was apparently after this that the Lord despatched

Nathan to speak to the king. By this time the palace gossip must have
been rife. Even if David's adultery was a well-kept secret at the time
(which is open to doubt), his hurried acquisition of Bathsheba as a wife
as soon as the formalities of her mourning were over must have raised
an eyebrow or two and the timing of the child's birth will certainly
have set tongues wagging. Palace servants can do the maths. In all
probability, Nathan stepped into a situation of public scandal rather
than merely private sin. The prophet comes apparently seeking the
king's judgment.

The dialogue between the king and his prophet breaks down into
five parts: first the prophet tells a parable (verses 1 to 4); then the king
gives an instant response (verses 5 to 6); Nathan follows this up with
the application (verses 7 to 12); to this, the king again makes an instant
response; and finally, Nathan declares the Lord's judgment on David
(verses 13b to 15).

The parable is about two men: one rich and one poor. In the English
translation, nine words suffice to introduce the rich man (verse 2). In
Hebrew, it is just six. Even this brief description is reminiscent of
Nabal (1 Samuel 25). A much fuller picture is given of the poor man.
It may also occupy only a single verse (verse 3); but it is 55 words long
in the NRSV (and 25 in Hebrew). He is the one with whom the reader
(and of course David) is invited to identify and sympathise. In David's
case, the account perhaps resonates with his own shepherd upbringing.
Nathan contrasts the one pet lamb with the rich man's 'many flocks
and herds'; but he goes on to set this lamb within the man's home and
family: 'it used to eat of his meagre fare and drink from his cup'. The
Hebrew sentence concludes, 'it was to him like – a daughter'. The
word for daughter there is *bat*, and the prophet teeters momentarily on
the brink of naming Bathsheba.

The parable turns on the obligations of hospitality in Middle Eastern
culture. A visitor comes calling on the rich man, who is therefore
expected to provide a meal. He is loath to deplete his own flock; so he
takes the poor man's lamb and serves that to his guest instead.

Nathan's story ends abruptly. It does not state the feelings of the
poor man, and so invites the listener to imagine them. The invitation
elicits David's outrage. Not realising that the parable is a fiction, the
king declares that 'the man who has done this deserves to die'. The
overreaction betrays the sensitivity of David's conscience. (For murder
or adultery in that culture a man might be condemned to death; but for
the theft of a lamb?) The reader senses the king is projecting onto the
rich man his own guilt. Still supposing himself to be dispensing justice
in his royal authority, David demands that the man restore the lamb

fourfold. (Christian readers will recall how in Luke 19.8, Zacchaeus responds to Jesus by promising to restore fourfold what he has stolen). What particularly outrages David is that the rich man had no pity and no empathy for the poor man.

'You are the man!' Nathan pronounces. The exclamation is just two words in Hebrew. Nathan effectively passes a sentence of death on the king: 'You say that the man who did this deserves to die: you are that man'.

There follows one of the most devastating denunciations in all Scripture. In six short verses, David's world is turned upside down. First, the oracle contrasts the generosity of the Lord who has given David so much, with David's greed in taking what did not belong to him. 'I *gave* you your master's house and your master's wives into your bosom, and *gave* you the house of Israel and of Judah; and if that had been too little, I would have added as much more... [but] you have struck down Uriah the Hittite with the sword and have *taken* his wife to be your wife... you have *taken* the wife of Uriah the Hittite to be your wife'. David has shown himself to be every bit as acquisitive as any king. He has not been able to break the mould set out in 1 Samuel 8 or to refrain from taking. The one responsible for justice in the land has been responsible for a great injustice; the one whose vocation it is to protect the people from exploitation has exploited others for personal gain. David's failure to execute justice (at which 8.15 suggests he formerly excelled) will again be his undoing later in the narrative (15.1-6).

Then the consequences of David's actions are spelt out. At one level, David is condemned for adultery and murder; his are sins of sex and violence. The punishment will therefore fit the crime. The violence David has wrought will bring rebound on him. The Lord declares (verses 9-10), '[Because] you have struck down Uriah the Hittite with the sword... and have killed him with the sword of the Ammonites, now therefore the sword shall never depart from your house' (compare David's callous words to Joab in 11.25). Similarly, David's adultery will recoil on his own head: 'Thus says the Lord: I will raise up trouble against you from within your own house; and I will take your wives before your eyes and give them to your neighbour, and he shall lie with your wives in the sight of this very sun' (verse 11). The terribly literal fulfillment of this prophetic judgment is recorded in 16.20-23.

Thirdly however the root of David's actions is exposed. Ultimately his sin is not against Uriah or Bathsheba, but against the Lord himself. His acts of murder and adultery are symptoms of a deeper malaise:

he has 'despised the word of the Lord', verse 9; he has 'despised [the Lord]', verse 10; he has 'utterly scorned the Lord', verse 14.

The two words of Nathan's initial Hebrew accusation in verse 7 ('You-are the-man') is matched by a two word confession by David in verse 13 ('I-have-sinned against-the-Lord'). This is one of the great dramatic moments in the David story and a defining one in terms of the story of David's downfall. The most attractive characteristic of David after he assumes the kingship of all Israel is his sincere and ready contrition. He is able to admit his fault. He does not seek to evade responsibility or to blame others or to excuse himself or to adopt any of the many other strategies human beings are prone to adopt when we are confronted with our wrongdoing.

In this respect David remains a model of godliness. The effect of the word of God is to subvert our defences and to open us up to the truth about ourselves and our limitations. It divests us of the masks behind which we hide, and the layers of pretence with which we cloak ourselves. It gets behind our dissembling and self-justifying, and our attempts to bolster our sense of our own rightness. It holds up for us a mirror in which we are able to see ourselves as we are and are able to accept the liberating truth that we are sinners. David's confession is familiar to every believer: *mea culpa.* I have sinned.

David's sincere and ready contrition stands in subtle but critical contrast with the response of Saul, when he was accused by God's prophet in very similar terms. Here David is rebuked by Nathan for 'despising the word of the Lord'. In 1 Samuel 15.23, 26 Saul is rebuked by Samuel for 'rejecting the word of the Lord'. It is absolutely true that Saul confessed his fault. To Samuel's repeated rebuke Saul twice replies, in words which are, after all, similar to David's, 'I have sinned' (verses 24, 30). Yet Saul says both much less and much more than David. He says less in the sense that David's confession is not 'I have sinned' but 'I have sinned against the Lord': Saul lacks that keen sense of the presence of God with which David is blessed. He says more in the sense that when David has said 'I have sinned against the Lord' he falls silent. He has said everything he has to say. For Saul however that phrase is just one he uses among many. Indeed, Saul's first 'I have sinned' only follows an initial denial of any wrongdoing (1 Samuel 15.20-21); then, that first 'I have sinned' is followed by an attempt to shift the blame for his behaviour onto others (1 Samuel 15.24). Furthermore, his second 'I have sinned' is followed by a request which shows that he is still preoccupied with the appearance of things and is anxious to avoid any public loss of face (1 Samuel 15.30). There is no such prevarication with David.

The first scene closes with a final utterance from Nathan, who then departs for his own house. Is David now forgiven? It appears that he is. Nathan's words are initially words of reassurance: 'The Lord has put away your sin. You shall not die' (verse 13). There is mercy here. If a sentence of death has been hanging over David since he himself pronounced judgment in verse 5, it is now removed. Yet David's sin still has terrible consequences, both for himself and for others around him. Nathan declares that because David has utterly scorned the Lord 'the child that is born to [him] shall die'.

This outcome seems extraordinarily harsh to a contemporary western reader. Why should a baby die for something David has done? Is God's judgment really so punitive? It may help to bear in mind two things. The first is that in Hebrew thought there are no 'secondary causes'. All that is, is attributable to God. If something happens, good or bad, it is because God did it. So Hebrew tends not to say 'the baby became sick', but rather (as in verse 15b) 'God struck the child' (compare 1 Samuel 25.38). This means that Hebrew theology can sound more punitive than it is, because it attributes directly to the hand of God events which in a Greek culture might be regarded as a more impersonal outworking of circumstances. Secondly, Hebrew culture was far less privatised and individualistic than our own and celebrated a far greater degree of solidarity between people. In such a culture, there is far less sense of unease about a child sharing in the punishment of a parent, or vice versa, since one is not easily isolated from the other.

David's confession may restore his relationship with the Lord. But his sin nevertheless still causes devastating consequences. His guilt may have been assuaged, but his distress is not yet over.

Scene Two (verses 15b-23): David's behaviour baffles his servants

The Lord struck the child that Uriah's wife bore to David, and it became very ill. 16 David therefore pleaded with God for the child; David fasted, and went in and lay all night on the ground. 17 The elders of his house stood beside him, urging him to rise from the ground; but he would not, nor did he eat food with them. 18 On the seventh day the child died. And the servants of David were afraid to tell him that the child was dead; for they said, 'While the child was still alive, we spoke to him, and he did not listen to us; how then can we tell him the child is dead? He may do himself some harm.'

19 But when David saw that his servants were whispering together, he perceived that the child was dead; and David said to his servants, 'Is the child dead?' They said, 'He is dead.'

20 Then David rose from the ground, washed, anointed himself, and changed his clothes. He went into the house of the Lord, and worshipped; he then went to his own house; and when he asked, they set food before him and he ate. 21 Then his servants said to him, 'What is this thing that you have done? You fasted and wept for the child while it was alive; but when the child died, you rose and ate food.' 22 He said, 'While the child was still alive, I fasted and wept; for I said, "Who knows? The Lord may be gracious to me, and the child may live." 23 But now he is dead; why should I fast? Can I bring him back again? I shall go to him, but he will not return to me.'

David's wholehearted acknowledgment of his own responsibility for what has happened is further demonstrated in his response to the circumstances, when the unnamed infant born of his affair with the woman who (despite 11.27) is still called 'Uriah's wife' becomes ill. He pleads with God for the life of the child, fasting from food and lying in prayer on the ground all night. The intensity of David's response worries the elders of his house, who urge him to get up and eat. But he will not. For a week, the text implies, he barely moves from the spot. On the seventh day, the child dies. When, in verse 18 it is said that 'David's servants were afraid to tell him that the child was dead', it is the first of five repetitions of the word 'dead' in just two verses. His servants cannot bring themselves to tell David that his distressed fasting and prayer have been in vain; but he infers as much from their whispers.

When they confirm that his worst fears are realised, David gets up, washes himself and goes to worship the Lord in his tabernacle – the same place, presumably, where he had sat and wondered at the goodness of God in chapter 7.18. He asks for food and eats it. Understandably, this behaviour baffles David's servants, who had been anxious that the child's death would tip David's distress over into despair and that he might even harm himself. Given the depth of David's grief at earlier moments in the story, particularly at the deaths of Saul and Jonathan in 1.17-27, his reaction is unexpected. His servants are so puzzled that they ask David to explain why, given that he had fasted and wept while the child lay sick, he is now acting as if all is well when the child has died. David's reply sounds harsh, not least to those who have suffered the tragedy of losing a child: 'While the child was alive', he says, 'I fasted and wept because it was still possible that the Lord would relent and let the child live. Now that he is dead there is no point in fasting any longer. It certainly won't bring the child back'. It is however only fasting that David says is now pointless – not weeping. His response doesn't necessarily imply any lack of love for either the dead child or his mother.

In fact verse 23 expresses a new and appropriate vulnerability in David. He has learned that in all the things that matter most to him, he is virtually powerless to secure what he wants. He has no control over matters of life and death. This is the first purely personal (that is, non-political) reflection by David in the story. From now on his speeches will frequently reiterate this sense of powerlessness and vulnerability.

Scene Three (verses 24-25): The Lord sends a second message to David via Nathan

24 Then David consoled his wife Bathsheba, and went to her, and lay with her; and she bore a son, and he named him Solomon. The Lord loved him, 25 and sent a message by the prophet Nathan; so he named him Jedidiah, because of the Lord.

Bathsheba is named here for only the second time in the story (see also chapter 11.3). The new naming serves, like the renewed affirmation after verse 15b that she is David's wife, to emphasise that a new start is being made.

Some time has passed, so that it is possible for Bathsheba to become pregnant again (perhaps two months or more). David consoles his wife (again a sign that his behaviour in the previous episode was not heartless), lies with her and she again conceives. Nine months later, she bears a second son, and David names him Solomon – meaning 'God's peace'. The name further underlines that the stormy events of the recent past have blown over.

This child, it is said, is especially loved by God, who sends his prophet to the king for a second time. This time there is no denunciation for David, but great reassurance. As a result of the message delivered by Nathan, David gives his new son an additional name: 'Jedidiah', which means 'beloved by Yahweh'. If the death of the first child somehow symbolised God's anger at David's adultery, then the birth of the second symbolises God's renewed blessing on David and his acceptance of the king's union with Bathsheba. Oddly, this name is never used again. The child now disappears from the story until 1 Kings 1. He re-emerges there as a central figure in the narrative (again in association with both Nathan and Bathsheba, who likewise disappear from the narrative in the meanwhile), but as Solomon rather than Jedediah.

Yet the significance of the second name is obvious: Solomon may be only David's tenth born son. But he is special. It is he who will succeed to his father's throne, rather than any of his older brothers, because he is loved by God.

Scene Four (verses 26-31): Joab sends messengers to David from Rabbah

26 Now Joab fought against Rabbah of the Ammonites, and took the royal city. 27 Joab sent messengers to David, and said, 'I have fought against Rabbah; moreover, I have taken the water city. 28 Now, then, gather the rest of the people together, and encamp against the city, and take it; or I myself will take the city, and it will be called by my name.' 29 So David gathered all the people together and went to Rabbah, and fought against it and took it. 30 He took the crown of Milcom from his head; the weight of it was a talent of gold, and in it was a precious stone; and it was placed on David's head. He also brought forth the spoil of the city, a very great amount. 31 He brought out the people who were in it, and set them to work with saws and iron picks and iron axes, or sent them to the brickworks. Thus he did to all the cities of the Ammonites. Then David and all the people returned to Jerusalem.

A further indication that normality is restored is the resumption of the account of the war against the Ammonites, now taken to its conclusion.

Joab (urged by David in 11.25 to 'press [his] attack against the city and overthrow it) has finally achieved his goal. Rabbah, royal city of the Ammonites, has fallen. At once Joab sends messengers to David with the good news. In fact the sequence of events is curiously unclear. Verse 26 suggests that the city had been taken; but Joab's message implies that at least the *coup de grace* has still to be delivered. The first part of the message ('I have fought against Rabbah, I have taken the water city') has verse-like properties about it, as if Joab composed a poem to his own power and glory. So it is hard to avoid the impression of an ultimatum, when (having urged David to leave Jerusalem and to come to the site 'with the rest of the people', to encamp against the city and take it in person) Joab's message concludes 'Otherwise I myself will take the city and it will be called by my name'.

On the one hand Joab is clearly still acting here as David's loyal servant. He seems genuinely concerned that David should receive the credit for an important, long-awaited and costly victory. On the other hand it is unsettling that Joab should express such concern for David's reputation. Is he no longer able to enhance his reputation by himself? Or is Joab even taunting David at some level in bringing him to the place where Uriah died? The relationship between Joab and David has never been easy. This is not the first time Joab has asserted himself (compare 3.26-39). One day the two will be on opposing sides (see 1 Kings 1), and this incident might be read as a step in that direction. David is paying a heavy price for the way he engineered Uriah's death.

But David did go to Rabbah and duly took it. He also took the crown of Milcom (weighing as much as 65 pounds, or about 30 bags of sugar), which was placed on his own head. At one level, his glory seems only to have been further enhanced by another great victory resulting in yet more spoil.

Yet the episode ends on another disquieting note. For the first time, there is explicit reference in the story to forced labour. David brings out the people of Rabbah 'and set them to work with saws and iron picks and iron axes, or sent them to the brickworks'. Previously, defeated cities and nations are said to have become David's servants (compare 8.2, 14). But this is something else, something more sinister. David, the Lord's anointed, has become hard to distinguish from any Pharaoh.

Conclusion

The consequences of our actions can be terrible. Sometimes we are fortunate and the results of our ignorance or our recklessness are modest. Sometimes a moment of madness has implications which seem disproportionately serious. That is David's experience here. His adultery with Bathsheba was a folly, compounded by his grievous sin in pursuing Uriah to death. What distress has already ensued, and what further distress is to follow.

Yet in the birth of Solomon, David knows himself forgiven. As countless Christians today can testify, to be forgiven is not to rewind the clock: the past cannot be undone. Nor is it to escape from the future: sin has consequences. Forgiveness is nevertheless transforming. It is to know that a relationship with the Lord has been re-established and that the burden of a guilty conscience has been lifted. To be forgiven is not to deny one's wrongdoing; but it is, in acknowledging wrongdoing, to escape the weight of its condemnation. David must forever live with what he has done. There is no redemption from the consequences of his sin. But the birth of Solomon symbolises the truth that there can be redemption even in the midst of the consequences of our sin. Thus by grace there is hope even when the outcome of our wrongdoing is very terrible indeed.

Chapter Nine
2 Samuel 13.1–39

Tamar and Absalom

Introduction

In this episode (as in chapter 11) a man lusts for a beautiful woman with whom he has no legitimate prospect of a sexual relationship and nevertheless takes her, with appalling consequences. A sexual transgression in David's palace results in a murder elsewhere. Thus although the chronological link between the previous episodes and this one is uncertain ('some time passed'), the theological link is not: what follows is in direct fulfillment of Nathan's prophecy.

This is the first of a series of seven chapters featuring Absalom (although he shares the limelight in this episode with his half-brother Amnon and his sister Tamar, and in the next episode with David's general Joab and an anonymous wise woman).

Amnon is David's oldest son; Absalom is third in line (2.2-3). While there was no established right of primogeniture to the throne of Israel, there are hints of an assumption that Amnon is the heir apparent (for instance, in verse 21). Once the birth of Solomon has been reported, it becomes important to establish how the succession will be managed and what will become of David's other sons.

The episode unfolds in four scenes. The first tells the dreadful story of the rape of Tamar. The second records David's surprisingly inadequate response; the third, after an interval of fully two years, relates Absalom's revenge and Amnon's murder; and the last recounts Absalom's subsequent exile.

Tamar is defined by her relationship to her brothers. At the beginning and ending of the first scene, she is Absalom's sister; in the middle, she is loved and then hated, taken and then rejected, by Amnon. Both Absalom and Amnon are defined by their relationship to David (verse 1).

Scene One (verses 1-20): The rape of Tamar

The first scene (compare Genesis 27) is made up of seven steps, in each of which only two people feature, with one of the two providing continuity with the following step. Thus step one features Jonadab and Amnon, step two Amnon and David, step three David and Tamar, step four Tamar and Amnon, step five Amnon and a servant, step six the servant and Tamar, and step seven Tamar and Absalom. The middle step (in which the critical and terrible act of rape is related) is by far the longest.

Step 1: Jonadab and Amnon

Some time passed. David's son Absalom had a beautiful sister whose name was Tamar; and David's son Amnon fell in love with her. 2 Amnon was so tormented that he made himself ill because of his sister Tamar, for she was a virgin and it seemed impossible to Amnon to do anything to her. 3 But Amnon had a friend whose name was Jonadab, the son of David's brother Shimeah; and Jonadab was a very crafty man. 4 He said to him, 'O son of the king, why are you so haggard morning after morning? Will you not tell me?' Amnon said to him, 'I love Tamar, my brother Absalom's sister.' 5 Jonadab said to him, 'Lie down on your bed, and pretend to be ill; and when your father comes to see you, say to him, "Let my sister Tamar come and give me something to eat, and prepare the food in my sight, so that I may see it and eat it from her hand." '

It is an indication of the prominence Absalom will play in the ensuing episodes rather than in this scene, that Tamar is introduced in such a roundabout way – not simply as David's daughter, but as the sister of David's third son.

Amnon 'fell in love' with Tamar. This is an oddly modern and romantic translation. It would be truer to say he developed an obsessive infatuation with Tamar or that he lusted after her. It is true that he becomes love-sick for her; but there is no indication in the story that he had any feelings of tenderness (contrast Genesis 34).

Amnon feelings for Tamar overwhelmed him and he did not know what to do. She was a virgin in a patriarchal culture in which a woman's virginity had matrimonial value. So it seemed impossible to Amnon to 'do anything to her'. It is a brutal euphemism, which perfectly conveys his view of Tamar as a merely sexual object.

'But', the text continues in verse 3, not everyone regarded Amnon's situation as hopeless. He had a friend – actually a cousin, the son of David's brother Shimeah (is this Shammah as in 1 Samuel 16.9, 17.13?). Jonadab had a reputation for craftiness, which is immediately demonstrated in the way the way he addresses the prince: 'O son of the king', he says, drawing attention to the contrast between Amnon's exalted status and his present dejection. 'Why do you look so haggard day after day?'. Jonadab's apparently instant proposal suggests that he suspected the answer to his question. He urges Amnon to take to his bed. When the king comes to see what ails his firstborn, as he surely must, then Amnon is to request him to send Tamar to prepare some special food for him. This way, Amnon will secure what has seemed so impossible: time alone with Tamar in his bedchamber with all the intimacy implied by eating from her hand.

Later in the story, when Amnon declares his lust to Tamar and she begs him not to rape her, she does so not on the basis of their kinship, but on the grounds that if proper procedures are only followed, King David would arrange their match. It is possible therefore that Jonadab thought he was facilitating not a rape but the possibility of a consensual encounter. On the other hand, given his own reputation for wisdom, and given Amnon's state of mind, he must surely have known the risks.

Step 2: Amnon and David

6 So Amnon lay down, and pretended to be ill; and when the king came to see him, Amnon said to the king, 'Please let my sister Tamar come and make a couple of cakes in my sight, so that I may eat from her hand.'

Jonadab's scheme works to perfection. Amnon takes to his bed and feigns illness and when David comes to visit him, Amnon makes his request.

The only improvisation in Amnon's request relates to the particular kind of food he wants his sister to prepare for him. He specifies 'a couple of cakes'. The Hebrew word used for 'cakes' here is *lebibot*, which appears to be derived from *lebab*, meaning 'heart'. This is presumably a Freudian slip on Amnon's part: an unintentional and revealing insight into his true feelings. The exact meaning of *lebibot* is not known; it may mean 'heart-shaped cakes' or 'cakes that will strengthen the heart', or even 'my favourite cakes' (in the sense of 'cakes that the heart longs for').

Step 3: David and Tamar

*7 Then David sent home to Tamar, saying, 'Go to your broth-
er Amnon's house, and prepare food for him.'*

David acts on Amnon's request without delay and apparently
without apprehension. Since David has himself been the master of
trickery (fooling Goliath with the use of a decoy staff in 1 Samuel
17.40-43, King Achish of Gath with his feigned madness in 1 Samuel
21.13-15 and entering into the ruses of Michal and Jonathan to
deceive their father in 1 Samuel 18 and 20), it is startling to find him
so easily taken in. Yet the king suspects no ploy – or he suppresses
any suspicions he may have. His instruction to Tamar is the first in a
series of four commands she is given, with which she complies with
varying degrees of willingness or reluctance (compare verses 10, 11
and 15).

Step 4: Tamar and Amnon

*8 So Tamar went to her brother Amnon's house, where he
was lying down. She took dough, kneaded it, made cakes
in his sight, and baked the cakes. 9 Then she took the pan
and set them out before him, but he refused to eat. Amnon
said, 'Send out everyone from me.' So everyone went out
from him. 10 Then Amnon said to Tamar, 'Bring the food
into the chamber, so that I may eat from your hand.' So
Tamar took the cakes she had made, and brought them into
the chamber to Amnon her brother. 11 But when she brought
them near him to eat, he took hold of her, and said to her,
'Come, lie with me, my sister.' 12 She answered him, 'No,
my brother, do not force me; for such a thing is not done in
Israel; do not do anything so vile! 13 As for me, where could
I carry my shame? And as for you, you would be as one of
the scoundrels in Israel. Now therefore, I beg you, speak to
the king; for he will not withhold me from you.' 14 But he
would not listen to her; and being stronger than she was, he
forced her and lay with her. 15 Then Amnon was seized with
a very great loathing for her; indeed, his loathing was even
greater than the lust he had felt for her. Amnon said to her,
'Get out!' 16 But she said to him, 'No, my brother; for this
wrong in sending me away is greater than the other that you
did to me.' But he would not listen to her.*

So Tamar is sent to her brother's quarters, where he lies in his bedchamber, from where it is possible for him to watch the baking process. At this point the narrative slows right down. It could so easily summarise 'She made the cakes'. But it dwells on the process: 'she took dough, kneaded it, made the cakes in his sight and baked the cakes'. This all takes time. All the while Amnon watches hungrily. But when Tamar brings him the pan and holds the cakes out for him, he does not eat. Instead he dismisses everyone else from the room. It is ambiguous whether the words 'Tell everyone to leave' are spoken to one of the servants or courtiers, who then leads the exodus or to Tamar who orchestrates it. Presumably while there were others present she felt no qualms about what was being asked of her. It may be at this moment that she sensed the first inkling of her vulnerability.

Then Amnon requested her to bring the food right to his bedside so that he could eat it from her hand. Tamar does as she is told. The moment she is close enough, he seizes her. The strength in his grip will at once have alerted Tamar to the pretence of his illness. His words confirm his intentions. He demands Tamar to lie with him. She refuses. Her rejection in verses 12-13 is polite ('No, my brother'); but it could not be more explicit. When she says 'do not force me', it makes clear that any sexual encounter will be an assault against her will. There is no consent. When she says 'Such a thing is not done in Israel. Do not do anything so vile [*nabalah* – foolish or morally senseless]', it is the one point in the story which might allude to the incestuous nature of the rape. Unlike Amnon (and unlike David with Bathsheba), she is aware that sexual encounters mostly have consequences. She is concerned for her own reputation ('where would I carry my shame?'), but also for his ('You would be as one of the scoundrels [*nebalim* – fools or immoral rogues] in Israel'). In both cases, where the consequences are concerned, her point of reference is the community to which they both belong rather than a personal moral code. Her categorical 'No' is not 'No, such a thing would violate my values' or 'No, such a thing would violate my body' (still less, 'No, I don't fancy you'). It's 'No, such a thing would violate our people'. Yet her final strategy plays down the taboo of their kinship. She urges Amnon not to rape her, but instead to seek formal permission from David to marry her. 'He will not withhold me from you'. The provisions of Leviticus 18.9 and Deuteronomy 27.22 prohibit precisely the kind of union Tamar envisages here. Even if her suggestion was just a ruse to buy time, it depends for its effectiveness on the genuine possibility of such an outcome. Perhaps the laws of the Pentateuch were not widely enforced at this point in

Israel's history; or perhaps there were occasional exemptions and a royal union might be an obvious case.

Her protests are to no avail. Amnon does not listen. He overwhelms her, coerces and rapes her. At once, having consummated the desire he has nurtured for so long, his lust is turned to loathing. The revulsion he feels is psychologically highly plausible. He projects his self-loathing and commands her to get out. In Hebrew, his order is 'Get up, go!' (verse 15), the exact opposite of his earlier invitation, 'Come, lie' (in verse 11). Again Tamar refuses. For the second time she says, 'No, my brother'. Again she is alert to the consequences of what Amnon is proposing. 'This wrong in sending me away is greater than the other [harrowingly unspecified, for she cannot bring herself to name it] that you did to me'. In a contemporary western culture it is hard to imagine a greater wrong than rape. But Tamar understands that Amnon has not just taken her virginity, but her eligibility for marriage. He has taken her future. If he rejects her now, he consigns her to a life of desolation. The rape is a terrible crime and will scar Tamar for life. But in her eyes, the practical social implications of being rejected by Amnon after he has had sex with her are even worse than the psychological personal implications of the physical assault. But again (compare verse 14) Amnon would not listen to her.

Step 5: Amnon and a servant

17 He called the young man who served him and said, 'Put this woman out of my presence, and bolt the door after her.'

An extraordinary contrast in this short verse between Amnon's scrupulous courtesy towards his servant and his utter indifference towards Tamar is obscured in the NRSV translation, which omits a word it might have supplied and supplies a word it might have omitted. In the Hebrew, Amnon's request to the servant actually begins with something like a 'Please'. But on the other hand, the Hebrew lacks a noun where the English has 'woman'. The sense is something like 'Please put this (or 'she' – the word is feminine) out and bolt the door after her' – as if Tamar is rubbish.

Step 6: The servant and Tamar

18 (Now she was wearing a long robe with sleeves; for this is how the virgin daughters of the king were clothed in earlier times.) So his servant put her out, and bolted the door after

*her. 19 But Tamar put ashes on her head, and tore the long
robe that she was wearing; she put her hand on her head,
and went away, crying aloud as she went.*

Of the seven steps which make up this first scene, this is the only
one without any dialogue. The servant has nothing to say to Tamar
and she has nothing to say to him. The speechlessness accentuates the
trauma. The servant complies carefully with his master's command: he
first puts her out, and then bolts the door.

Only now does the text refer to Tamar's clothing. She is wearing
a special robe, which testifies to her status as a virgin daughter of the
king. (The robe is the same sort as that given by Jacob to Joseph in
Genesis 37.3, where it constituted a mark of favouritism.) But virgin
robes are no longer appropriate for Tamar, so she tears them. She puts
ashes on her head and tears her robe and puts her hand on her head in
the classic cultural expressions of grief (compare Jeremiah 2.37 and 1
Samuel 4.12). As she makes her way (through the palace to her own
quarters?) she cries aloud. She weeps. Her cry is not merely a cry of
pain and sorrow; it is a cry of protest and a cry for justice.

Step 7: Tamar and Absalom

*20 Her brother Absalom said to her, 'Has Amnon your
brother been with you? Be quiet for now, my sister; he is
your brother; do not take this to heart.' So Tamar remained,
a desolate woman, in her brother Absalom's house.*

Absalom quickly infers what has happened without being told.
Whereas David was slow to discern the implications of Amnon's request, Absalom grasps the situation at once.

Absalom's words seem pastorally crass. His question shows that
he knows exactly what has happened. But his response is first to tell
Tamar to stop her fuss ('Be quiet now') and then to imply that Amnon's
status as a member of the family can help her not to take to heart what
has happened.

The sequel however proves that Absalom was not dismissing his
sister's experience lightly. For one thing (unlike David who did nothing
in verse 21), Absalom took his forlorn and devastated sister into his
own house to ensure she was provided for. Moreover, whatever he
meant by telling Tamar not to take the matter to heart, he did not mean
that it was to be forgotten. On the contrary, it transpires that he took the
assault very much to heart himself (compare verse 22).

Scene Two (verses 21-22): The responses of David and Absalom

*21 When King David heard of all these things, he became
very angry, but he would not punish his son Amnon, because
he loved him, for he was his firstborn. 22 But Absalom spoke
to Amnon neither good nor bad; for Absalom hated Amnon,
because he had raped his sister Tamar.*

David hears about all these things. He hears that Amnon (his son)
has raped Tamar (his daughter). He hears no doubt about her distress
and desolation, her torn robe and her loud crying, and the refuge she
has taken in Absalom's house. And he presumably realises that he
himself has been used in the process as a pimp – procuring sex for his
own son by means of his own daughter. He becomes angry.

Anger in the Bible (particularly in the face of wrongdoing) is not
a vice. It can be a virtue when it results in the energetic pursuit of
justice. But anger can lead to vice (as in 1 Samuel 17.28 for example,
or 1 Samuel 20.30). It can do so when it fuels careless action; but it can
also do so when it results in no action at all. Incredibly, angry as David
is with what has happened to Tamar, he does nothing. Both as a father
and as a king, he should act. He is after all the one responsible for the
administration of justice (compare 8.15), the one who not so very long
ago had a reputation for ruling in justice and equity.

The reason for his inaction is straightforward: he cannot bring
himself to punish Amnon because he loves him for being his firstborn.
David is not often said in the narrative to love another person. In fact,
Jonathan is the only person David has previously been said to love
(1.26). But this love for Absalom is barely a more wholesome kind of
love than the kind Amnon was said to have for Tamar in verse 1. True
love rebukes vice; it does not indulge it.

This is a sharp decline from the shrewdness and decisiveness with
which he was capable of acting in the days before he became king.
Here David stands in an ignoble tradition of Israelite leaders who
found themselves unable to control their adult sons – men like Jacob
himself (compare Genesis 34.30) and Eli (1 Samuel 2.22-25). David
seems unaware that to do nothing is to sow the seeds of further trouble.
Much later in life he will similarly fail Adonijah by the poverty of
his parenting (1 Kings 1.6). In a culture which had an exceptionally
high view of fatherhood (as the names of so many in this cast betray),
this was a serious weakness in David. (The prefix or suffix 'Ab' in a
Hebrew name stems from the word for 'father', as in Abishai, Abigail,
Abishag, Joab, Abiathar, Abner and so on).

For the time being, Absalom also did nothing except break off all contact with his brother. He refused to speak to him either in peace or hostility. But whereas in doing nothing David was nurturing a misguided love and was hoping that in time the problem would go away, Absalom was nurturing an equally misguided hatred and was hoping that in time he would have the opportunity to take revenge.

Scene Three (verses 23-29): The murder of Amnon

23 After two full years Absalom had sheepshearers at Baal-hazor, which is near Ephraim, and Absalom invited all the king's sons. 24 Absalom came to the king, and said, 'Your servant has sheepshearers; will the king and his servants please go with your servant?' 25 But the king said to Absalom, 'No, my son, let us not all go, or else we will be burdensome to you.' He pressed him, but he would not go but gave him his blessing. 26 Then Absalom said, 'If not, please let my brother Amnon go with us.' The king said to him, 'Why should he go with you?' 27 But Absalom pressed him until he let Amnon and all the king's sons go with him. Absalom made a feast like a king's feast. 28 Then Absalom commanded his servants, 'Watch when Amnon's heart is merry with wine, and when I say to you, "Strike Amnon", then kill him. Do not be afraid; have I not myself commanded you? Be courageous and valiant.' 29 So the servants of Absalom did to Amnon as Absalom had commanded. Then all the king's sons rose, and each mounted his mule and fled.

Absalom was a patient man. The expression 'after two full years' nicely creates the impression that Absalom had been counting the days since Tamar's rape, biding his time. There is no indication what changed to make him confident that this was the moment he had waited for. But at the season of sheep-shearing (which was a traditional time of community celebration, compare 1 Samuel 25.2, Genesis 38.12) Absalom threw a party at Baal-hazor. He invited his father (perhaps banking on David's inertia and reluctance to leave his palace). David refuses, politely citing a concern that with all his household, his presence would be burdensome. Absalom presses him, but David still refuses, while giving his blessing to the festivities. This is probably the outcome Absalom had intended. He has used his father as an intermediary to get access to Amnon, just as Amnon had himself done to get access to Tamar.

He then asks the king to send Amnon instead. David's suspicions are evidently aroused. How odd that Absalom should single out among all his brothers the one he hates, the one he has not spoken to for two full years! 'Why should he go with you?', he asks. No explanation is offered. Absalom just presses his father further. Despite his misgivings and perhaps inhibited by the fact that he has already resisted his son's urgings by refusing to attend in person, David concedes. Perhaps he naively hopes that Absalom is holding out an olive branch to his brother and offering the possibility of a reconciliation.

In the event not just Amnon but all the king's sons go with Absalom, who prepares a feast fit for a king (just as the fool Nabal had done in 1 Samuel 25.36). This is the first indication of Absalom's own ambitions. He wants to be king. It may be that two full years of brooding have led him to see that murdering Amnon will not only avenge the wrong done to his sister, but will eliminate the heir apparent to his father's throne.

Much more attention is given (in verse 28) to the build up than to the assassination of Amnon itself (in verse 29). Absalom instructs his servants what they are to do and when they are to do it: when the feast is in full swing and Amnon is 'merry with wine', when Absalom gives the command 'Strike Amnon!' they are to kill him. It is worth noting that with the exception of Goliath in 1 Samuel 17, in the whole of this narrative David never kills anyone with his own hands. He orders the execution of numerous unfortunate victims (see for example 1.15, 4.12), but always gets others to do the dirty work for him. Absalom follows that example here. He doesn't shed his brother's blood himself; he gets his men to do that. But Absalom is not yet a leader of Israel, and his intended victim is not a misguided messenger as David's often were. Absalom is asking his servants to do something dangerous so he urges them not to be afraid, assures them that this really is what he wants and bids them to be courageous and valiant. As so often in Hebrew narrative, it is in the dialogue that the plot moves forward.

The actual moment of the assassination by contrast could hardly be reported in less detail: 'the servants of Absalom did to Amnon as Absalom had commanded'. The text does not even say in so many words that Amnon was killed, although that is clear enough. The immediate sequel confirms it: in the ensuing panic, 'all the king's sons rose, and each mounted his mule and fled'.

Scene Four (verses 30-39): The Flight of Absalom

30 While they were on the way, the report came to David that
Absalom had killed all the king's sons, and not one of them

*was left. 31 The king rose, tore his garments, and lay on
the ground; and all his servants who were standing by tore
their garments. 32 But Jonadab, the son of David's brother
Shimeah, said, 'Let not my lord suppose that they have killed
all the young men the king's sons; Amnon alone is dead. This
has been determined by Absalom from the day Amnon raped
his sister Tamar. 33 Now therefore, do not let my lord the
king take it to heart, as if all the king's sons were dead; for
Amnon alone is dead.'*

*34 But Absalom fled. When the young man who kept watch
looked up, he saw many people coming from the Horonaim
road by the side of the mountain. 35 Jonadab said to the king,
'See, the king's sons have come; as your servant said, so it
has come about.' 36 As soon as he had finished speaking, the
king's sons arrived, and raised their voices and wept; and
the king and all his servants also wept very bitterly.*

*37 But Absalom fled, and went to Talmai son of Ammihud,
king of Geshur. David mourned for his son day after day. 38
Absalom, having fled to Geshur, stayed there for three years.
39 And the heart of the king went out, yearning for Absalom;
for he was now consoled over the death of Amnon.*

A report reaches David in Jerusalem before the fleeing princes.
David is told that all his sons are dead and that Absalom has killed
them. It says something about the extent of David's weakness and lethargy, both that such a report should be credible at all and that David
himself should accept it at face value. At once he is overwhelmed by
grief. He lies on the ground as he had done in response to the death of
the son born to Bathsheba (see 12.16). He and his servants tear their
robes, as Tamar had done in response to her rape (see 13.19).

But Jonadab, about whom nothing has been heard since he gave
crafty advice to Amnon (see 13.3), is wise enough to know how misleading initial reports of a traumatic event can be. He urges the king not
to jump to conclusions. 'Amnon alone is dead', he says twice over. It is
clear to him, as it was apparently not clear to David, that Absalom has
been plotting this outcome determinedly ever since the day Amnon had
violated his sister and that this was a highly predictable consequence
of Amnon's attendance at the feast.

Sure enough as soon as Jonadab has finished speaking, the look-
out sees a crowd approaching by the Horonaim road. 'There you are',

Jonadab continues, 'I told you so. It's your sons'. When the kings' sons arrive, they raise their voices in weeping. The king and all his servants also weep bitterly. Presumably they are weeping partly in relief at their escape; but they are also weeping for the loss of the king's first-born and beloved son. But Jonadab is oblivious to, or is at least unaffected by, all this distress. For all that Amnon was his special friend, he is too busy congratulating himself on his superior perspective.

Meanwhile as the king's sons had already done (compare verse 29), Absalom fled. The fact is repeated three times over in verses 34, 37 and 38 (as the words 'David fled' had similarly been repeated at an earlier point in the narrative; see 1 Samuel 19.10, 12, 18). He flees because he chooses not to count on his father's inaction. This time, he senses, the king will be bound to execute justice: the rape of a princess is one thing; the murder of a beloved first-born prince is another.

Absalom took refuge in Geshur with King Talmai his grandfather (see 3.3). He stayed there for three years – longer even than he had waited after the rape of Tamar for the moment to exact his revenge on Amnon. If he was harbouring political ambitions of his own, he was willing to take the long-term view.

The text of the final verse, like the second half of verse 37 is ambiguous. When verse 37b states that 'David mourned for his son day after day', is the son the recently killed Amnon or is it Absalom whose flight is being recorded? The final verse states unambiguously that after those three years David 'was consoled over the death of Amnon'. But it is not clear whether the earlier clause means, as the NRSV translates it, that 'the heart of David went out, yearning for Absalom', or simply that he gave up on any attempt to pursue him. The Hebrew literally states, 'his spirit was spent for Absalom'. It could mean that the passage of time had indeed taken the edge off David's fury – but only within limits. As a father he longs to see his son again. As a king he cannot justly recall him.

Conclusion

It has occasionally been suggested that Amnon's death was in some ways politically convenient to David, as well as to Absalom. Amnon was the son of a wife of David's called 'Ahinoam of Jezreel' (see 3.2). But Ahinoam ('daughter of Ahimaaz') happens also to be the name of one of Saul's wives (see 1 Samuel 14.50). Since David is said to have inherited Saul's wives and concubines (12.8), it is at least possible that

Ahinoam was both his wife and Saul's and that Amnon was therefore, not only his son, but also Saul's posthumous step-son (or at least, a son in some sense uniting David's house with Saul's). But David would surely have regarded this as an asset, not a liability; and in any case it is stressed that David loved Amnon.

There are a number of literary features linking scenes one and two on the one hand, with scenes three and four on the other. The murder in the latter corresponds to the rape in the former. In both, Jonadab is a wise counsellor. In both there is a cunning deceit involving food to make the victim vulnerable to the violator. In both there is a grief-stricken tearing of robes. In both the grief-stricken one is urged not to take the matter to heart. At the end of both David is exposed as passive and powerless. In both (for the first time in this story of David's fall) there is not a single reference to God.

Chapter Ten
2 Samuel 14.1–33

David and the Wise Woman

Introduction

Family relationships can create the most complicated circumstances a person ever has to navigate. For a parent, there are few experiences harder to bear than estrangement from a child. For a Christian, called to the way of peace and reconciliation, such situations can represent the most severe spiritual challenges. If the example of David is anything to go by, they can ruthlessly expose vulnerabilities and limitations of character.

Three years have passed. During that time, David's grief at the death of Amnon has eased, and his anger with Absalom has given way to longing. But how can he possibly declare the amnesty, without which Absalom cannot return from exile? David is trapped between his emotions as a father and his duties as a king. Indeed, it emerges by the end of the episode that his duties as a king complicate his feelings as a father.

This episode is something of an interlude – a moment of light relief in an otherwise relentlessly dark section of the narrative in which David's domestic and political worlds unravel and his success gives way to failure. There is comedy in the encounter first between David and the wise woman of Tekoa (in two scenes in verses 1 to 20); and subsequently between Absalom and Joab (in the single scene in verses 21 to 33).

In the first scene it is tempting to suppose that Joab has taken a leaf out of Nathan's book. But the truth is that David is repeatedly hoodwinked at this stage in his career: to good effect by Nathan in chapter 12, and here by Joab and the wise woman of Tekoa; but to more sinister effect by his two sons in the previous episode, first by Amnon and then by Absalom. He will be similarly fooled by Absalom in the following chapter too. That being said, there is a parallel in verses 1 to 20 with Nathan's parable in chapter 12. David is invited, as the one responsible for the administration in the nation, to pronounce judgment on what is presented as an actual case, only to discover that, in responding to a parable, he has effectively given a verdict against himself. The result is that Absalom returns to Jerusalem. But while Joab is successful in engineering matters thus far, the final two scenes only demonstrate how far David and Absalom remain from complete reconciliation.

Scene One (verses 1-3): Joab recruits a wise woman to trick the king

Now Joab son of Zeruiah perceived that the king's mind was on Absalom. 2 Joab sent to Tekoa and brought from there a wise woman. He said to her, 'Pretend to be in mourning; put on mourning garments, do not anoint yourself with oil, but behave like a woman who has been mourning many days for the dead. 3 Go to the king and speak to him as follows.' And Joab put the words into her mouth.

If David has become lethargic, the same cannot be said for Joab. He is the one who gets things done, who sees things as they really are, who finds effective strategies for every situation.

On this occasion, it is Joab who perceives that the king is preoccupied with Absalom. The NRSV mirrors the slight ambiguity of the Hebrew. It states, 'the king's mind was on Absalom'. But it isn't explicit whether he longed for him or was still seething with anger at him. The outcome of this episode will show that David was utterly torn.

The way in which the previous episode ended (with David yearning for Absalom) and especially David's eventual raw distress at Absalom's death leaves no real doubt as to the reality and depth of the love that he had for his son. But matters are not straightforward. On the one hand, David longs to have his son home; on the other hand, he feels constrained by his judicial responsibilities to withhold a pardon.

Joab perceives this and seeks to provide David with a way out. He recruits a wise woman from Tekoa (see Amos 7.14) and enlists her help. She is to pretend that she has been tragically bereaved; and she is to seek an audience with the king. Unusually in Hebrew narrative, the reader is not given a first airing of what the woman's words are to be.

No clue is given about Joab's motivation here. Most likely, he is concerned about the succession. It may be that he is anxious to ensure the stability of the kingdom and has become convinced that, with Amnon dead, Absalom is the most obvious successor to David.

(He will eventually, fatally, throw his support behind Adonijah rather than Solomon, in 1 Kings 1). Absalom has exhibited ruthlessness – a characteristic Joab himself also shared (3.39) and which he may have regarded as a virtue in a potential future king. In the following scene, when David discerns the hand of Joab behind the woman's charade, it may indicate that Joab has been banging this particular drum (the need for a reconciliation with Absalom in order to secure the succession) so repeatedly that David detects his voice behind that of the woman.

Scene Two (verses 4-20): The woman of Tekoa sets her case before the king

4 When the woman of Tekoa came to the king, she fell on her face to the ground and did obeisance, and said, 'Help, O king!' 5 The king asked her, 'What is your trouble?' She answered, 'Alas, I am a widow; my husband is dead. 6 Your servant had two sons, and they fought with one another in the field; there was no one to part them, and one struck the other and killed him. 7 Now the whole family has risen against your servant. They say, "Give up the man who struck his brother, so that we may kill him for the life of his brother whom he murdered, even if we destroy the heir as well." Thus they would quench my one remaining ember, and leave to my husband neither name nor remnant on the face of the earth.' 8 Then the king said to the woman, 'Go to your house, and I will give orders concerning you.' 9 The woman of Tekoa said to the king, 'On me be the guilt, my lord the king, and on my father's house; let the king and his throne be guiltless.' 10 The king said, 'If anyone says anything to you, bring him to me, and he shall never touch you again.' 11 Then she said, 'Please, may the king keep the Lord your God in mind, so that the avenger of blood may kill no more, and my son not be destroyed.' He said, 'As the Lord lives, not one hair of your son shall fall to the ground.'

12 Then the woman said, 'Please let your servant speak a word to my lord the king.' He said, 'Speak.' 13 The woman said, 'Why then have you planned such a thing against the people of God? For in giving this decision the king convicts himself, inasmuch as the king does not bring his banished one home again. 14 We must all die; we are like water spilled on the ground, which cannot be gathered up. But God will not take away a life; he will devise plans so as not to keep an outcast banished for ever from his presence. 15 Now I have come to say this to my lord the king because the people have made me afraid; your servant thought, "I will speak to the king; it may be that the king will perform the request of his servant. 16 For the king will hear, and deliver his servant from the hand of the man who would cut both me and my son off from the heritage of God." 17 Your servant thought, "The word of my lord the king will set me at rest"; for my lord the king is like the angel of God, discerning good and evil. The Lord your God be with you!' 18 Then the king answered the woman, 'Do not withhold from me anything I ask you.' The woman said, 'Let my lord the king speak.' 19 The king said, 'Is the hand of Joab with you in all this?' The woman answered and said, 'As surely as you live, my lord the king, one cannot turn right or left from anything that my lord the king has said. For it was your servant Joab who commanded me; it was he who put all these words into the mouth of your servant. 20 In order to change the course of affairs your servant Joab did this. But my lord has wisdom like the wisdom of the angel of God to know all things that are on the earth.'

This wise woman of Tekoa is a further example (to add to the list which includes Michal, Abigail, the witch of Endor and Bathsheba) of a female character in this narrative who exercises a disproportionately significant influence over its shape and progress, given how few words in the story relate to her.

She is one more citizen who witnessed that David's primary responsibility is for justice in Israel (for all the trappings of monarchy, he remains the very much a ruler in the image of the Judges). It appears that David is still only too keen to respond to his subjects when they appeal to him. The woman (as far as we know, a stranger to the king) shouts, 'Help!' and he immediately asks, 'What's the problem?'.

The woman explains that (like Naomi in the book of Ruth), she was a wife with two sons. But her men-folk began to expire on her: first her husband died; then (like Cain with Abel) one of her sons set about the other in the field and killed him. Now the family is divided. The woman's relatives want justice for the son who was killed – but they have also worked out that if he is sentenced to death for the murder of his brother, the woman will have no heir and her husband's property will devolve to them. (Like the characters in Jesus' later parable, they are telling one another, 'This is the heir. Come let us kill him and the inheritance will be ours'; Mark 12.7).

Although the woman tells the king her story, she does not say in so many words what it is she wants the king to do. The king gives what is (in verse 8), on the face of it, a positive response. But the woman could be forgiven for supposing that the king is barely interested in the matter. He dismisses the woman with a vague undertaking to attend to her case.

She is not to be thrust aside so easily. She speaks a second time. (In an unusually extended dialogue for this narrative, she will speak no fewer than eight times in all, and the king will respond no fewer than seven. Still more unusually, the longest speeches belong to the woman, particularly in verses 13-17.) She acknowledges that she is guilty of special pleading: for the king to pronounce in favour of her surviving son will require the ordinary course of justice to be suspended. She calls for this on the grounds that responsibility for it will be hers, and not that of the king. Again the king gives what appears to be a favourable response: he says that if anyone should take action against her, she should report it to him. But still this is not enough for the woman: she realises this might be too late. She is not asking for the assurance that if anyone kills her son, they will be brought to justice; she is asking for the assurance that no-one will kill her son. In verse 11 she makes this clear; and the king at last explicitly concedes what she has requested. Surely she has now got what she came for?

It is therefore something of a surprise when the woman speaks again in verse 12. She knows that this is the most delicate point in her encounter with the king. So she carefully asks for permission to speak on. David gives it. Then the woman abandons her fiction and confronts the king directly: 'How can it be?', she demands, 'that you can agree to pardon my son, who has killed his brother, and yet refuse to pardon your own son in the same circumstance. It's a miscarriage of justice against the whole people of God! (This is a rare phrase, and it is startling that she should introduce it out of nowhere. The woman is clearly speaking about Absalom, even though Absalom is not named. Does she mean that Absalom is an obvious successor to David and that by his intransigence the king risks depriving God's people of a rightful successor to himself? Does Absalom's exile create a problem for the nation and threaten its security?)

Her speech reaches its climax with an affirmation of the merciful goodness of God: 'God will not take away a life. He will devise plans so as not to keep an outcast banished forever from his presence'. The woman's view of God is extraordinary. It is not merely that she speaks often of God and appeals to the king (in verse 11) to keep the Lord God in mind. It is rather that she understands God to be the kind of god who would sooner spare a life than take it. She has evidently learned that 'the Lord is gracious and merciful, slow to anger and abounding in steadfast love' (Exodus 34.6, Joel 2.13, Jonah 4.2, Psalms 86.5, 103.8, 145.8 and Nehemiah 9.17).

It is odd that, having abandoned her cover in verse 13, the woman seems to retreat to the refuge of her fiction in verse 15. She speaks again (especially in verse 16) of 'the man who would cut both me and my son off from the heritage of God'. It is almost as odd as if Nathan, having declared to David, 'You are the man', had suddenly begun to speak again about the poor man and his lamb. But in fact verses 15-17 are wonderfully ambiguous. At one level it does seem that the woman has reverted to her parable. Perhaps she feels that unlike Nathan, the prophet of God, she has no authority to rebuke the king even indirectly. Or perhaps she is seeking to protect Joab. And yet at another level her words (in verses 15 and 17, if not in verse 16) are utterly relevant to the issue of David's relationship with Absalom. 'Your servant thought', she tells him, "I will speak to the king. It may be that the king will perform the request of his servant…" Your servant thought, "The word of my lord the king will set me at rest"; for my lord the king is like the angel of God, discerning good and evil. The Lord is with you'.

She is not the first person to compare David to 'the angel of God' (see 1 Samuel 29.9); nor is she the first (though she is the last) to state that the Lord is with David (see 5.10; also 1 Samuel 16.18; 18.12, 14, 28).

But the wise woman is only as wise as Jonadab, or as cunning as Joab. When Nathan used a parable, it was to prick David's conscience, to bring him to his senses and to circumvent his passion. In this case the situation is reversed: Joab's ruse is intended to by-pass David's conscience and to arouse his affection for his son. Besides, the situation between Absalom and Amnon is not parallel to that of the two sons in the woman's story: for one thing, her story implies a case of manslaughter, rather than outright cold-blooded and premeditated murder (verse 6); and for another, David would not be left childless by the loss of Absalom as well as Amnon, as the woman would be if her fictive second son were killed.

At this point the woman has said everything that she has to say and the tables are turned. King David effectively seeks her permission to speak. As in verse 12, what is sought is licence to broach a new layer of truthfulness. David asks, 'Is this Joab's work?'. The woman concedes that it is, but hopes by flattery to disarm the king from any fury he may feel on this account. She begins by asserting that David's wisdom is so great that it is not possible to turn either to the left or to the right in defiance of him. Then in verses 19b-20a she first admits that Joab has set up this contrivance, but then adds why he did so. Finally (from verse 20b) she acknowledges that it was a forlorn hope if it was ever expected that such a ruse should hoodwink the king: for 'my lord has wisdom like the wisdom of the angel of God to know all things that are on the earth'. If David believes this, it only confirms quite the opposite: in his old age, the king has become naïve and gullible and susceptible even to the flattery of strangers.

The woman then disappears from the narrative even more swiftly than she appeared: this time there is no reply from the king. It is striking because there has been a remarkably sustained toing and froing in speech between the king and herself since verse 20. Here there is not even a statement of the woman's departure from David's presence. The end of her speech marks the end of her part in the story.

Scene Three (verses 21-24): Joab brings Absalom back to Jerusalem

> *21 Then the king said to Joab, 'Very well, I grant this; go, bring back the young man Absalom.' 22 Joab prostrated himself with his face to the ground and did obeisance, and blessed the king; and Joab said, 'Today your servant knows that I have found favour in your sight, my lord the king, in that the king has granted the request of his servant.' 23 So Joab set off, went to Geshur, and brought Absalom to Jerusalem. 24 The king said, 'Let him go to his own house; he is not to come into my presence.' So Absalom went to his own house, and did not come into the king's presence.*

The narrative focus moves on at once to David's instruction to Joab to fetch Absalom home. The shift in scene is so swift that it is tempting to imagine that Joab has been waiting in the wings, eavesdropping on the king and the wise woman from just outside the room. Even though neither David nor Joab refer to the woman or to her part in proceedings, the very abruptness of the transition serves to emphasise that when David accedes to Joab's request, the king's concession is itself his response to her. In his 'Very well' there is perhaps a veiled acknowledgment of her contribution. It is also a clear if oblique recognition that what he is granting really is Joab's wish rather than the woman's.

When David speaks of his son as 'the young man Absalom', it may be that there is a note of reservation in the mode of address. No family tie is admitted. David will use the same phrase again, in conversation with Joab but also with others, during the period of Absalom's rebellion (18.5, 12, 29, 32). It contrasts sharply with the way David will speak of his son after he is dead (18.33, 19.4).

Joab greets the king's decision with proper deference, prostrating himself and referring to the king in the third person and to himself, twice, as a servant. In this context there is presumably nothing presumptuous in his blessing the king, even though it is usually the greater who blesses the lesser and not the other way around.

His journey to Geshur (an independent city-state close to Syria in the modern-day Golan Heights) and back is recounted in a few words. His errand is successful. Absalom returns to Jerusalem.

But there is a sting in the tail of this scene. It emerges that David is far from reconciled to his son. He gives an order: Absalom is to go to his own house. He is not to enter the king's presence. The text then reports this as an accomplished fact: Absalom went to his own house and did not come into the king's presence. The repetition alerts the reader to the significance of this development.

The outcome is surely not what Joab had in mind. It may be the worst of both worlds: Absalom is back in Jerusalem, but not quite back in favour. He is back in the public eye, but banished from the king's house. If he is disaffected, he is now sufficiently close by to be a threat.

The text gives no clues as to David's intentions here or what he hoped to achieve. The decision has the feel of one made impulsively, perhaps even at the news of Absalom's arrival in Jerusalem, rather than of one made carefully and fully thought through. Politically, the compromise is foolish. Personally, it seems petty. At an earlier stage it appeared that the conflict was between his longing for his son as a father and his sense of responsibility to act justly as a king. Yet the efficacy of the woman's parable has demonstrated that Absalom's return may serve the interests of justice and of the nation too.

How differently the sequel might have been if David had welcomed Absalom fully into his presence. What a contrast between the part played by David here and the part played by the father in Jesus' parable of the prodigal son (see Luke 15.20-23; but of course, there is no indication that Absalom was as contrite as the prodigal in Jesus' story).

Scene Four (verses 25-33): Absalom and David are apparently reconciled

25 Now in all Israel there was no one to be praised so much for his beauty as Absalom; from the sole of his foot to the crown of his head there was no blemish in him. 26 When he cut the hair of his head (for at the end of every year he used to cut it; when it was heavy on him, he cut it), he weighed the hair of his head, two hundred shekels by the king's weight. 27 There were born to Absalom three sons, and one daughter whose name was Tamar; she was a beautiful woman.

28 So Absalom lived two full years in Jerusalem without coming into the king's presence. 29 Then Absalom sent for Joab to send him to the king; but Joab would not come to him. He sent a second time, but Joab would not come. 30 Then he said to his servants, 'Look, Joab's field is next to mine, and he has barley there; go and set it on fire.' So Absalom's servants set the field on fire. 31 Then Joab rose and went to Absalom at his house, and said to him, 'Why have your servants set my field on fire?' 32 Absalom answered Joab, 'Look, I sent word to you: Come here, that I may send you to the king with the question, "Why have I come from Geshur? It would be better for me to be there still." Now let me go into the king's presence; if there is guilt in me, let him kill me!' 33 Then Joab went to the king and told him; and he summoned Absalom. So he came to the king and prostrated himself with his face to the ground before the king; and the king kissed Absalom.

To this point in the story Absalom has been a somewhat shadowy figure. Here he is properly introduced for the first time. Like his father David (1 Samuel 16.12), his sister Tamar (13.1) and his daughter by the same name (verse 27) he is fabulously beautiful. Unlike them (as far as the text indicates), he was also vain. His beauty was a thing to be praised. His pride and joy was his luxuriant hair. Once a year, he would cut it. Evidently this was an event. In this pride, he would weigh the clippings, glorying in its heaviness as a mark of his virility. (It amounts to five or six pounds in weight, or two to three kilos.) His three sons likewise testify to his potency.

This is not much of a character reference. He is good looking, with especially lovely hair; and he has children. Nothing at all is said about any particular skills or abilities, nor about any faith or trust in God. It is an especially empty portrait in comparison with the way in which David was introduced, as a skilful musician, a man of valour, prudent in speech and full of presence (1 Samuel 16.18). Absalom would have been at home in the western world today, where in politics as popular culture, appearances triumph over aptitude and style over substance.

This beautiful hirsute Absalom lived 'two full years' in Jerusalem without coming into the king's presence. 'Two full years' is not a common phrase in the Hebrew bible, so it can be no coincidence that this is exactly the length of time he waited before exacting revenge on Amnon (see 13.23). It is now seven years since the rape of Tamar. If Absalom has a particular talent, perhaps it is for patient plotting.

After two full years then Absalom feels sufficiently confident or impatient to press for a resolution to his predicament. He sends for Joab 'to send him to the king'. He wants Joab once again to act as an intermediary. But Joab refuses to respond, not once but twice. Joab is a powerful agent in chapters 12 to 20, frequently intervening decisively. There has been a shift in the balance of power since David solicited Joab's help in killing Uriah. Yet Joab remains loyal to the king. If David will not see Absalom, nor will Joab.

But there is a limit to Absalom's patience. He is not a man to take 'No' for an answer. He is content to wait; but not to be thwarted. He instructs his servants to commit an act of vandalism. They are to set on fire a field of barley belonging to Joab, which happens to be adjacent to Absalom's own field. As Absalom anticipated, this gets Joab's attention. Perhaps the only way to get the ear of a man of violence (see 3.39) is with an act of violence. In person Joab goes to Absalom's house and confronts him. 'Why have your servants set my field on fire?'. Absalom explains: 'What's the good of my having come from Geshur. Either I am guilty [of my brother's murder], in which case let the king kill me. Or [particularly in the light of the king's failure to do anything at all], what I did was justifiable in the circumstances, in which case I should not be punished. I should be free to enter the king's presence'.

Joab is persuaded, and goes at once to David. The king is persuaded and summons his son. At last there is a physical, and presumably public, reconciliation. Absalom prostrates himself before the king and David kisses his son.

Conclusion

There are three bowings before David in this episode: first the wise woman (verse 4), then Joab (verse 22) and finally Absalom (verse 33) prostrate themselves before David and do obeisance. The series is climactic and only Absalom is received with a kiss.

Yet the reconciliation described in the final verse of the episode is threadbare. Statutory categories take precedence here over personal ones. This is the king becoming formally reconciled to a troublesome subject rather than David becoming reconciled to a wayward son. There is no dialogue (which, in Hebrew narrative, is always a mark that what transpires is somehow superficial and fails to engage the emotions). There is no real meeting of minds or hearts here even when Absalom gets the face to face meeting with the king that he has waited two years to achieve. No forgiveness has truly been offered by David or received by his son.

The consequences of this will be tragic. Absalom will dominate the next few chapters, and his actions will plunge the kingdom of Israel into costly civil war. Yet this episode is also a story about David being charged with wrongdoing and responding contritely. Between the first act of obeisance in the chapter and the second, the woman declares that the king has convicted himself (verse 13) of wrongdoing. The king might have responded to this charge in any number of ways. He might certainly have responded more defensively and defiantly. But it is typical of the meekness which David manifests throughout the narrative in the story of his fall that he responds not in self-righteousness by protesting his innocence, but in humility by agreeing with the woman's proposal.

The Rebellion of Absalom

Introduction

It is striking how often adversity brings out the best in a person. As long as circumstances are essentially easy, it is possible to coast. It is only when things go wrong that it becomes necessary to dig deep and to tap reserves of character and strength that might not otherwise have been drawn upon at all.

The reconciliation between David and Absalom proves to have been superficial. The vague chronological reference in verse 1 suggests that these events followed quite swiftly on the close of the previous episode. It will be another four years (verse 7) before Absalom is sufficiently confident of his powerbase to embark on rebellion outright; but he begins to build that powerbase without delay. Perhaps he is encouraged in his designs by his father's languor. David has been a shadow of his former self since Nathan denounced him in chapter 12. Once Absalom rebels however something of the old David (which is to say, the young David) returns. By the end of this episode, David is once again exercising the faith and generosity which had previously characterised him.

The episode comprises five scenes. In the first, Absalom deliberately adopts some of the trappings of kingship and sets out to woo support among the Israelites. In the second, he visits Hebron, ostensibly to worship the Lord, but in reality to launch an uprising. In the third, the rebellion gathers momentum. In the fourth (easily the longest), events are described in some detail as David surprisingly opts to abandon his capital city. In the final scene, the king begins his counter-attack, sending an ally back to Jerusalem as a spy.

Scene One (verses 1-6): Absalom steals the hearts of the people of Israel

After this Absalom got himself a chariot and horses, and fifty men to run ahead of him. 2 Absalom used to rise early and stand beside the road into the gate; and when anyone brought a suit before the king for judgement, Absalom would call out and say, 'From what city are you?' When the person said, 'Your servant is of such and such a tribe in Israel', 3 Absalom would say, 'See, your claims are good and right; but there is no one deputed by the king to hear you.' 4 Absalom said moreover, 'If only I were judge in the land! Then all who had a suit or cause might come to me, and I would give them justice.' 5 Whenever people came near to do obeisance to him, he would put out his hand and take hold of them, and kiss them. 6 Thus Absalom did to every Israelite who came to the king for judgement; so Absalom stole the hearts of the people of Israel.

The wise woman of Tekoa credited David (14.20) with having the wisdom to know 'all things that are on the earth' (or more probably, 'everything taking place in the land'). But either David was oblivious to what Absalom was up to or he foolishly chose to turn a blind eye to it.

Absalom acquires a chariot and horses and men to run before him, heralding his presence. It is unmistakably the act of a man who would be king (see 1 Kings 1.5) – and a king like one from the neighbouring nations at that (see 1.6; 8.3-4; Exodus 14.7-29).

But Absalom was capable of the subtle manouevre as well as the blatant one. However vain he may have been, he was not a lazy man. He is as energetic as his father is lethargic. Day after day, in pursuit of his goal, he rose early and made his way to the city gate in order to be in the place where legal disputes were traditionally heard, at the time it was conventional to hear them (see Ruth 4.1-11; Jeremiah 21.12).

It was not simply in succession to 'the judges' that Israelite kings were appointed, but in order to put right a judicial system which had gone wrong (see 1 Samuel 8.1-2). David at his best dispensed justice and equity in Israel. And if Absalom is to become king, he must first convince the people that he can fulfil the judicial function more effectively than his father. So he loiters at the place of justice and curries favour among those who seek the king's intervention there. Either David has become slow and ineffective at hearing the cases which are brought to him (which would be entirely consistent with the impression of indolence he gives at this stage of his reign) or Absalom is able to create the impression that it is so and to exaggerate the problems. He assures supplicants that their cases are strong (which is easy enough to do if judgment has only to be dispensed in theory not practice). It is always easier to be the party of opposition than the party of government. 'Oh, if only I were judge', he sighs. 'I wouldn't keep people waiting like my father. I'd make sure people had prompt hearings – and favourable ones'. It is not necessary for him to declare openly his desire to be king. Everyone knows that it is the king's job to exercise justice.

So the narrator says 'Absalom stole the hearts of the people of Israel'. The surprise here is not that Absalom succeeded in his objective, but that David lost people's hearts so easily. The expression surely means that Absalom won not just the affection of the Israelites, but their political loyalty and commitment also. How did David alienate his subjects? Perhaps there was a widespread loss of public confidence in his leadership partly on account of what he did (in relation to Bathsheba and Uriah) and partly on account of what he failed to do (in relation to Amnon and then Absalom). Perhaps his sins of commission and of omission have undermined his credibility as the nation's judge.

It may be that Absalom's efforts were focused on the Israelites in the narrow, rather than the broad, sense of that word. Was he especially seeking to cultivate support among the northern tribes, who might be quick to feel disadvantaged by David's administration of justice? David's Judean origins possibly made his support precarious among the former subjects of Ishbaal (2 Samuel 2-4) so that these were only too eager to transfer their allegiance to Absalom (especially given his political affiliation to Geshur). Interestingly, the wise woman of Tekoa, who succeeded in getting David's ear readily enough when she brought her case to be heard by him, came from the south.

In a sense of course Absalom had already usurped David's role as judge when he took matters into his own hands and killed Amnon for what he had done to Tamar. But that act of usurpation was isolated and personal; now he is usurping his father's role systematically and publicly. There remains but one step and that is for him to usurp his father's throne.

Scene Two (verses 7-9): Absalom proposes to worship the Lord in Hebron

7 At the end of four years Absalom said to the king, 'Please let me go to Hebron and pay the vow that I have made to the Lord. 8 For your servant made a vow while I lived at Geshur in Aram: If the Lord will indeed bring me back to Jerusalem, then I will worship the Lord in Hebron.' 9 The king said to him, 'Go in peace.' So he got up, and went to Hebron.

Absalom's request – or rather David's apparent lack of unease about it – is intriguing for two reasons. First there is the timing. On any reading of verse 7 (it is impossible to be certain about the chronology because the Hebrew manuscript tradition is confusing), it is clear in the light of 14.28 that it took Absalom an inordinately long time to get round to honouring a vow he made in Geshur. He has been back in Jerusalem at least two years and probably six. One possibility is that it is now seven years since he killed his brother (taking verse 7 to mean 'four years after he returned from Geshur' and adding the three years he spent in exile there, 13.38). It may be that that was a requisite period of penance for a crime such as Absalom's and that the worship to which he refers is the sacrifice which will expiate his transgression. Yet it seems not to have occurred to David to question his son's motivation or to ask, 'Why now?'.

Absalom's request is intriguing secondly because he specifies that he wishes to go to worship the Lord in Hebron. At least twice already in this story an occasion to worship the Lord has been used as a cover for some ulterior purpose. When Samuel first went to Bethlehem (in 1 Samuel 16.1-5) to anoint David, his fear of Saul was such that the Lord encouraged his prophet to pretend that the purpose of his journey was to make a sacrifice. When David himself fled from Saul's presence, Jonathan claimed that his friend was absent from the king's table only because he had returned to his home town to join his family in offering a sacrifice. So David can hardly be unaware of the risk that Absalom's request is sinister. Moreover there is no evidence that Hebron was regarded as a particularly holy place or served as a traditional centre of worship in Israel. What better place for worship than Jerusalem, where the ark of the Lord was stationed? Conversely Hebron was Absalom's birthplace and the place where David himself had first been acclaimed as king. It was therefore an obvious power base for Absalom, especially if there was any lingering sense of betrayal by David among its citizens after he moved his capital city to Jerusalem. Yet it seems not to have occurred to David to ask, 'Why Hebron?'.

David's complete lack of suspicion is all the more surprising given that Absalom had deceived his father with a similar, ostensibly innocent, request in the run up to Amnon's murder. If David had any qualms about these developments there is no hint of it in the text. Rather he dismissed his son in peace and Absalom went at once to Hebron.

It transpires that these were the last words exchanged between father and son. Absalom speaks repeatedly of the Lord but with deceitful intent. David speaks of peace but with almost willful naivety.

Scene Three (verses 10-12): Absalom's conspiracy grows in strength

10 But Absalom sent secret messengers throughout all the tribes of Israel, saying, 'As soon as you hear the sound of the trumpet, then shout: Absalom has become king at Hebron!' 11 Two hundred men from Jerusalem went with Absalom; they were invited guests, and they went in their innocence, knowing nothing of the matter. 12 While Absalom was offering the sacrifices, he sent for Ahithophel the Gilonite, David's counsellor, from his city Giloh. The conspiracy grew in strength, and the people with Absalom kept increasing.

Hebron may provide a convenient platform for Absalom's rebellion in the short-term. But he has been building support 'throughout all the tribes of Israel' for several years and now sends secret messengers to his supporters to tell them to await the proclamation of his kingdom. (On the use of the trumpet to herald a new king, compare 1 Kings 1.34, 39, 2 Kings 9.13, 11.14.) It must have been a considerable logistical feat to dispatch sufficient messengers. This was a substantial conspiracy.

Meanwhile Absalom takes with him two hundred men from Jerusalem – all apparently innocent of his intentions and as unsuspecting as David. If the king has authorised the expedition, after all, what concern can there be?

From Hebron Absalom sends for a key recruit to his cause. Ahithophel is described as 'David's counsellor'. He was apparently a principal member of his team (although this is the first time he has been mentioned and his name does not feature in the list of officers in chapter 8.16-18). He may have been grandfather to Bathsheba, since he had a son by the name of Eliam (included in the list of the Thirty of David's most valiant warriors, 23.34), which was also the name of her father (11.3). It could be that his defection to Absalom reflects a sense of betrayal by David and a lingering loyalty to Uriah and resentment over the treatment of his granddaughter.

At some point the trumpets were presumably duly sounded. At any rate the conspiracy became a matter of public knowledge, so that it became possible to speak of it growing and of people flocking to join it. What happened to the two hundred innocent participants in Absalom's act of 'worship' is not clear.

Scene Four (verses 13-31): David abandons Jerusalem

13 A messenger came to David, saying, 'The hearts of the Israelites have gone after Absalom.' 14 Then David said to all his officials who were with him at Jerusalem, 'Get up!

*Let us flee, or there will be no escape for us from Absalom.
Hurry, or he will soon overtake us, and bring disaster down
upon us, and attack the city with the edge of the sword.' 15
The king's officials said to the king, 'Your servants are ready
to do whatever our lord the king decides.' 16 So the king
left, followed by all his household, except ten concubines
whom he left behind to look after the house. 17 The king left,
followed by all the people; and they stopped at the last house.
18 All his officials passed by him; and all the Cherethites,
and all the Pelethites, and all the six hundred Gittites who
had followed him from Gath, passed on before the king.*

*19 Then the king said to Ittai the Gittite, 'Why are you also
coming with us? Go back, and stay with the king; for you are
a foreigner, and also an exile from your home. 20 You came
only yesterday, and shall I today make you wander about
with us, while I go wherever I can? Go back, and take your
kinsfolk with you; and may the Lord show steadfast love and
faithfulness to you.' 21 But Ittai answered the king, 'As the
Lord lives, and as my lord the king lives, wherever my lord
the king may be, whether for death or for life, there also
your servant will be.' 22 David said to Ittai, 'Go then, march
on.' So Ittai the Gittite marched on, with all his men and
all the little ones who were with him. 23 The whole country
wept aloud as all the people passed by; the king crossed
the Wadi Kidron, and all the people moved on towards the
wilderness.*

*24 Abiathar came up, and Zadok also, with all the Levites,
carrying the ark of the covenant of God. They set down the
ark of God, until the people had all passed out of the city.
25 Then the king said to Zadok, 'Carry the ark of God back
into the city. If I find favour in the eyes of the Lord, he will
bring me back and let me see both it and the place where it
remains. 26 But if he says, "I take no pleasure in you", here
I am, let him do to me what seems good to him.' 27 The king
also said to the priest Zadok, 'Look, go back to the city in
peace, you and Abiathar, with your two sons, Ahimaaz your
son, and Jonathan son of Abiathar. 28 See, I will wait at the
fords of the wilderness until word comes from you to inform
me.' 29 So Zadok and Abiathar carried the ark of God back
to Jerusalem, and they remained there.*

30 But David went up the ascent of the Mount of Olives, weeping as he went, with his head covered and walking barefoot; and all the people who were with him covered their heads and went up, weeping as they went. 31 David was told that Ahithophel was among the conspirators with Absalom. And David said, 'O Lord, I pray you, turn the counsel of Ahithophel into foolishness.'

News of the conspiracy reaches David in Jerusalem. In verse 6 the reader was told that Absalom was stealing the hearts of the people of Israel. Now a messenger tells David, 'the hearts of the Israelites have gone after Absalom' (verse 13).

The king's response is urgent. 'Quick!', he calls, 'we must flee'. His instinct is to revert to the pattern of flight he knew under Saul. Why does he not plan to fight in defence of Jerusalem and the throne? Is he really so fearful and so pessimistic about his chances of victory? Does he not still have the upper hand – possession of the capital city (which, until David took it was considered almost impregnable, compare 5.6), the loyalty of a large and experienced army, and ample wealth and resources?

But there is another possibility. It may be that what he wants to avoid is not defeat but a bloody conflict in Jerusalem. It may be that his response is not one of panic and fear, but one of political pragmatism or even of spiritual courage. Perhaps he wants to spare the city the trauma of battle and the 'collateral damage' that such conflicts inevitably entail. Perhaps, just as David had earlier refused to snatch at the crown (2.1-4), he now refuses to cling to it.

Certainly no-one advises against the course of action the king suggests. His officers assure him of their loyal support. So David evacuates, together with all his household; that is, all except for ten concubines who are left 'to look after the house' – a decision he would later come to regret (16.20-22). Why does the house need 'looking after'? And if this piece of property were deemed worthy of care, how on earth did David imagine ten females associated with himself would be safe to provide it? Did he really not foresee their fate? Or were they in fact left as some sort of lightening conductor to 'earth' the wrath of God prophesied by Nathan in 12.11-12. If there was a degree of calculation about David's decision to leave Jerusalem, it is likely there was also a degree of calculation about his decision to abandon his concubines to their fate.

So the king leads his officials into exile. At the edge of the city, at the last house, David stops and the procession marches past him, including the Pelethites and the Cherethites (see 8.18) and six hundred 'Gittites who had followed him from Gath'. Presumably the latter are his most longstanding troops, who were with him when he sought refuge with King Achish, and thus followed him first into Gath in 1 Samuel 27.1-4 and then out again afterwards as implied by 1 Samuel 30.9; see also 2 Samuel 6.11).

Then the king speaks to Ittai, leader of the Gittites. This is the first in a series of five encounters David has as he leaves Jerusalem which will in due course be balanced by a series of four on his return (in 2 Samuel 19). After Ittai, Abiathar and Zadok together (15.24-29), then Hushai (15.32-37), Ziba (16.1-4) and Shimei (16.5-8) will encounter the king as he departs; the last two of these (19.16-23), plus Mephibosheth (19.24-30) and Barzillai (19.31-40) will do so on his return.

It is no coincidence that it is in speaking with one of his oldest allies that David first recovers his old tone of faith and trust in God. As Ittai marches past, David urges him to turn back and remain in the city. 'After all', he says, 'you owe me nothing. You're a foreigner who joined my ranks only yesterday'. He gives Ittai every opportunity to withdraw with honour. In fact, if the six hundred men led by Ittai are indeed the six hundred referred to in 1 Samuel 27.1-4, then he has been with David something over 20 years – certainly from a time before Absalom was even born (3.2). At the climax of this generous invitation to Ittai, David prays that the Lord might show the Gittite his steadfast love and faithfulness. What he seeks for Ittai is what he most needs himself. It is a piety David has not shown since before his affair with Bathsheba.

Presumably to help Ittai feel free to choose to stay in Jerusalem, David goes as far in verse 19 as to call Absalom 'the king'. The title is all the more startling because of the studied emphasis on David's kingship in the surrounding verses. Verse 15 is typical: 'The king's officials said to the king, "Your servants are ready to do whatever our lord the king decides"'. David may be ready to concede his crown to his son; but his faithful officials are not.

Ittai chooses to stay with David. (The Hebrew *'iti* means 'with me'.) He promises solemnly, with an invocation of the Lord, that he (and his men and all the little ones with them, verse 22) will remain with David whatever the cost. His words are reminiscent of those of Ruth to Naomi in Ruth 1.16-17. Ittai is a man of war. He understands that there may be a cost. His commitment is 'for death or for life'. The pledge is not lightly made.

It is a symbolically highly charged moment when (in verse 23) David crosses the Wadi Kidron and the exodus begins to head out towards the wilderness. At the sight, 'the whole country wept aloud'. As David leaves Jerusalem in the company of his faithful followers but under threat, Christian readers are reminded of the journey made by Jesus with his disciples on the night before he died (see John 18.1).

Now a critical decision has to be made. Is the ark of God to go into exile with David or to remain in Jerusalem? Is it destined to cross not just the Wadi Kidron but the Jordan River out of Israel, as David will do in 17.22 (in a reversal of what had happened at the conquest in Joshua 3.14-17)? Abiathar and Zadok present themselves before David 'with all the Levites' (to whom this, in verse 24, is one of only two references in 1 and 2 Samuel; compare 1 Samuel 6.15, also in association with the ark). But the priests say nothing. Perhaps they dare not express a preference. Again David is first to speak. Addressing himself to Zadok, he again urges his followers to turn back. Again his words are full of trust in the providence of God. Perhaps, if he finds favour with the Lord, the Lord will restore him to Jerusalem and will enable him to see the ark in its rightful place once again. But if not, 'Let him do to me what seems good to him' he says. If in bringing the ark to Jerusalem in 2 Samuel 6, David was in danger of identifying the purpose and will of God with his own, then here in refusing to take the ark out of Jerusalem, he is correcting his mistake. Remarkably, David is able to distinguish between knowing that *God* is with him and having the *symbol* of God's presence with him. He is also ready to run the risk that not all his opponents or supporters will be able to make that distinction. Some must surely have supposed that the one in possession not just of Jerusalem, but of the ark of God, was the one with divine legitimation.

There is no word of protest from the priests, nor any word of acceptance or sorrow. Instead David speaks again. He tells Zadok that he and Abiathar, together with their sons (also priests) are to go back to the city 'in peace'. He then adds a commission. It isn't immediately obvious that his words are an instruction to the priests to act covertly as spies on his behalf. The sequel in 17.15-21 however leaves no doubt at all that that is what is meant when he tells them that he will wait at the fords of the wilderness 'until word comes from you to inform me' (verse 28). Again this is more like the old David, who typically combined real faith with shrewd political acumen (see for example the two contrasting questions about fighting Goliath which are David's very first words in this story, in 1 Samuel 17.26).

As the priests and the ark of God turn back, David continues his *Via Dolorosa*. He stands weeping on the Mount of Olives as a descendant (also rejected by the people, although the rightful king) would do under

difference circumstances many centuries later (see Luke 19.41). He
walks barefoot, with his head covered. His followers also weep, with
covered heads (see Ezekiel 24.17, 23). Then comes a bitter blow as
David learns that Ahithophel is among the defectors. But he responds
in a simple prayer that God might thwart any counsel Ahithophel offers
Absalom and turn it 'into foolishness'. This is the first time David
has been recorded in prayer since his response to Nathan's oracle in 2
Samuel 7.

**Scene Five (verses 32-37): David sends Hushai the Archite back to
Jerusalem**

> *32 When David came to the summit, where God was wor-
> shipped, Hushai the Archite came to meet him with his coat
> torn and earth on his head. 33 David said to him, 'If you go
> on with me, you will be a burden to me. 34 But if you return to
> the city and say to Absalom, "I will be your servant, O king;
> as I have been your father's servant in time past, so now I
> will be your servant", then you will defeat for me the counsel
> of Ahithophel. 35 The priests Zadok and Abiathar will be
> with you there. So whatever you hear from the king's house,
> tell it to the priests Zadok and Abiathar. 36 Their two sons
> are with them there, Zadok's son Ahimaaz and Abiathar's
> son Jonathan; and by them you shall report to me everything
> you hear.' 37 So Hushai, David's friend, came into the city,
> just as Absalom was entering Jerusalem.*

David's prayer is effectively answered at once, although it will be
some time before he knows it. As he reaches the summit, a high place
where God is worshiped, he meets another of his faithful followers.
Hushai the Archite is in mourning, with his coat torn and with earth on
his head, in complete solidarity with the king. Hushai is another, like
Ahithophel, who is evidently ones of the king's most trusted allies,
but of whom there has been no mention in the story until now. Indeed
when in verse 37 he is described as 'David's friend' this seems to be
an official title (which recurs for example at 1 Kings 4.5) rather than
a merely personal statement: he is David's Friend, his confidant and
adviser, perhaps a longstanding rival to Ahithophel for the king's ear.
    Again David is first to speak and again his intention is to urge his
friend to turn back. This time his political strategy is unmistakable: 'If
you come with me, you'll only be in the way', David tells Hushai. 'But

if you return to Jerusalem, you can ingratiate yourself with Absalom and position yourself to render useless any advice given by Ahithophel. I want you to be a double agent'. David explains to Hushai how he can use the priests and their sons as part of an intelligence network of trusted couriers to provide David with inside information about Absalom's plans.

So Hushai's return to the city coincides perfectly and providentially with the arrival of Absalom.

Conclusion

The crucial question when times are hard is this: on whom will I rely? When my own resources are stretched and I am barely coping, where will I turn? It is an extraordinary mark of grace that in this episode David rediscovers that ultimately he can only rely on God. Family is not to be relied upon and friends are fickle.

It is in this sense that Christians have found over and over again that adversity can be good for the soul. When all else is taken away, there is nothing for it but to cast oneself on the mercy of God, who is faithful.

So it is that David's three encounters with Ittai, Zadok and Abiathar together, and Hushai share two features. The first is a renewed sense of trust on David's part in the purpose of God. To Ittai and to his priests, he speaks of the Lord. Immediately before his encounter with Hushai, he prays. Face to face with these potential allies, David finds himself still more directly face to face with God himself.

The second feature is his invitation to them to 'go back'. All three parties are invited to return to Jerusalem. David is not relying on them, but on God to provide. Nevertheless, it is clear that David has not abandoned his cunning. He is still planning shrewdly, though now against his own son. The upshot is that David has taken the soldier Ittai with him into the wilderness, but has deployed the priests and the diplomat behind enemy lines.

This combination of faith and trust in God with astute strategy is hard to achieve: it is much easier to combine faith and trust in God with political naivety, or expedient shrewdness with self-reliance.

Chapter Twelve
2 Samuel 16.1–23

David and Absalom

Introduction

To know who your friends are is a wonderful comfort. To know who your enemies are is some kind of defence. Unfortunately not everyone falls neatly into one category or the other.

In the previous episode David, fleeing, met with a series of friends: Ittai the Gittite, Zadok and Abiathar the priests and Hushai the Archite. Their intentions were sincerely loyal and he was able to speak with them frankly; and he spoke often of Yahweh.

In this episode David meets with two others. Both are associates of King Saul. The second is openly hostile; but the first is friendly, at least superficially. In the first scene, he meets with Ziba, the servant of Mephibosheth, whose life was probably impoverished by David's generosity to Jonathan's son in 2 Samuel 9. In the second scene, he meets with Shimei in one of the defining encounters in this story and stands accused of being a man of blood.

Then the spotlight in this episode shifts from David to Absalom. In the final scene, David's decision in the previous episode to leave his concubines 'to care for the house' has truly terrible repercussions.

Scene One (verses 1-4): David and Ziba

> When David had passed a little beyond the summit, Ziba the servant of Mephibosheth met him, with a couple of donkeys saddled, carrying two hundred loaves of bread, one hundred bunches of raisins, one hundred of summer fruits, and one skin of wine. 2 The king said to Ziba, 'Why have you brought these?' Ziba answered, 'The donkeys are for the king's household to ride, the bread and summer fruit for the young men to eat, and the wine is for those to drink who faint in the

wilderness.' 3 The king said, 'And where is your master's son?'
Ziba said to the king, 'He remains in Jerusalem; for he said,
"Today the house of Israel will give me back my grandfather's
kingdom."' 4 Then the king said to Ziba, 'All that belonged
to Mephibosheth is now yours.' Ziba said, 'I do obeisance; let
me find favour in your sight, my lord the king.'

As David begins his descent of the Mount of Olives, he is met by
a fifth person: Ziba the servant of Mephibosheth, with a couple of
donkeys and a considerable supply of provisions. The gift is greatly
reminiscent of the one brought to David by Abigail in 1 Samuel 25.
As Ziba is now doing, Abigail was attempting to ingratiate herself
with David. But whereas Abigail was seeking to atone for a blatant
transgression on the part of her husband Nabal, who was openly hostile
to David, this scene turns on the ambiguity as to whether Mephibosheth
is guilty of an equivalent hostility and transgression. Given the sequel
in 19.24-30, it seems more likely that Ziba is here acting duplicitously
to further his own interests.

David apparently suspects as much. He asks a wary question,
'What's all this for?'. Ziba (comically exaggerating the usefulness of
the donkeys) states the obvious: 'The food is for your men to eat, and
the wine is for those who might become weary in the wilderness'.
David remains cautious. 'Where is your master's son?' he asks. It now
becomes clear why Ziba has really come to find David. He relates that
Mephibosheth has chosen to remain in Jerusalem and regards David's
exile as the opportunity to recover his grandfather's kingdom.

David accepts this report at face value and at once confers on
Ziba all his master's property. Of course, it is possible that Ziba is
telling the truth: Mephibosheth has become convinced that a civil war
between David and Absalom, dividing the royal house, might end
in a restoration of the house of Saul; Ziba by contrast has decided
he would rather throw in his lot with the fleeing David than remain
with Mephibosheth or present himself to Absalom. David might have
feared all along that his generosity to Mephibosheth would ultimately
be spurned. It may be that he is so quick to credit Ziba's story because
it corresponds to his suspicions. It is even possible that the gift Ziba is
bringing to the king is the freely offered harvest of his own fields and
not produce stolen from Mephibosheth.

This is all possible, but not likely; and it is hard to escape the
impression that David has been deceived. Apparently on impulse, he
has broken the vow he made to his dearest friend to provide for his
descendants (see 1 Samuel 20.14-17).

Scene Two (verses 5-14): David and Shimei

*5 When King David came to Bahurim, a man of the family
of the house of Saul came out whose name was Shimei son
of Gera; he came out cursing. 6 He threw stones at David
and at all the servants of King David; now all the people and
all the warriors were on his right and on his left. 7 Shimei
shouted while he cursed, 'Out! Out! Murderer! Scoundrel! 8
The Lord has avenged on all of you the blood of the house
of Saul, in whose place you have reigned; and the Lord has
given the kingdom into the hand of your son Absalom. See,
disaster has overtaken you; for you are a man of blood.'*

*9 Then Abishai son of Zeruiah said to the king, 'Why should
this dead dog curse my lord the king? Let me go over and
take off his head.' 10 But the king said, 'What have I to do
with you, you sons of Zeruiah? If he is cursing because the
Lord has said to him, "Curse David", who then shall say,
"Why have you done so?" ' 11 David said to Abishai and
to all his servants, 'My own son seeks my life; how much
more now may this Benjaminite! Let him alone, and let him
curse; for the Lord has bidden him. 12 It may be that the
Lord will look on my distress, and the Lord will repay me
with good for this cursing of me today.' 13 So David and
his men went on the road, while Shimei went along on the
hillside opposite him and cursed as he went, throwing stones
and flinging dust at him. 14 The king and all the people who
were with him arrived weary at the Jordan; and there he
refreshed himself.*

If Ziba's allegiance and motivations are open to question, the same
cannot be said for the last of those who approach David on his flight
from Jerusalem. When he reached Bahurim (the place where Michal's
second husband Paltiel, weeping pitifully, was finally kept from
following his wife in 3.15-16), a member of Saul's family, Shimei son
of Gera, suddenly appeared and began to abuse David.

He threw stones and hurled insults, cursing the while. 'Get out! Get
out!', he cried, 'This is the Lord's doing. He has given your kingdom
into the hand of your son Absalom. He is punishing you for all the
blood of the house of Saul that you have shed!' (verses 7-8).

What is the reader to make of this tirade? If only because of the
way the story develops, it is clear that Shimei is quite wrong in his

assertion that David's flight signifies that his kingdom is about to be handed by God to his son. But other parts of his outburst are not so easily refuted.

When Shimei calls David a murderer, a scoundrel and a man of blood the context suggests that he has in mind the violent and untimely deaths of Saul, Jonathan and Ishbaal. The charge that David was somehow complicit in these deaths is something from which the story of his rise is at great pains to protect him. Throughout the narrative from 1 Samuel 16.1 to 2 Samuel 5.10, David is presented as refusing to lift his hand against the Lord's anointed (e.g. 1 Samuel 24.6, 26.11), and as wholly innocent of involvement in the deaths of Saul and Jonathan (1.15-16), Abner (Saul's chief general, 3.37) and Ishbaal (4.9-12). So much emphasis is placed on this point that some scholars have suspected a cover up. On the other hand, there is the story in 21.1-9, clearly chronologically displaced, in which David plainly is implicated in the deaths of members of Saul's house.

Even if Shimei is wrong to accuse David of responsibility for those particular deaths, the reader knows that in his treatment of Uriah, David really has been a murderer, a scoundrel and a man of blood. (In the alternative tradition documented in 1 Chronicles 22.8, the reason given by the Lord why Solomon and not David himself would build the temple is that David has blood on his hands.) Even if Shimei is wrong that this civil war will end in triumph for Absalom, he is right that this disaster is the Lord's doing and is an avenging of David's wrongdoing – and David knows it.

David's response is telling and is in complete contrast to the utterly predictable and ferocious reaction of Abishai, one of the savage sons of Zeruiah, whose instinct is to attack Shimei and chop off his head. But the king distances himself from his general. 'What have I to do with you, you sons of Zeruiah?', he asks (see 19.22 and 3.39; the plural 'sons of Zeruiah' is common even when David is only addressing one of them).

What strikes David is the sense in which Shimei is right, or may be right, rather than the sense in which he is quite wrong. Again in his distress David is moved to speak of the Lord and to express his trust in the Lord's good purpose and providence. He intuits that the Lord has prompted Shimei to curse. He notes that his own son has turned against him, so why not 'this Benjaminite' (i.e., this member of the tribe to which Saul belonged')?

'It may be', he concludes (and this is the resignation of faith, not of despair) 'that the Lord will look on my distress and repay me with good for what I am suffering today'. Indeed, there are grounds to prefer a variant reading here: 'It may be that the Lord will look upon my iniquity and repay me with good for this cursing of me today'. David's sin in relation to Bathsheba and Uriah is without doubt the defining act in the story of his fall; but the saving grace in the story is his readiness to confess his sin and his refusal to assert his innocence. The 'it may be' signifies David's readiness to accept whatever the Lord has in store for him. (The expression has parallels in the Old Testament: compare for example the faith of king Hezekiah in 2 Kings 19.4 [=Isaiah 37.4].) David does not presume that it is God's will to honour him and does not seek to dictate terms to the Almighty.

So the narrative depicts David and his entire entourage (probably in the region of a thousand strong) wearily trudging their way along the road from Jerusalem to the Jordan accompanied by Shimei, still flinging stones and dirt and abuse, presumably causing both physical and emotional injury. The ordeal only ends at the Jordan where David is able to refresh himself in its cool waters.

Scene Three (verses 15-23): Ahithophel's advises Absalom to appropriate David's concubines

15 Now Absalom and all the Israelites came to Jerusalem; Ahithophel was with him. 16 When Hushai the Archite, David's friend, came to Absalom, Hushai said to Absalom, 'Long live the king! Long live the king!' 17 Absalom said to Hushai, 'Is this your loyalty to your friend? Why did you not go with your friend?' 18 Hushai said to Absalom, 'No; but the one whom the Lord and this people and all the Israelites have chosen, his I will be, and with him I will remain. 19 Moreover, whom should I serve? Should it not be his son? Just as I have served your father, so I will serve you.'

20 Then Absalom said to Ahithophel, 'Give us your counsel; what shall we do?' 21 Ahithophel said to Absalom, 'Go in to your father's concubines, the ones he has left to look after the house; and all Israel will hear that you have made yourself odious to your father, and the hands of all who are with you will be strengthened.' 22 So they pitched a tent for Absalom upon the roof; and Absalom went in to his father's concubines in the sight of all Israel. 23 Now in those days the counsel that Ahithophel gave was as if one consulted the oracle of God; so all the counsel of Ahithophel was esteemed, both by David and by Absalom.

For the first time since the second scene of the previous episode (15. 12), the focus of the narrative shifts back to Absalom and to his arrival in Jerusalem, with Ahithophel prominent among his followers. He is greeted at once by Hushai, but in amusingly ambiguous words: 'Long live the king!'. In fact, he repeats the phrase (a unique occurrence in the writings of the Hebrew Bible). It is as if the duplication mirrors the political muddle: is there one king in Israel or two? And to which of the two candidates is Hushai referring? Absalom proves to be as credulous as his father. After an initially sceptical question, with its deliberate emphasis on Hushai's role ('Is this your loyalty to your friend? Why did you not go with your friend?') he is surprisingly quick to accept Hushai's explanation – once more amusingly ambiguous. Hushai manages to convince Absalom of his allegiance without ever lying outright: 'No', he says, 'the one whom the Lord and this people and all the Israelites have chosen, his I will be and with him I will remain'. It doesn't occur to Absalom that Hushai might be speaking of his father. His final words are admittedly more deceitful: 'Whom should I serve? Should it not be his son? As I have served your father, so I will serve you'. But even then the first two parts of his assurance are framed as questions rather than assertions. In the final phrase he is repeating words fed to him by David in chapter 15.34. Hushai is applying for the role of 'king's friend' to Absalom, so that he will be in a position to rival Ahithophel. Ahithophel (who has presumably been party to this conversation) fails to register any protest.

It is however first and foremost to Ahithophel that Absalom still turns for advice. Presumably the new king had not expected to take control of Jerusalem so easily. David has gone, leaving only his ten concubines in residence at the palace. Absalom is at a loss. So he turns to his counsellor who advises a bold course of action. 'Go in to your father's concubines' he says.

It is shrewd advice. It is calculated to show 'all Israel' that Absalom means business. Those who have supported him will realise there is no way back; waverers will be forced to choose sides. There will be no prospect of a reconciliation between father and son after this. It is a public, symbolic and potent act, laying claim to his father's role. (Abner in 3.7-10 and Adonijah in 1 Kings 2.13-25 take similar action.) Ahithophel is banking on a hardening of the lines of division.

It is also a fulfillment of Nathan's prophecy. When they pitch a tent for Absalom on the palace roof, it is the very roof on which David was walking when he first saw Bathsheba (see 11.2). When Absalom went into his father's concubines 'in the sight of' all Israel, the narrative picks up a phrase Nathan had used in his denunciation of David (see

12.11-12). It is ironic that a man who was so incensed by his brother's sexual crime against his sister, should so readily commit a sexual crime against his father. He does so on the advice of the man who may well have been the grandfather of Bathsheba (see the comments on 15.12, page 101).

The scene concludes with an affirmation of the value of Ahithophel's advice. This is the first recorded example of his counsel and it is essential to the plot that Absalom will follow it: Ahithophel's counsel was regarded in those days (not just by Absalom but also previously by David) as an oracle of God.

Conclusion

There is precious little truth-telling in the three scenes in this episode. There is none in the third scene, certainly, in which Absalom is deceived by Hushai (though the latter avoids telling an outright lie). There is probably none in the first scene, in which David is apparently deceived by Ziba (who on this reading is guilty of an outright lie). Even in the central scene, in which Shimei denounces David, the truth-telling is inadvertent. David is most likely innocent of the specific crimes Shimei had in mind (the deaths of Saul and Jonathan); but he cannot defend himself because his conscience convicts him of a crime his accuser knows nothing about. On occasions, the Truth of God may even be spoken by those who are not only malicious but also entirely ignorant of the truths they utter.

Chapter Thirteen
2 Samuel 17.1–29

Absalom and Ahithophel

Introduction

There is a certain arbitrariness about this chapter break. There is hardly even a scene break here: the first verse of chapter 17 continues directly on the last verse of chapter 16. Ahithophel is still dispensing advice to Absalom. There is however an interlude, summarised in 16.22, in which Absalom duly acts on the first advice Ahithophel had given. And whereas that advice was political, the advice Ahithophel proceeds to offer in this episode is military.

This chapter is made up of six scenes in all. In the first, Ahithophel tells Absalom how he to prosecute the war against David. In the second, Hushai opposes this advice. In the third, Hushai then briefs his informers, who in the fourth, duly pass their intelligence to David. In the brief and pathetic fifth scene, Ahithophel takes his own life – the first indication that the rebellion of Absalom has overreached itself. The episode closes with a further shift in the balance of power towards David: the sixth scene resumes the account of Absalom's pursuit of David, who finds new allies.

Scene One (verses 1-4): Ahithophel advises Absalom to target David in person

> Moreover, Ahithophel said to Absalom, 'Let me choose twelve thousand men, and I will set out and pursue David tonight. 2 I will come upon him while he is weary and discouraged, and throw him into a panic; and all the people who are with him will flee. I will strike down only the king, 3 and I will bring all the people back to you as a bride comes home to her husband. You seek the life of only one man, and all the people will be at peace.' 4 The advice pleased Absalom and all the elders of Israel.

The previous episode closed with a reminder to the reader that the counsel of Ahithophel was so highly regarded in Israel in those days that it was treated (not just by Absalom, but by David as well) as the oracle of God. So it is no surprise that when he suggests how Absalom might best proceed with his coup, 'the advice pleased Absalom and all the elders of Israel'. (David doesn't seem to have worked much with 'all the elders of Israel'. It may be significant that they have not appeared in the story since, with Abner's encouragement, they anointed David as their king in 5.3; though compare 'the elders of his house' in 12.17.)

Ahithophel's proposal is twofold: he advises Absalom to act at once, and to focus his efforts on the elimination of David in person. In addition, he envisages a leading role for himself. 'Let me choose twelve thousand men', he says (or perhaps twelve battalions of men). 'I will set out and pursue David tonight. I will come upon him while he is weary and discouraged (see 16.14). I will strike down only the king'. The effect will be that those who are with David will flee in panic, and 'I will bring all the people back to you as a bride comes home to her husband'. Kill just one man, Ahithophel urges – and let the general population be left in peace. The current civil strife could yet be as quickly resolved as a first row between a newly married couple.

Scene Two (verses 5-14): Hushai opposes the counsel of Ahithophel

5 Then Absalom said, 'Call Hushai the Archite also, and let us hear too what he has to say.' 6 When Hushai came to Absalom, Absalom said to him, 'This is what Ahithophel has said; shall we do as he advises? If not, you tell us.' 7 Then Hushai said to Absalom, 'This time the counsel that Ahithophel has given is not good.' 8 Hushai continued, 'You know that your father and his men are warriors, and that they are enraged, like a bear robbed of her cubs in the field. Besides, your father is expert in war; he will not spend the night with the troops. 9 Even now he has hidden himself in one of the pits, or in some other place. And when some of our troops fall at the first attack, whoever hears it will say, "There has been a slaughter among the troops who follow Absalom." 10 Then even the valiant warrior, whose heart is like the heart of a lion, will utterly melt with fear; for all Israel knows that your father is a warrior, and that those who are with him are valiant warriors. 11 But my counsel is that all Israel be gathered to you, from Dan to Beer-sheba, like the sand by the sea for multitude, and that you go to battle in person. 12 So we shall come upon him in whatever place he may be found, and we shall light on him as the dew falls on the ground; and he will not survive, nor will any of those with him. 13 If he withdraws into a city, then all Israel will bring ropes to that city, and we shall drag it into the valley, until not even a pebble is to be found there.' 14 Absalom and all the men of Israel said, 'The counsel of Hushai the Archite is better than the counsel of Ahithophel.' For the Lord had ordained to defeat the good counsel of Ahithophel, so that the Lord might bring ruin on Absalom.

For some undisclosed and thoroughly providential reason, Absalom seeks a second opinion. He sends for Hushai, who has evidently quickly won Absalom over. Hushai arrives and Absalom explains Ahithophel's advice. His question seems to imply he somehow knew that Hushai would not be in agreement. Sure enough, Hushai dares to question even the Oracle himself: 'This time the counsel Ahithophel has given is not good'. (In fact of course the advice is perfectly 'good' as the narrative makes clear in verse 14: it is 'good' in the sense of being sound, but 'not good' in the sense of opposing the will of God.)

Such a bold rejection of an esteemed authority meets with complete silence, into which Hushai speaks again, improvising brilliantly. For a start, he says, Ahithophel is wrong to suppose that David and his men will panic easily. They are warriors and in battle will be like a bear robbed of its cubs. Moreover Ahithophel is wrong to suppose David will be found so easily. David is an experienced soldier, who won't be waiting around in the open. He will be hiding in one of the hundreds of caves or pits in the wilderness. And thirdly how will the twelve thousand men on our side cope when the fighting starts? It's all too easy to imagine that when the first few casualties occur, the panic will be on our side, not David's. 'All Israel knows that your father is a warrior and that those who are with him are valiant warriors'.

So Hushai has an alternative strategy to put forward, but subtly undermines Ahithophel as much by adopting a different tone. Where Ahithophel had couched his remarks in the first person singular, Hushai speaks of 'you' and 'we'. Where Ahithophel had reserved a leading role for himself, Hushai appeals to Absalom's vanity and so casts himself as the loyal retainer. 'First', he says, 'muster all Israel. Summon as many troops as possible so that we are like sand on the seashore. Second, you take command; never mind Ahithophel leading

us, you do it in person. Then we can march on David at our leisure and
defeat him and all his men. Even if he retreats into a city for refuge,
we'll have sufficient forces to destroy the city'.

There is even something symbolic about the length of Hushai's
speech. Ahithophel had argued for immediate action in a speech that is
appropriately swift and direct. Hushai's first objective is to buy time,
so that the weary and discouraged David (Ahithophel is absolutely
right about this) can rest and refresh himself. But he not only counsels
delay; he effects it. His speech is nearly three times as long as that of
Ahithophel. His four vivid similes ('like a bear robbed of her cubs',
'like the heart of a lion', 'like the sand by the sea', and 'as the dew
falls') slow down the narrative, like the time-wasting antics of an
unscrupulous sportsman.

As soon as Hushai has finished speaking, and without allowing
Ahithophel any right of reply, Absalom and his colleagues declare that
his advice is superior. This, the text states, was the Lord's doing: 'for
the Lord had ordained to defeat the good counsel of Ahithophel, so
that the Lord might bring ruin on Absalom'. Whether or not Hushai
foresaw the consequences, in Ahithophel's plan Absalom would not
himself have been at risk. In adopting Hushai's alternative, Absalom
had placed himself fatally in the line of fire. This too, the narrator
seems to imply, was the Lord's doing.

**Scene Three (verses 15-20): Hushai passes intelligence to the two
spies**

*15 Then Hushai said to the priests Zadok and Abiathar, 'Thus
and so did Ahithophel counsel Absalom and the elders of
Israel; and thus and so I have counselled. 16 Therefore send
quickly and tell David, "Do not lodge tonight at the fords of
the wilderness, but by all means cross over; otherwise the
king and all the people who are with him will be swallowed
up." ' 17 Jonathan and Ahimaaz were waiting at En-rogel; a
servant-girl used to go and tell them, and they would go and
tell King David; for they could not risk being seen entering
the city. 18 But a boy saw them, and told Absalom; so both
of them went away quickly, and came to the house of a man
at Bahurim, who had a well in his courtyard; and they went
down into it. 19 The man's wife took a covering, stretched
it over the well's mouth, and spread out grain on it; and
nothing was known of it. 20 When Absalom's servants came*

to the woman at the house, they said, 'Where are Ahimaaz and Jonathan?' The woman said to them, 'They have crossed over the brook of water.' And when they had searched and could not find them, they returned to Jerusalem.

The intelligence network established by David in 15.24-29, 33-36, is now put to use. Hushai at once tells the priests Zadok and Abiathar what has happened and urges them to get a message to David as quickly as possible, telling him not to loiter at the Jordan but to cross over at once. Hushai assumes nothing: he passes on both Ahithophel's counsel and his own and in exhorting David not to delay he appears to be taking precautions lest, after all, it is Ahithophel's counsel rather than his own which prevails.

In an attempt to prevent them from being spotted, this message is passed from Zadok and Abiathar to their sons, who are waiting at En-rogel, by a servant girl. But the subterfuge fails. A boy sees them and reports them to Absalom. Aware of the threat however, Jonathan and Ahimaaz escape to a safe house in Bahurim belonging to a man with a well in his courtyard. Evidently not everyone in that place shared Shimei's views about David (see 16.5). The two spies hide in the well with the help of the man's wife. Like a latter-day Rahab (who also once hid two spies under stalks of flax, compare Joshua 2.6), she places a covering over the mouth of the well and spreads grain on it. Sure enough Absalom's men come in search. Now like a latter-day Michal (compare 1 Samuel 19.14-17) she misleads them with an outright lie. They don't believe the woman for a moment, but after a fruitless search they return to Jerusalem.

Once again (as in 2 Samuel 14) anonymous women play a critical role in the narrative.

Scene Four (verses 21-22): The two spies pass intelligence to David

21 After they had gone, the men came up out of the well, and went and told King David. They said to David, 'Go and cross the water quickly; for thus and so has Ahithophel counselled against you.' 22 So David and all the people who were with him set out and crossed the Jordan; by daybreak not one was left who had not crossed the Jordan.

As soon as the spies are safe, they emerge from the well to go directly to David on the banks of the Jordan (see 16.14) and give him their message. Perhaps because it represents the worst case scenario from David's point of view, they report only Ahithophel's advice, as if it was this and not the advice of Hushai that Absalom intended to follow (see verses 15-16).

David responds at once. Overnight he and his troops cross the Jordan so that by daybreak not one of them was left west of the river.

Scene Five (verse 23): Ahithophel takes his own life

> *23 When Ahithophel saw that his counsel was not followed, he saddled his donkey and went off home to his own city. He set his house in order, and hanged himself; he died and was buried in the tomb of his father.*

Despite the seriousness with which Hushai and his men are taking Ahithophel's counsel, Ahithophel himself knows that the moment has passed. His advice has not been followed.

In a pitiful series of personal pronouns, his predicament is spelt out: because *his* counsel was not followed, he saddled *his* donkey and went home to *his* city, he set *his* house in order, hanged himself and was buried in the tomb of *his* father. It echoes the emphasis on the role he himself intended to play in the plan he outlined to Absalom (compare the fourfold repetition of 'I will' in verses 1-3).

Why does Ahithophel despair so completely? Presumably it isn't just because he has lost face in relation to Hushai. It is rather because he senses that the only chance Absalom had of victory was by a swift attack. He realises it is now inevitable that David will recover the kingdom. The tide has turned. News of this suicide must surely have spread through the ranks of Absalom's army and may have reached David's ears as well.

Scene Six (verses 24-29): New allies bring support to David

> *24 Then David came to Mahanaim, while Absalom crossed the Jordan with all the men of Israel. 25 Now Absalom had set Amasa over the army in the place of Joab. Amasa was the son of a man named Ithra the Ishmaelite, who had married Abigal daughter of Nahash, sister of Zeruiah, Joab's mother. 26 The Israelites and Absalom encamped in the land of Gilead.*

27 When David came to Mahanaim, Shobi son of Nahash from Rabbah of the Ammonites, and Machir son of Ammiel from Lo-debar, and Barzillai the Gileadite from Rogelim 28 brought beds, basins, and earthen vessels, wheat, barley, meal, parched grain, beans and lentils, 29 honey and curds, sheep, and cheese from the herd, for David and the people with him to eat; for they said, 'The troops are hungry and weary and thirsty in the wilderness.'

Oddly, it now emerges that Ahithophel's advice was not completely disregarded, though it was disastrously compromised. If Absalom delayed to muster 'all the men of Israel' (rather than setting off at once with only the 12,000 men recommended by Ahithophel), it seems he didn't delay long. He is hot on David's heels. But Absalom has not moved quickly enough and his own life is now on the line. As he crosses the Jordan, David has only reached as far as Mahanaim, about ten miles to the east (formerly Ishbaal's base; see 2.8). Once across the river, the Israelites and Absalom (an odd reversal of the expected order this – is he already a mere afterthought?) encamped at Gilead (compare 2.9).

It also now emerges that Absalom has chosen as his chief general Amasa, the son of Ithra the Ishmaelite and of 'Abigal daughter of Nahash, sister of Zeruiah, Joab's mother'. If the tradition in 1 Chronicles 2.16-17 is to be relied upon (the difficulty being that here Abigal is described as the daughter of Nahash; there she is the daughter of Jesse), then Amasa was not only Joab's cousin, but (like Joab) David's nephew. Equally related to David and Absalom, Joab and Amasa are perhaps obvious rivals.

At Manahaim, meanwhile, David is once again provisioned. Just as Ziba had come to him on the west side of the river, so now three more allies come to him on the east: Shobi son of Nahash from Rabbah of the Ammonites, Machir son of Ammiel of Lo-debar, and Barzillai the Gileadite from Rogelim.

Shobi, son of Nahash, must be a chastened (or more discerning) brother of King Hanun, who so badly miscalculated in humiliating David's emissaries in 10.1-5. It was Rabbah that Joab had successfully besieged before summoning David to deliver the coup de grace (see 12.26-31). (It is possible that the word 'Nahash' only truly belongs here, and has been confusingly written into verse 25 in place of 'Jesse' by copyist error.) Machir, son of Ammiel of Lo-debar, was the one who had formerly offered hospitality to Mephibosheth (see 9.4-5). In a small way, his readiness to associate himself with David and not Absalom further strengthens the case for suspecting that Ziba was lying in chapter 16.3. Barzillai the Gileadite, finally, is a newcomer to the narrative who will feature again (see 19.31-37).

These three, apparently working in collaboration, brought not only food for David, but equipment too. Once again there is acknowledgment of David's weariness and that of his men.

Conclusion

Such an explicit statement of divine intervention as occurs in verse 14 is rare in this narrative (though compare another significant turning point in the narrative at 11.27). Mostly the providence of God is something more hidden. In this case the Lord's action is a direct answer to David's prayer in 15.31. What David feared most about Absalom's rebellion was the power of Ahithophel's advice. He prayed that it might be confounded and so it has been. The 'good' counsel of Ahithophel (meaning his sound and effective counsel) has been defeated and Hushai's weaker advice has been preferred. Only the direct intervention of the Lord explains this turn of events.

However, the unfolding of the Lord's purpose is no less to be celebrated in the other important developments in this episode: in the escape of the spies with the help of the anonymous women and in the appearance of some unlikely allies (including a foreigner and a former supporter of the house of Saul). These providential contributions are far more typical of the way in which the good purpose of God unfolds in this story – as indeed in the lives of most Christian believers today. It is often only in hindsight that it is possible to discern it at all.

Chapter Fourteen
2 Samuel 18.1–33

The Death of Absalom

Introduction

David has not routinely led his troops into combat since the distant days before his adultery with Bathsheba (8.1-14). He had more recently made a brief battlefield appearance, but only to preside over the finalities of the siege of Rabbah and at the summons of Joab (12.26-31). But civil war has changed everything and in this episode David intends to resume command of the army. His generals have other ideas, however.

Surprisingly, the narrator's attention in this episode is not on the battle or its outcome, but on the fate of Absalom and even more on the response of David to it. The sequence of four scenes makes this focus clear. The first scene, in which David agrees to leave the fighting to his generals, concludes with the king ordering them 'to deal gently with Absalom'. The second scene summarises the ensuing battle – but it does so, almost dismissively, in just three verses. The third scene, in which Absalom's death is reported, is longer than the earlier two scenes put together. And the final scene, which recounts David's reaction on hearing the news, is almost as long as all three previous scenes combined.

Scene One (verses 1-5): David orders his generals to deal gently with Absalom

Then David mustered the men who were with him, and set over them commanders of thousands and commanders of hundreds. 2 And David divided the army into three groups: one-third under the command of Joab, one-third under the command of Abishai son of Zeruiah, Joab's brother, and one-third under the command of Ittai the Gittite. The king said to

the men, 'I myself will also go out with you.' 3 But the men
said, 'You shall not go out. For if we flee, they will not care
about us. If half of us die, they will not care about us. But you
are worth ten thousand of us; therefore it is better that you
send us help from the city.' 4 The king said to them, 'Whatever
seems best to you I will do.' So the king stood at the side of
the gate, while all the army marched out by hundreds and
by thousands. 5 The king gave orders to Joab and Abishai
and Ittai, saying, 'Deal gently for my sake with the young
man Absalom.' And all the people heard when the king gave
orders to all the commanders concerning Absalom.

At first the king appears to be fully in control. He marshalls his
troops. He appoints commanders over platoons and battalions. He
divides the army into brigades and appoints three brigadiers: the two
surviving sons of Zeruiah, Joab and Abishai, and in addition loyal
Ittai.

But David's failure to respond adequately to the rape of Tamar and
to the insubordination of Absalom has undermined his authority to the
extent that in this episode, on the two occasions when he speaks, his
words carry no weight. First he proposes to lead his men into battle.
His men find a diplomatic way of doing so, but in effect they reject
his plan. They tell him he is much too highly prized an asset to put
himself (and them) at risk. Of course a political leader is always at risk
on the battlefield, as Absalom will soon discover. But that argument
was never made in earlier years, when David's military reputation was
at its height and the people liked nothing more than for him to 'lead
Israel out and bring it in' (see 5.2). Those years are past, however, and
one wonders if other reservations are unspoken here: that he is not
longer valiant enough, swift enough and practised enough to lead them
well. In his heart of hearts he knows it and he complies readily enough
with the men's wishes.

Secondly David instructs his men to 'deal gently' with 'the young
man' Absalom. David seems to have foreseen that there might be
circumstances outside the heat of battle in which his troops might
be in a position to show mercy towards Absalom or to withhold it.
In fact David himself is 'dealing gently' with his rebellious son by
speaking of him as 'the young man': Saul was much harsher with
Jonathan under far less provocation (compare 1 Samuel 20.30). But
it is an inappropriate gentleness. It is an unfair expectation of his
officers. It might interfere operationally in the task he has delegated
to them and demonstrates on the eve of battle that military concerns

are not David's priority: private ones are. Just as he was ready to risk lives in pursuit of a purely personal goal to eliminate Uriah the Hittite (11.14-21), so he is apparently ready to do so again to protect his son.

The final sentence of the scene leaves no doubt that the commanders heard David's instruction. When Joab later dispatches Absalom, it will be an act of outright defiance.

Scene Two (verses 6-8): The battle is summarised

> *6 So the army went out into the field against Israel; and the battle was fought in the forest of Ephraim. 7 The men of Israel were defeated there by the servants of David, and the slaughter there was great on that day, twenty thousand men. 8 The battle spread over the face of all the country; and the forest claimed more victims that day than the sword.*

Battle is joined. David's troops are fighting 'against Israel' – something he avoided one way or another even when he was retained as bodyguard by the king of Gath (1 Samuel 29). It is a tragic moment. It represents a return to the years of civil war before the death of Ishbaal (see 3.1) and a foreshadowing of the years of civil war which will follow the death of Solomon (see 1 Kings 12.21). It is odd that Absalom, who had arranged to have himself proclaimed king in Hebron (David's capital when he was king only over the southern kingdom of Judah), should now be in command of 'the men of Israel' (that is, the usual designation of what was and would be again the northern kingdom). There are indications later in the narrative that 'the men of Israel' are indeed to be understood here as meaning the ten northern tribes (see 19.11-15, 41-43).

Scene Three (verses 9-18): The Death of Absalom

> *9 Absalom happened to meet the servants of David. Absalom was riding on his mule, and the mule went under the thick branches of a great oak. His head caught fast in the oak, and he was left hanging between heaven and earth, while the mule that was under him went on. 10 A man saw it, and told Joab, 'I saw Absalom hanging in an oak.' 11 Joab said to the man who told him, 'What, you saw him! Why then did*

you not strike him there to the ground? I would have been glad to give you ten pieces of silver and a belt.' 12 But the man said to Joab, 'Even if I felt in my hand the weight of a thousand pieces of silver, I would not raise my hand against the king's son; for in our hearing the king commanded you and Abishai and Ittai, saying: For my sake protect the young man Absalom! 13 On the other hand, if I had dealt treacherously against his life (and there is nothing hidden from the king), then you yourself would have stood aloof.' 14 Joab said, 'I will not waste time like this with you.' He took three spears in his hand, and thrust them into the heart of Absalom, while he was still alive in the oak. 15 And ten young men, Joab's armour-bearers, surrounded Absalom and struck him, and killed him.

16 Then Joab sounded the trumpet, and the troops came back from pursuing Israel, for Joab restrained the troops. 17 They took Absalom, threw him into a great pit in the forest, and raised over him a very great heap of stones. Meanwhile all the Israelites fled to their homes.

18 Now Absalom in his lifetime had taken and set up for himself a pillar that is in the King's Valley, for he said, 'I have no son to keep my name in remembrance'; he called the pillar by his own name. It is called Absalom's Monument to this day.

One of the victims of the forest (see verse 8) was Absalom himself. Mounted on a mule, the king's son 'happened' (a word which subtly implies the providence of God at work) to meet the servants of David on the battlefield. Presumably riding at speed through thick forest to escape, with his enemies pursuing him, Absalom's mount took him 'under the thick branches of a great oak'. Somehow (it is hard to imagine that his extravagantly long and thick hair was not a contributory factor), Absalom's head got stuck in the branches and he was left dangling 'between heaven and earth' (that is, suspended in mid-air, but also between life and death) as the mule rode on.

One of those who saw it took a report to Joab. Joab is furious with him. As a man of violence (3.39), Joab can scarcely credit what he is hearing: 'You had Absalom at your mercy, and you let him be? Why did you not kill him?' he asks. 'I'd have rewarded you with ten pieces of silver – and a belt'.

But the messenger is not as naïve as Joab might suppose. For two reasons, he would not have killed Absalom for any amount of silver. First there is the fact that David had expressly requested Joab and his colleagues to protect 'the young man Absalom'. And secondly the messenger is wise enough to know that if he had killed Absalom, Joab (far from rewarding him) would have distanced himself from the deed, giving the killer up to face the full fury of the king. (His restraint in refusing to 'raise his hand' against Absalom recalls David's refusal to raise his hand against Saul, 'the Lord's anointed'; see 1 Samuel 24.10; 26.9-11.)

Joab's response concedes the strength of the man's argument. He doesn't attempt a rebuttal. He simply states he can't afford to waste time debating the issue. Impatient as ever, he takes matters into his own hands. Where he previously had Uriah killed strictly in accordance with David's instructions (11.15-17), he now has Absalom killed strictly in defiance of them. He himself strikes the first blows while Absalom is still alive, before involving his own ten armour-bearers in the coup de grace (as he had previously involved David in the taking of Rabbah). For the killers there is strength in numbers (or at least a measure of anonymity and of protection against the king's predictable wrath). For Absalom there may be a grisly retribution in the fact that his killers numbered ten: just as he had gone in to his father's ten concubines (15.16, 16.21), so ten stabbings 'go into' him. For Joab the killing may or may not have been an act of revenge (see 14.30). What is clear is that the man who was once Absalom's chief advocate has become his executioner.

But violent as he is, Joab too is capable of restraint. As soon as Absalom is dead, he sounds the trumpet (there is a pun here: in the Hebrew text, the 'blow' of the trumpet in verse 16 is the same word as the 'blows' inflicted on Absalom by Joab in verse 14), and calls off the pursuit of the men of Israel. Enough blood has been shed. Joab is apparently as wise a politician as Ahithophel had been: he knows that the fewer casualties, the greater the prospects of reconciliation between the warring factions.

At the end of the scene, while all the Israelites flee from the battlefield, the burial of Absalom is recorded with some care. He is thrown callously into a big pit and a great heap of stones is erected over him. This turns out to be the second monument to Absalom: the vain young man had 'in his lifetime' (there is a scandalised emphasis here) earlier erected a pillar 'for himself in the King's Valley'. He had done so to keep his name alive, because (so he said), 'I have no son to keep my name in remembrance'. The notice creates a small difficulty in the narrative. In 14.27 it is said that in addition to the beautiful daughter he named after his sister, there were three sons born to Absalom. One harmonising possibility is that the sons all predeceased their father.

At the time of the conquest it was apparently a convention to execute a king by hanging him on a tree and then burying him under a heap of stones (or in a cave, covering the entrance with a heap of stones) as a monument (compare Joshua 8.29, 10.27). To hang from a tree is a particular curse in the Hebrew Scriptures (Deuteronomy 21.23). If Absalom's death evokes these earlier executions, for Christian readers it will also evoke the execution and burial of Jesus, 'the king of the Jews'.

Scene Four (verses 19-33): News of Absalom's death is carried to David

19 Then Ahimaaz son of Zadok said, 'Let me run, and carry tidings to the king that the Lord has delivered him from the power of his enemies.' 20 Joab said to him, 'You are not to carry tidings today; you may carry tidings another day, but today you shall not do so, because the king's son is dead.' 21 Then Joab said to a Cushite, 'Go, tell the king what you have seen.' The Cushite bowed before Joab, and ran. 22 Then Ahimaaz son of Zadok said again to Joab, 'Come what may, let me also run after the Cushite.' And Joab said, 'Why will you run, my son, seeing that you have no reward for the tidings?' 23 'Come what may,' he said, 'I will run.' So he said to him, 'Run.' Then Ahimaaz ran by the way of the Plain, and outran the Cushite.

24 Now David was sitting between the two gates. The sentinel went up to the roof of the gate by the wall, and when he looked up, he saw a man running alone. 25 The sentinel shouted and told the king. The king said, 'If he is alone, there are tidings in his mouth.' He kept coming, and drew near. 26 Then the sentinel saw another man running; and the sentinel called to the gatekeeper and said, 'See, another man running alone!' The king said, 'He also is bringing tidings.' 27 The sentinel said, 'I think the running of the first one is like the running of Ahimaaz son of Zadok.' The king said, 'He is a good man, and comes with good tidings.'

28 Then Ahimaaz cried out to the king, 'All is well!' He prostrated himself before the king with his face to the ground, and said, 'Blessed be the Lord your God, who has delivered up the men who raised their hand against my lord the king.' 29 The king said, 'Is it well with the young man Absalom?' Ahimaaz answered, 'When Joab sent your servant, I saw a great tumult, but I do not know what it was.' 30 The king said, 'Turn aside, and stand here.' So he turned aside, and stood still.

31 Then the Cushite came; and the Cushite said, 'Good tidings for my lord the king! For the Lord has vindicated you this day, delivering you from the power of all who rose up against you.' 32 The king said to the Cushite, 'Is it well with the young man Absalom?' The Cushite answered, 'May the enemies of my lord the king, and all who rise up to do you harm, be like that young man.' 33 The king was deeply moved, and went up to the chamber over the gate, and wept; and as he went, he said, 'O my son Absalom, my son, my son Absalom! Would that I had died instead of you, O Absalom, my son, my son!'

The final scene is the most significant of the whole episode: far more important to the narrative than the death of Absalom in scene three (let alone than the outcome of the battle in scene two) is David's reaction afterwards.

The story resumes in Joab's presence. After a battle, there is always a need for news of the outcome to be carried to those awaiting it (see 1 Samuel 4.12, 2 Samuel 11.18-19). In this case, Ahimaaz son of Zadok volunteers to carry to David the news that 'the Lord has delivered him from the power of his enemies'. He is an obvious candidate to do so. He had previously been entrusted with a responsibility for relaying important messages to the king (15.27-28, 35-36) and had evidently remained with David's forces after doing so (see 17.15-22). But Joab is cautious. He knows that sometimes a miserable end awaits a messenger who bears bad tidings (see 1.1-16) and he knows that for David the bad news of Absalom's death will weigh more heavily than the good news of Joab's victory.

Instead Joab commissions a Cushite for the task. Without delay, off he runs.

But Ahimaaz is determined. He presses Joab for permission to run as well. Joab queries Ahimaaz's motivation – he guesses there will be no reward for the messenger. Ahimaaz does not care. In what is plainly a tacit acknowledgement of the risk involved, he repeats that he wishes to run 'come what may'. So Joab authorises him and Ahimaaz is able to outrun the Cushite by taking a different route.

David meanwhile is sitting at Manahaim, between the city gates. It was the place where the judge sat to dispense justice (compare Ruth 4.1-16, 2 Samuel 15.2). The sentinel sees a man running alone. In the ancient near east, a man only ever runs in the heat of the day when there is urgent news to deliver. 'If he is alone', the king says, 'he has tidings to deliver'. Before the first runner arrives, however, the second one is sighted. 'He also is bringing news', the king concludes.

As he approaches, Ahimaaz is recognised by his running style. He is in a familiar role. David, clutching at straws, draws comfort from the identity of the messenger: 'he's a good man, he'll bring good news'. At one level of course, David's instinct is true and is immediately confirmed by the first words uttered by Ahimaaz: 'All is well' – *shalom*, peace and prosperity. Ahimaaz then amplifies his message by blessing the God who has delivered up those who rebelled against the king. But this is not the news David has been waiting to hear. 'Is it well', he asks, 'with the young man Absalom?'. Is it *shalom* for Absalom? David is frankly unconcerned with the bigger picture. Once before he had awaited news of the outcome of a battle and on that occasion too what really concerned him was the fate of a particular individual he loved (compare 1.5).

This is the moment Joab had foreseen and from which he had wanted to protect Ahimaaz, who now prevaricates in the face of the king's question. He can't bring himself to tell the king that his son is dead, because he knows how devastating this news will be to David (and presumably also because he anticipates the king's fury that his command has been disobeyed). So Ahimaaz says that although he was aware of a commotion, he does not know what it was about. This is a lie. Joab had told him in verse 20.

But if Ahimaaz does not know what has become of Absalom then he is of no use to David. So the king tells him to step aside. So Ahimaaz steps out of the narrative, never to step back in.

Meanwhile the Cushite has arrived. 'Good news!', he cries – again amplifying his opening by attributing the outcome to the Lord. But this is not news to the king. His question picks up the term introduced by Ahimaaz: 'Is it *shalom* with the young man Absalom?'. Even the Cushite cannot bear to state the facts in so many words. He cannot bring himself to mention Absalom by name. Instead, he uses David's preferred epithet for his son: 'the young man'. And he can't bring himself to say 'he is dead'. Resorting to circumlocution he simply states the wish that all David's enemies may 'be like that young man'.

But David knows that in this instance 'no news' is 'bad news'. If Absalom were alive and well, there would be no hesitation on the part of the messengers in telling him so. Overwhelmed with grief, the king hurries out of sight. But even before he reaches the privacy of 'the chamber over the gate', his weeping spills out. In one of the most poignant speeches in all Scripture, David repeats again and again not just Absalom's name, but his relationship: my son, my son, my son – five times over in the final verse of the episode.

This is the fourth time in the story that David's grief has surfaced. In 2 Samuel 1 he grieved for Saul and for his beloved Jonathan. In 2 Samuel 3 he grieved for Abner. In 2 Samuel 12 he grieved in advance for his unnamed newborn son. But there is something particularly desperate and unrestrained about David's grief here. The death of this son, like the earlier death of the infant, represents the outworking of Nathan's prophecy in 12.10. This is why David expresses the wish that he had died instead of Absalom (verse 33): there is an element of contrition in this grief which is new. He knows he is at fault for what has come to pass.

Conclusion

It can be difficult to translate Hebrew names precisely. But while scholars do not agree exactly on the meaning of the name 'Absalom' (is it 'Peace to my father'? 'My father is peace'? 'Father of peace'?), it is perfectly clear that the name comprises two components (father and peace) such that it is hard to avoid a sense of irony. For the king, in his public role, there is peace: those who rebelled against him have been roundly defeated and the kingdom is safe once again. For the father, in his private role, there is no peace, but only a terrible distress at the loss of his son.

Chapter Fifteen
2 Samuel 19.1–43

David Resumes his Kingship

Introduction

The new episode begins where the previous one left off, with David grieving for Absalom in the immediate aftermath of hearing the news. The continuity is emphasised by the recurrence of his heart-rending cry: 'O my son Absalom, O Absalom, my son, my son'. If grief is by definition overwhelming, the grief which follows the death of a beloved child is especially so.

But, as noted at the end of the previous episode, in this situation David is not just a private individual, mourning the loss of a son. He is a king, victorious over a rebel. As such he lacks the time and space in which to come to terms with his bereavement: the responsibilities of his office clamour for attention. Thus in the first ten verses there is no reference to David by name. He is simply, repeatedly, 'the king'.

In the first scene of this episode, Joab confronts David with his royal responsibilities. 'The king' accepts the point and embarks on a journey back to the kingship. In the second scene, he engineers an invitation to return from his closest allies in Judah. In the following three scenes on the banks of the Jordan, David encounters in turn Shimei (see 16.5-14), Mephibosheth (see 16.1-4) and Barzillai (see 17.27-29). Shimei shares the limelight in scene three with Ziba, although in Ziba's case (unlike each of the other encounters) no dialogue is reported with the king. The episode concludes in scene six with a sharp dispute between the elders of Judah and those of Israel about their respective relationships to the king.

Scene One (verses 1-8a): Joab confronts David

It was told Joab, 'The king is weeping and mourning for Absalom.' 2 So the victory that day was turned into mourning for all the troops; for the troops heard that day, 'The king is grieving for his son.' 3 The troops stole into the city that day as soldiers steal in who are ashamed when they flee in battle. 4 The king covered his face, and the king cried with a loud voice, 'O my son Absalom, O Absalom, my son, my son!' 5 Then Joab came into the house to the king, and said, 'Today you have covered with shame the faces of all your officers who have saved your life today, and the lives of your sons and your daughters, and the lives of your wives and your concubines, 6 for love of those who hate you and for hatred of those who love you. You have made it clear today that commanders and officers are nothing to you; for I perceive that if Absalom were alive and all of us were dead today, then you would be pleased. 7 So go out at once and speak kindly to your servants; for I swear by the Lord, if you do not go, not a man will stay with you this night; and this will be worse for you than any disaster that has come upon you from your youth until now.' 8 Then the king got up and took his seat in the gate. The troops were all told, 'See, the king is sitting in the gate'; and all the troops came before the king.

This first scene is one of the most vivid in the whole narrative. A great sense of urgency and immediacy is conveyed by the repetition in the early verses first of the phrase 'that day' (three times in verses 2-3) and then of the word 'today' (four times in verses 5-6).

David may have taken himself into a private chamber (see 18.33), but his grief is no secret. His crying is audible. As his army approaches Mahanaim, walking wearily but exultantly in the footsteps of Ahimaaz and the Cushite, the king's reaction is reported to Joab. Meanwhile news filters through to the soldiers more generally. The impact is catastrophic. Their mood is transformed from joy into mourning as if their victory had been a defeat and they creep into the city in shame, as if they had fled from the battle.

Joab acts at once – and then urges the king to do the same. He has no recourse to any wise woman here: the situation is too urgent for any elaborate devices. He confronts the king bluntly. His speech in verses 5b-7 is lengthy and eloquent. He rebukes David for despising the sacrifices of those who had risked their lives for him in battle and for putting the welfare of his enemies before that of his allies ('for love of those [like Absalom] who hate you and for hatred of those [like Ittai?] who love you'). David's grief, where there should have been gratitude, demonstrates that he places no value on the lives not only of his foot soldiers but even of his officers and commanders. Joab perceives that if David's son had survived and his generals had died, the king would have been pleased.

Having delivered his diagnosis, Joab provides a prescription. David is to go out 'at once' to speak to his troops. He then adds a prognosis. Swearing by the Lord, he warns that if David does not do this, his army will abandon him, precipitating a crisis 'worse for you than any disaster that has come upon you from your youth until now'. 'Now' is exactly the right word on which to end the translation. Joab's words are intended to jolt David into immediate action. It may well be that this is wise counsel in David's best interests. But Joab's speech serves his own best interests as well. His robust attack on the king is also the very best form of defence: David never gets around to enquiring more closely into the circumstances of Absalom's death or to questioning why his instruction to his commanders had not been heeded.

David does as he is told. He obeys Joab where Joab had not obeyed him. The significant shift in the balance of power between these two men, which had been underway since David instructed Joab to contrive Uriah's death, is now complete.

The king leaves the upstairs chamber and returns to the place at the gate where he had received the messengers only hours before. His troops gather around him. Where Joab hoped David would rally his men, they rally around him.

Scene Two (verses 8b-15): The people of Judah invite David to return as king

> *Meanwhile, all the Israelites had fled to their homes. 9 All the people were disputing throughout all the tribes of Israel, saying, 'The king delivered us from the hand of our enemies, and saved us from the hand of the Philistines; and now he has fled out of the land because of Absalom. 10 But Absalom, whom we anointed over us, is dead in battle. Now therefore why do you say nothing about bringing the king back?'*
>
> *11 King David sent this message to the priests Zadok and Abiathar, 'Say to the elders of Judah, "Why should you be the last to bring the king back to his house? The talk of all Israel has come to the king. 12 You are my kin, you are my bone and my flesh; why then should you be the last to bring back the king?" 13 And say to Amasa, "Are you not my bone*

and my flesh? So may God do to me, and more, if you are not
the commander of my army from now on, in place of Joab."'
14 Amasa swayed the hearts of all the people of Judah as
one, and they sent word to the king, 'Return, both you and
all your servants.' 15 So the king came back to the Jordan;
and Judah came to Gilgal to meet the king and to bring him
over the Jordan.

Meanwhile, as Joab and his men had returned from the battlefield to Manahaim, the defeated army of Absalom had fled across the Jordan and dispersed. As a result there was commotion 'throughout all the tribes of Israel'. What was to happen next? All (the word is used three times in verses 8b-9) can recall a time when David was the king and a highly successful one at that. Yet he had fled before Absalom. But Absalom is now dead. Is David to resume his kingship? (The reference to the 'anointing' of Absalom in verse 10 fills out what is only implicit in 15.10).

Joab's instinct is that unless David acts at once, someone else will step into the vacuum. David apparently sees the danger and uses his trusted agents, the priests Zadok and Abiathar, to get a message to his core supporters, the elders of Judah. He is himself a Judahite from Bethlehem (see Judges 17.7, Ruth 1.1, Matthew 2.1) and it was they who had first anointed him king (in 2.4). But to galvanise their support, David plays on their insecurity. The northerners ('all Israel') are talking about inviting David home – wouldn't it be better if his own people were first to do so? (The fact that in verse 11 'all Israel' is to be interpreted as a reference to the ten northern tribes is established by the quotation in verse 12 of the words with which those tribes had finally invited David to become their king in 5.2.)

Verse 13 comes as a considerable shock. Joab is to be replaced as David's commander in chief. It seems David has not overlooked Joab's failure to 'deal gently' with Absalom after all. Spurring David into action has been more effective than Joab intended. But if the sacking of the 'son of Zeruiah' is shocking, the choice of his replacement is still more so. Amasa had been commander of Absalom's army (replacing Joab on that occasion also; 17.25). But Amasa is David's nephew (17.25, 1 Chronicles 2.16-17), so truly (compare verse 13) David's 'bone and flesh'. Besides, Amasa's association with Absalom's rebellion may be politically advantageous: his appointment has the capacity to unite David's divided kingdom.

The gesture has the desired effect. Amasa is able to canvas the necessary support and an official invitation is issued by 'Judah' to

David to return as king. So David makes his way to the river Jordan (crossings of which are always symbolically loaded in Scripture) and 'Judah' (the two southern tribes) meets him there to provide an escort and reception committee.

Scene Three (verses 16-23): David and Shimei again

16 Shimei son of Gera, the Benjaminite, from Bahurim, hurried to come down with the people of Judah to meet King David; 17 with him were a thousand people from Benjamin. And Ziba, the servant of the house of Saul, with his fifteen sons and his twenty servants, rushed down to the Jordan ahead of the king, 18 while the crossing was taking place, to bring over the king's household, and to do his pleasure.

Shimei son of Gera fell down before the king, as he was about to cross the Jordan, 19 and said to the king, 'May my lord not hold me guilty or remember how your servant did wrong on the day my lord the king left Jerusalem; may the king not bear it in mind. 20 For your servant knows that I have sinned; therefore, see, I have come this day, the first of all the house of Joseph to come down to meet my lord the king.' 21 Abishai son of Zeruiah answered, 'Shall not Shimei be put to death for this, because he cursed the Lord's anointed?' 22 But David said, 'What have I to do with you, you sons of Zeruiah, that you should today become an adversary to me? Shall anyone be put to death in Israel this day? For do I not know that I am this day king over Israel?' 23 The king said to Shimei, 'You shall not die.' And the king gave him his oath.

There on the banks of the Jordan, David has a series of personal encounters, balancing those he had had on his flight out of Jerusalem and involving some of the same cast of characters. The first two men to step forward are members of the household of Saul. Both hasten to ingratiate themselves with David. Shimei (who had cursed the king on his way into exile in 16.5-14) 'hurries' to David 'with a thousand men of Benjamin' (Saul's tribe). Ziba (who had dubiously protested his loyalty to David in 16.1-4) 'rushes down' to the river ahead of the king, to help David and his household with the crossing.

Nothing more is said about Ziba at this point, but Shimei falls down before David and makes a confession. David is not the only one in the narrative capable of contrition. Shimei too says, 'I have sinned' (verse 20; compare 12.13). He acknowledges that in cursing the David 'on the day my lord the king left Jerusalem' he did wrong. He comes 'as the first of the house of Joseph' (as a representative of the northern tribes of Israel) to beg for mercy.

As predictable as a pantomime villain, Abishai will hear none of it. Shimei deserves to die 'because he cursed the Lord's anointed'. Once more, using precisely the phrase with which he had rebuked Abishai on the day of Shimei's cursing, David distances himself from 'the sons of Zeruiah' and their violent instincts (see 16.10; 3.39). David has repeatedly found himself at odds with these brothers. They have often seemed more like adversaries (literally, 'satans') than allies to him. Amasa may have become David's commander in chief, but 'the sons of Zeruiah' are still prominent (the plural hints at the fact that Joab is still actively involved in David's entourage). It is worth noting that Abishai was not always so particular about protecting the Lord's anointed (see 1 Samuel 26.6-12).

David chooses to show mercy to Shimei at least for the time being (though the sequel in 1 Kings 2.8-9 is to be noted). No-one 'in Israel' is to die on this day when David is once more 'king over Israel'. If for no other reason David will be merciful for political reasons, to consolidate the support of those who are least inclined to support his kingship.

Scene Four (verses 24-29): David and Mephibosheth again

24 Mephibosheth grandson of Saul came down to meet the king; he had not taken care of his feet, or trimmed his beard, or washed his clothes, from the day the king left until the day he came back in safety. 25 When he came from Jerusalem to meet the king, the king said to him, 'Why did you not go with me, Mephibosheth?' 26 He answered, 'My lord, O king, my servant deceived me; for your servant said to him, "Saddle a donkey for me, so that I may ride on it and go with the king." For your servant is lame. 27 He has slandered your servant to my lord the king. But my lord the king is like the angel of God; do therefore what seems good to you. 28 For all my father's house were doomed to death before my lord the king; but you set your servant among those who eat at your table. What further right have I, then, to appeal to the king?' 29 The king said to him, 'Why speak any more of your affairs? I have decided: you and Ziba shall divide the land.'

30 Mephibosheth said to the king, 'Let him take it all, since my lord the king has arrived home safely.'

Next to present himself before David is another member of Saul's house – Jonathan's son. It is at once clear that one of either Mephibosheth or Ziba is misleading David. Ziba had told David (16.1-4) that 'his master's son' had chosen to use Absalom's rebellion as a means to recover his grandfather's kingdom. But now it is reported that out of loyalty to David, Mephibosheth had not trimmed his beard, or washed his clothes or (and it is not quite clear what this means, except that it presumably relates directly to his disability) 'taken care of his feet' from the day the king had left Jerusalem until now. If Mephibosheth is lying, he is prepared to go to extreme lengths to maintain his charade.

David challenges Mephibosheth. 'Why did you not go with me when I left Jerusalem?', he asks. Mephibosheth explains that he had asked Ziba to saddle a donkey for him, so that he could do just that, but that his servant had deceived him. The implication seems to be that Ziba fled to David with the donkey, knowing that his lame master would not be able to follow. At some point, Mephibosheth has got wind of the story Ziba has told David and now protests that he has been slandered.

Mephibosheth then throws himself upon David's mercy. 'My lord the king is like the angel of God', he says. This is a compliment David is repeatedly paid. King Achish of Gath thought so (see 1 Samuel 29.9) and so did the wise woman of Tekoa (see 14.17, 20). It seems to imply perfect innocence and wisdom. Acknowledging the unexpected generosity he has already received from David, Mephibosheth refuses to defend himself further. 'Do what seems good to you', he tells the king.

David makes an instant decision to divide Saul's land between the two men. Mephibosheth brushes the offer aside: 'Let Ziba have it all', he says (like the true mother of the disputed son in the story of Solomon's wisdom in 1 Kings 3.16-28, but without the vindicating consequence). 'It is enough for me', he concludes, 'that my lord the king' (it is the fifth time in as many verses that he has used the phrase) 'has come home in safety'.

There the scene closes. The narrative never returns to either Ziba or Mephibosheth again (with the brief and probably chronological displaced exception of 21.7-8) to put beyond doubt with whom the right lay. It is not even clear whether David's compromise reflects his judicial uncertainty as to where the truth lies or whether he is simply giving the guilty party the benefit of the doubt (whoever that might be), just as he had earlier refused to punish Shimei. In other words, like the appointment of Amasa, this may be a further example of David's determination to bring reconciliation to his divided kingdom. If as seems most likely it is Mephibosheth who is telling the truth and Ziba who is lying, it is possible that David's *hesed* (compare 9.1-7) here embraces not only his natural enemy (Mephibosheth), but even his enemy's enemy (Ziba).

Scene Five (verses 31-40): David and Barzillai again

> *31 Now Barzillai the Gileadite had come down from Rogelim; he went on with the king to the Jordan, to escort him over the Jordan. 32 Barzillai was a very aged man, eighty years old. He had provided the king with food while he stayed at Mahanaim, for he was a very wealthy man. 33 The king said to Barzillai, 'Come over with me, and I will provide for you in Jerusalem at my side.' 34 But Barzillai said to the king, 'How many years have I still to live, that I should go up with the king to Jerusalem? 35 Today I am eighty years old; can I discern what is pleasant and what is not? Can your servant taste what he eats or what he drinks? Can I still listen to the voice of singing men and singing women? Why then should your servant be an added burden to my lord the king? 36 Your servant will go a little way over the Jordan with the king. Why should the king recompense me with such a reward? 37 Please let your servant return, so that I may die in my own town, near the graves of my father and my mother. But here is your servant Chimham; let him go over with my lord the king; and do for him whatever seems good to you.' 38 The king answered, 'Chimham shall go over with me, and I will do for him whatever seems good to you; and all that you desire of me I will do for you.' 39 Then all the people crossed over the Jordan, and the king crossed over; the king kissed Barzillai and blessed him, and he returned to his own home. 40 The king went on to Gilgal, and Chimham went on with him; all the people of Judah, and also half the people of Israel, brought the king on his way.*

The final individual to speak with David as he crosses the Jordan is the old Gileadite, Barzillai. It emerges in verse 32 that the hospitality he had shown David when he first arrived at Mahanaim in 17.27-29

was not an isolated occurrence. He had continued to provide David
with food while he stayed in that city.

Now David wishes to repay the debt. 'Come over the Jordan with
me', he invites him. 'I will provide for you in Jerusalem'. Perhaps the
treachery of his own son has taught him the value of a loyal ally.

But Barzillai is too old for such a major upheaval. At eighty years
old, his senses are failing him to such an extent that he can no longer
derive any enjoyment from food and drink or music. He is not in
any position to offer the king any active service and would only be
a burden. He would rather die in familiar surroundings, close to the
graves of his parents. So he requests to be allowed to return home.
But he adds a request on behalf of Chimham (presumably his son).
'Let him go over with my lord the king', he proposes, 'and do for him
whatever seems good to you'. In sincere gratitude (which the dying
David still felt many years later; see 1 Kings 2.7), the king turns the
words around: 'Chimham shall go over with me', he promises, 'and I
will do for him whatever seems good to you'.

Finally the crossing of the river Jordan follows. First all the
people cross over and then David follows suit. He kisses Barzillai
and blesses him and dismisses him to his home. He makes his way
to Gilgal (the site of Saul's decisive offences against the Lord; see
1 Samuel 13.8-15, 15.10-33), accompanied by Chimham and also
by 'all the people of Judah' but (curiously) only 'half the people of
Israel'. If David has been attempting to reconcile a divided kingdom
the work is not yet complete.

Scene Six (verses 41-43): Continued tension between Judah and Israel

*41 Then all the people of Israel came to the king, and said
to him, 'Why have our kindred the people of Judah stolen
you away, and brought the king and his household over the
Jordan, and all David's men with him?' 42 All the people of
Judah answered the people of Israel, 'Because the king is
near of kin to us. Why then are you angry over this matter?
Have we eaten at all at the king's expense? Or has he given
us any gift?' 43 But the people of Israel answered the people
of Judah, 'We have ten shares in the king, and in David also
we have more than you. Why then did you despise us? Were
we not the first to speak of bringing back our king?' But the
words of the people of Judah were fiercer than the words of
the people of Israel.*

There is an ambiguity in the narrative where the phrases 'all Israel' or 'all the men of Israel' are concerned. Sometimes (for example in 8.15 or 10.17) they are clearly inclusive phrases, meaning all the twelve tribes of Israel, the whole kingdom over which David ruled. Sometimes however, as in this scene, the reference is clearly narrower: it refers only to the ten northern tribes, as distinct from 'the men of Judah' comprising the two southern tribes.

It is not always clear which sense is meant. This is particularly so during the rebellion of Absalom. He has the support of 'all Israel' and his forces are 'all the men of Israel'; but it is not certain that the narrower sense is intended. David's army is consistently described in neutral terms, and not as 'the men of Judah' (for example as 'the servants of David' in 18.7, 9, or more often simply, as in verse 41, 'the men who were with him' or elsewhere 'the army', 'the troops').

However what is clear is that the unity of the kingdom under David since he was anointed by the elders of Israel in 5.3 has remained fragile. In this context it is understandable if members of the household of Saul (the Benjaminite) had hoped that with David in exile 'the house of Israel' would restore the former's kingdom (see 16.3). In this context it is understandable likewise if, now that David is returning to Jerusalem, 'the people of Israel' feel threatened by the king's personal allegiance to the tribe of Judah.

A quarrel thus breaks out between representatives of what during the civil war had been Ishbaal's northern kingdom and David's southern one (2 Samuel 2-4). The people of Israel accuse the people of Judah of stealing David away (as Absalom had 'stolen the hearts of the people of Israel' in 15.6). The people of Judah respond that they have not done anything underhand: David is their near kin. But the people of Israel feel that their greater numerical strength earns them some rights in relation to the king: they have ten shares in the throne (and by implication, Judah has just two). They rightly point out that in scene two, before David had sent his messengers to the elders of Judah to prompt negotiations over his return, they had already begun to talk about that possibility (19.9-11).

It is not an auspicious end to the scene or the episode when it is stated, 'the words of the people of Judah were fiercer than the words of the people of Israel'.

Conclusion

It is hard to imagine that as a father David was quickly able to come to terms with the loss of Absalom. But for the king, the rebel has disappeared entirely from the narrative. The forlorn and pathetic monarch who had to be roused by Joab has become a real leader again: sending and receiving emissaries, dispensing pardon and blessing, making appointments and judicial decisions. He is once more worth petitioning for favour and quarreling over.

Yet David's position is still precarious. Despite his considerable political generosity and diplomatic skill, it will never again be as strong as it had been before his affair with Bathsheba. The division of his kingdom is not so quickly or completely healed.

Chapter Sixteen
2 Samuel 20.1–26

The Scoundrel Sheba

Introduction

If David had hoped that the death of Absalom would at least represent
the death of opposition to his rule of a united kingdom, he is quickly
disabused of his opinion. The period before David's adultery with
Bathsheba had created the impression that the whole kingdom was
securely united under David's rule. But cracks in the edifice have
subsequently become all too apparent. Without energetic leadership,
it threatens to revert to the same north-south divide that existed
immediately after Saul's death.

Moreover there is a new twist in this episode. In the previous four
episodes the only threat to David (assuming, that is, that it is Ziba
rather than Mephibosheth who has been deceitful) has come from
his own family. Now it emerges that there is no assumption that the
vigorous leadership required to hold Israel together need come from
David's house or that when he himself ceases to rule, David will be
succeeded by a son. The northern tribes have retained a sense of their
own independence.

The episode consists of four scenes. A trumpet is sounded both at
the beginning of this episode (verse 1) and close to the end (verse 22).
At the beginning David's control of his kingdom seems once again to
be precarious; by the end his power is restored. The first two scenes are
exceptionally brief: in the first, 'Sheba son of Bichri' is introduced; in
the second, the king's return to Jerusalem is noted. The final episode
is also short, and summarises the arrangements made by David for the
administration of his government at the end of this period of turmoil.
The real drama in this episode is related in scene three, as Sheba's short-
lived uprising is quashed and Joab returns to prominence. The key
action is Joab's pursuit of Sheba (the word *radap*, pursue, is repeated
in verses 6, 7, 10 and 13); almost incidentally, his killing of Amasa is
also related. There is then a clear attempt by the narrator to suggest in

the closing verses of this episode that David's power is as it was not just before Sheba's rebellion, or (more critically) Absalom's, but even before David's adultery with Bathsheba and murder of Uriah.

Scene One (verses 1-2): The people of Israel withdraw from David

Now a scoundrel named Sheba son of Bichri, a Benjaminite, happened to be there. He sounded the trumpet and cried out, 'We have no portion in David, no share in the son of Jesse! Everyone to your tents, O Israel!'

2 So all the people of Israel withdrew from David and followed Sheba son of Bichri; but the people of Judah followed their king steadfastly from the Jordan to Jerusalem.

There is no doubt where the loyalties of the narrator lie in this story. Sheba is the third figure in the narrative to be called a scoundrel; but he is the first to whom that epithet is applied by the narrator. When Amnon was beseeched not to behave as a scoundrel, it was by Tamar his sister (13.13). When David was accused of being a scoundrel it was by Shimei (16.7). When the narrator uses the word here it is a rare editorial value judgment (although see 'worthless fellows' in 1 Samuel 30.22).

Sheba is a scoundrel. He is also 'son of Bichri'. He is consistently named in this way, eight times in all in the course of the episode (in verses 1, 2, 6, 7, 10, 13, 21 and 22); he is also a Benjaminite. The tribe of Benjamin occupied a territory on the border been Judah and Israel: it belonged to Israel, but geographically only just. Since this was also the tribe from which Saul came, it is possible that Sheba is a member of his house. (There is no hard evidence of this, although the name 'Bichri' may relate to the name 'Becorath' in 1 Samuel 9.1)

When the text states that Sheba 'happened to be there', it may imply that he was not a prince of Saul's house who has been biding his time, waiting for the right moment to assert a claim to the throne, but a more unlikely rebel, acting spontaneously. He sounds the trumpet (as Absalom had done before him, 15.10) and calls the people of Israel to withdraw from David. 'We have no share in David', he cries – although in only the previous verse (19.43) the people of Israel had claimed to have ten shares (that is, ten-twelfths on the basis that the northern kingdom of Israel comprised ten tribes and the southern kingdom of Judah only two). But fickle as the northern tribes may have been, the people of Judah followed their king 'steadfastly' (an equally rare positive value judgment on the part of the narrator) from the Jordan to Jerusalem.

Scene Two (verse 3): The fate of David's concubines

> *3 David came to his house at Jerusalem; and the king took the ten concubines whom he had left to look after the house, and put them in a house under guard, and provided for them, but did not go in to them. So they were shut up until the day of their death, living as if in widowhood.*

Meanwhile David arrives home. The ten concubines in whose care he had left his house when he fled in panic (15.16) and who had since been so abused by Absalom (16.22) are waiting for him. Their status is sensitive. Through no fault of their own, they are forever defiled by what Absalom had done. The outcome is unspeakably sad. Although he provides for them, David ceases to have any intimacy with them. Instead they are 'shut up until the day of their death', condemned to a permanent house arrest and to an involuntary 'widowhood' (as Michal in 6.23 and Tamar in 13.20 had been before them). The plight of women is often desperate in this story.

It is unclear whether any other course of action was open to David and whether the report of this decision amounts to a negative judgment. At the least it represents a dark and permanent shadow cast by David's earlier folly and precisely the consequence prophesied by Nathan (12.11-12).

Scene Three (verses 4-22): Joab defeats Sheba

> *4 Then the king said to Amasa, 'Call the men of Judah together to me within three days, and be here yourself.' 5 So Amasa went to summon Judah; but he delayed beyond the set time that had been appointed him. 6 David said to Abishai, 'Now Sheba son of Bichri will do us more harm than Absalom; take your lord's servants and pursue him, or he will find fortified cities for himself, and escape from us.' 7 Joab's men went out after him, along with the Cherethites, the Pelethites, and all the warriors; they went out from Jerusalem to pursue Sheba son of Bichri.*

8 When they were at the large stone that is in Gibeon, Amasa came to meet them. Now Joab was wearing a soldier's garment and over it was a belt with a sword in its sheath fastened at his waist; as he went forward it fell out. 9 Joab said to Amasa, 'Is it well with you, my brother?' And Joab took Amasa by the beard with his right hand to kiss him. 10 But Amasa did not notice the sword in Joab's hand; Joab struck him in the belly so that his entrails poured out on the ground, and he died. He did not strike a second blow.

Then Joab and his brother Abishai pursued Sheba son of Bichri. 11 And one of Joab's men took his stand by Amasa, and said, 'Whoever favours Joab, and whoever is for David, let him follow Joab.' 12 Amasa lay wallowing in his blood on the highway, and the man saw that all the people were stopping. Since he saw that all who came by him were stopping, he carried Amasa from the highway into a field, and threw a garment over him. 13 Once he was removed from the highway, all the people went on after Joab to pursue Sheba son of Bichri.

14 Sheba passed through all the tribes of Israel to Abel of Beth-maacah; and all the Bichrites assembled, and followed him inside. 15 Joab's forces came and besieged him in Abel of Beth-maacah; they threw up a siege-ramp against the city, and it stood against the rampart. Joab's forces were battering the wall to break it down. 16 Then a wise woman called from the city, 'Listen! Listen! Tell Joab, "Come here, I want to speak to you." ' 17 He came near her; and the woman said, 'Are you Joab?' He answered, 'I am.' Then she said to him, 'Listen to the words of your servant.' He answered, 'I am listening.' 18 Then she said, 'They used to say in the old days, "Let them inquire at Abel"; and so they would settle a matter. 19 I am one of those who are peaceable and faithful in Israel; you seek to destroy a city that is a mother in Israel; why will you swallow up the heritage of the Lord?' 20 Joab answered, 'Far be it from me, far be it, that I should swallow up or destroy! 21 That is not the case! But a man of the hill country of Ephraim, called Sheba son of Bichri, has lifted up his hand against King David; give him up alone, and I will withdraw from the city.' The woman said to Joab, 'His head shall be thrown over the wall to you.' 22 Then the woman

> *went to all the people with her wise plan. And they cut off*
> *the head of Sheba son of Bichri, and threw it out to Joab. So*
> *he blew the trumpet, and they dispersed from the city, and*
> *all went to their homes, while Joab returned to Jerusalem*
> *to the king.*

David summons Amasa, his newly-appointed commander in chief (19.13-14) and entrusts him with his first (and only) commission. He is to muster the men of Judah and is commanded to do so in three days. At once he departs. As he goes the reader inevitably wonders where Joab might be and how he is responding to this news. He had murdered the last general to bring the hearts of the northern tribes over to David's side (Abner, in 3.27; compare 3.21-22).

Amasa fatally delays or is himself delayed. The deadline given by David expires. But in dealing with Sheba son of Bichri, speed is of the essence. So David at once calls up Abishai and tells him to take David's standing army and to go in pursuit. He foresees that unless he moves swiftly Sheba's rebellion will prove more damaging than that of Absalom.

Sure enough, crack troops (including the Cherethites and the Pelethites, presumably under the authority of Benaiah, son of Jehoida, compare 8.18) are immediately led out of Jerusalem – only it is Joab who leads them. He is more easily dismissed than he is sidelined.

They get as far as Gibeon, when Amasa meets them – presumably keen to resume command. If Amasa knew how Abner had died, he didn't learn from it. Indeed if Amasa (who was their nephew after all) knew how Joab's brother Asahel had died, he didn't learn from that either. Joab had fought at Gibeon before. Asahel had died there from a blow to the stomach delivered by Abner (2.23). Abner had then himself been killed in revenge by Joab, again by a blow to the stomach – and in this case as Joab feigned friendship (3.27; compare also the deception of Ehud in Judges 3.16-23). Given the history Amasa might have been on his guard, but it seems he wasn't. (The deaths of Amasa and Abner are linked in 1 Kings 2.5.) Joab was wearing 'a soldier's garment' (a short cloak perhaps), tied with a belt from which was slung the sheath for his sword. Somehow as he stepped forward, the sword fell out. Subtly Joab picked it up. As he approached Amasa to greet him, his nephew never noticed the sword in his hand. Grasping Amasa by the neck to pull him into an embrace, Joab thrust the dagger into his belly. Amasa died bloodily and swiftly. No second blow was necessary.

When, in verse 10b, the text states that 'Joab and his brother Abishai' ('the sons of Zeruiah') pursued Sheba, it is clear from the order in which they are named (if it wasn't already clear from his initiatives in verses 7 and 8) that Joab is once more in charge of David's army. But for the troops there is still an issue of loyalty to resolve. They know that David had replaced Joab with Amasa. Now Amasa is not only dead, but has been killed by Joab. Immediately one of Joab's henchmen seizes the moment: he takes a stand over Amasa's dead body and calls the troops to follow Joab – cynically presenting loyalty to Joab as loyalty to David. But Amasa's dead body is an obstacle. 'Wallowing in his blood in the highway', it is causing the troops to hesitate. So the man removes the obstacle: he carries Amasa's corpse off the road and into a field and for good measure covers it with a garment. Psychologically and symbolically as well as literally the way is then clear for the troops to follow Joab (Abishai has for the moment slipped once again into the background) in pursuit of Sheba.

Sheba has meanwhile taken refuge with all his clan in the city of Abel of Beth-maacah. Joab's intelligence is good and he is promptly able to besiege it with overwhelming force, throwing up a siege ramp and threatening to batter down the wall.

A wise woman intervenes to minimise the bloodshed. Calling from the city wall, she succeeds in securing a semi-private audience with Joab. If Joab suspected a trap or was wary of finding himself crushed by a millstone thrown from the city wall (compare 11.21), the text glosses over it. He comes near enough to have at least a shouted conversation with the woman. She reminds Joab that hers is a city with a noble tradition as a centre of wisdom. When she herself claims to be 'one of those who are peaceable and faithful in Israel', the reader cannot help contrasting these virtues with Joab's treachery and violence. She accuses Joab of seeking to destroy a city 'that is a mother in Israel' and asks why he would 'swallow up' the Lord's heritage in this way.

Joab denies that that is his intention. He explains the nature of his errand. If the city will give up Sheba son of Bichri, who has raised his hand against king David, Joab will withdraw. In a grisly pact, the woman promises that 'his head will be thrown over the wall'. Sure enough, Sheba is the last in a series of figures in this story who suffer decapitation – an ignoble line stretching back to Goliath (1 Samuel 17.51), and including Saul (1 Samuel 31.9) and Ishbaal (4.8). Sheba's short-lived rebellion is over. His head is tossed to Joab, who blows the trumpet to call an end to hostilities (compare 2.28 and 18.16) and lift the siege. The troops return home and Joab (not Abishai, it is worth noting) returns to king David in Jerusalem.

Once again an anonymous woman plays a decisive role in the story.

Scene Four (verses 23-26): David's government re-established

23 Now Joab was in command of all the army of Israel; Benaiah son of Jehoiada was in command of the Cherethites and the Pelethites; 24 Adoram was in charge of the forced labour; Jehoshaphat son of Ahilud was the recorder; 25 Sheva was secretary; Zadok and Abiathar were priests; 26 and Ira the Jairite was also David's priest.

The text passes in silence over the reception Joab received when he got back to Jerusalem. No indication is given of David's reaction to the news of Amasa's death. If he was weary of the sons of Zeruiah and felt powerless to restrain them when they assassinated Abner (3.39), what must he have felt at this reprise? Perhaps he felt that the death of Sheba was some compensation. At any rate Joab is re-established as commander of 'all the army of Israel'.

Verses 23-25 invite direct comparison with 8.15-18. The parallels are so clear that these two summary sections effectively divide up the narrative, like a pair of 'book-ends' either side of what has become known in academic scholarship as 'the succession narrative' of 2 Samuel 9-20. The first list brings to an end Act One; this sequel brings to an end Act Two. In both cases, Joab is the first person listed among the servants of David and commands the army. In both cases (though not listed in exactly the same order) Benaiah son of Jehoiada commands the Cherethites and the Pelethites, while Jehoshaphat son of Ahilud is 'the recorder'.

There are also a number of small differences between the two lists, however. Although Zadok appears as priest in both summaries, for instance, in the earlier one he is listed alongside 'Ahimelech son of Abiathar', whereas here his colleagues are Abiathar (who presumably relates somehow to the aforementioned Ahimelech) and the newly introduced 'Ira the Jairite'. In the earlier list the secretary is a man called Seraiah; here it is Sheva.

But there are also two more significant and sinister developments. In this list, there is a new appointee: Adoram, who is in charge of the forced labour. This is a glimpse into the darker side of David's kingdom. There have been hints of this practice before (first perhaps at 8.6 and 8.14 and later more certainly at 12.31), but no such official was previously listed. Forced labour has now become a government department in David's kingdom: this is an Israel that resembles Pharaoh's Egypt. Secondly in this list David's own name is missing. In the earlier list he is named as administering 'justice and equity to all his people'. Here the fact that he is not named tallies with his neglect of precisely these duties during the course of Act Two. Where was his concern for 'justice and equity' in his treatment of Uriah the Hittite after his adultery with Bathsheba or of his own son Amnon after the rape of Tamar? His neglect of justice created the vacuum which Absalom was able to exploit (15.1-4).

The first passage (8.15-18) records a consolidation of David's empire at its strength. It comes after a series of campaigns in which David has apparently with ease defeated external enemies. This parallel passage comes after a pair of campaigns in which he has with difficulty (at least in the case of Absalom's rebellion) defeated internal enemies.

Conclusion

Most of the lowest moments in David's career fall within Act Two of the story. This is where his fall and its consequences are recounted. Classically, it is at the height of his power that David is corrupted. It is when the nation is at rest (7.1) and he himself has been at rest (11.2), that David's vulnerability is exposed.

Yet Act Two also includes some of David's moments of greatest self-awareness. He knows himself to be a sinner. Ultimately, this is a saving grace. In some respects, the narrative has at this point run its full course. All that remains is a pair of endings: first a set of appendices to his reign in 2 Samuel 21-24, and then the story of his final decline and death in 1 Kings 1-2.

ACT THREE

The Rule of David Reviewed

2 Samuel 21.1–24.25

Chapter Seventeen
2 Samuel 21.1–14

David and the Gibeonites

Introduction

The last four chapters of 2 Samuel amount to an appendix. The narrative arc is interrupted and is only resumed in 1 Kings 1-2 with an account of David's decline and his death. The distinctive tone of these chapters, as well as their chronological scheme, is obvious even to a casual reader.

However these are not a random collection of scraps of the David story. They have a coherence of their own and a neatly 'chiastic' (essentially, symmetrical) structure: there is a narrative (21.1-14), a synopsis (21.15-22) and a poem (22.1-51), followed by a poem (23.1-7), a synopsis (23.8-39) and a narrative (24.1-25). The parallelism can be developed further: in chapters 21-22, there is an account of a national disaster in which David intervenes decisively, a catalogue of some battles he and his chief warriors fought against the Philistines and a song sung by David. This is then mirrored in chapters 23-24 by a song sung by David, a catalogue of some battles he and his chief warriors fought against the Philistines, concluding with an account of a national disaster in which David intervenes.

The careful literary structure suggests that this section of the narrative may function as a résumé of the story as a whole: at the centre, in the two songs, is a statement of faith by David that God was at work in and through himself. Either side of those songs are two inventories of occasions when God was indeed at work in and through David and his associates to deliver them from their archetypal enemy; and at the margins is a concession that God was at work by grace, despite the sinfulness, and in view of the contriteness, of David and his people.

The present episode is thus the first in a series of six. It consists of three scenes. The story tells of a time when there was a famine in Israel. It emerges in the first scene that the cause of the famine is an unresolved act of bloodshed committed by Saul against the

Gibeonites, for which David is required to make expiation. He does this in the second scene, by handing over to the Gibeonites for execution seven members of the house of Saul (emphatically not including Mephibosheth). In the final scene, an act of mourning by the mother of two of those who were killed inspires David to do something which had apparently been overlooked: he gives the bones of Saul and Jonathan a decent burial, along with the bodies of those who have just been killed. As a result, the famine is ended.

The story contains a number of puzzling and challenging features. For example, David has previously only 'enquired of the Lord' via the ephod, which basically gave only a 'yes' or 'no' answer (see 1 Samuel 23.2, 4, 10-12; 30.8; 2 Samuel 2.1; 5.19, 23). Here (verse one), the response David receives from the Lord is so full that it suggests some other medium of communication. It is puzzling also that the slaughter of the Gibeonites by Saul (on which this story turns) is not recorded earlier in 1 and 2 Samuel. Again, the burial of the remains of Saul and Jonathan in Jabesh-gilead was previously presented as something noble and final, and without shortcoming (see 1 Samuel 31.1-13; 2 Samuel 2.4b-7); here (in verses 12-14) it is put right. It is theologically challenging that David is apparently contending with the consequences here not of his own wrongdoing, but of Saul's. It is disconcerting that David attributes to the Gibeonites the power to bless (and implicitly to withhold blessing from) 'the heritage of the Lord'. Perhaps it is most demanding of all for the Christian reader that although the Lord is not anywhere explicitly said to approve the execution of the members of Saul's household, these grisly impalings are nevertheless said to be 'before the Lord' (verses 6, 9). Such a concentration of puzzling and challenging features suggests that this appendix sits theologically, as well as chronologically, outside the framework of the narrative proper.

Scene One (verses 1-6): Famine in Israel and the Gibeonite's demand

Now there was a famine in the days of David for three years, year after year; and David inquired of the Lord. The Lord said, 'There is blood-guilt on Saul and on his house, because he put the Gibeonites to death.' 2 So the king called the Gibeonites and spoke to them. (Now the Gibeonites were not of the people of Israel, but of the remnant of the Amorites; although the people of Israel had sworn to spare

> *them, Saul had tried to wipe them out in his zeal for the*
> *people of Israel and Judah.) 3 David said to the Gibeonites,*
> *'What shall I do for you? How shall I make expiation, that*
> *you may bless the heritage of the Lord?' 4 The Gibeonites*
> *said to him, 'It is not a matter of silver or gold between us*
> *and Saul or his house; neither is it for us to put anyone to*
> *death in Israel.' He said, 'What do you say that I should do*
> *for you?' 5 They said to the king, 'The man who consumed*
> *us and planned to destroy us, so that we should have no*
> *place in all the territory of Israel – 6 let seven of his sons*
> *be handed over to us, and we will impale them before the*
> *Lord at Gibeon on the mountain of the Lord.' The king said,*
> *'I will hand them over.'*

It is difficult to place this story in the chronological framework provided by 2 Samuel 5-20. On the one hand it can be argued that the question David first puts to Ziba in 9.1 ('Is there anyone still left of the house of Saul to whom I may show kindness for Jonathan's sake?') presupposes an extermination along the lines of this episode. It may be that the cursing of David by Shimei in 16.7-8 presupposes this story too. On the other hand David's apparent lack of awareness of Mephibosheth's existence in 9.3 is odd, if he had already spared him in the way this passage relates.

There has certainly been no hint anywhere earlier in the story of a national disaster along the lines of the famine referred to here. David's reaction to the crisis is exactly right. He inquires of the Lord as to the cause of the problem. (The last previous recorded instance of David inquiring of the Lord is in 5.19-23, which may be a further indication that this incident took place early in his reign.)

The Lord tells David that the famine results from 'blood-guilt' on the part of king Saul 'because he put the Gibeonites to death'. The Gibeonites were Hivites (or according to verse 2, Amorites), who conned Joshua into making a treaty with them 'guaranteeing their lives' (Joshua 9). It is said here that Saul had broken this covenant and had tried to wipe them out. Again, there has been no hint earlier in the story of such an atrocity.

What David does next is to speak to the Gibeonites. By the end of the episode the reader is left wondering if David might not have done better to inquire of the Lord further what he ought to do about Saul's blood-guilt. That is to say, there is an uncertainty from verse 2 onwards whether or not David is acting in accordance with the will of God or against it. Is it in obedience to divine instruction or

156   Talking the Talk

on his own initiative that he asks the Gibeonites what they would
like him to do in order to make expiation, so that they 'may bless
the heritage of the Lord'. The exchange which follows is a typical
piece of ancient near eastern negotiation, reminiscent for example
of Abraham's discussion with Ephron the Hittite over a price for the
cave of Machpelah (Genesis 23.10-16). The Gibeonites tell David
not what they want, but what they do not want. They don't want
money and it is not for them to put any Israelites to death. The last
phrase hints at what they do want. David repeats his question: 'What
do you say I should do for you?'.

The reader's sense of concern, how far the story is unfolding in
harmony with God's purpose, deepens in verse 5. The Gibeonites
stipulate that David should hand over to them seven sons of Saul. 'We
will impale them before the Lord', they declare, 'on the mountain of
the Lord'. Later in Israel's history there was a holy place at Gibeon
certainly: it was here at 'the principal high place' that Solomon sacrificed
to the Lord, before the Lord appeared to him in a dream (1 Kings
3.4). It was also here that, according to the biblical tradition, the sun
had stood still when Joshua led the armies of Israel into battle against
the five kings of the Amorites (Joshua 10.12). But it is nevertheless
odd to find Gibeon referred to here as 'the mountain of the Lord' and
especially on the lips of the Gibeonites. Apparently without qualms,
David agrees to their demand. Perhaps from a political point of view
the request suits his own interests. Presumably if there are seven 'sons
of Saul' left alive, these are seven potential threats to David's own
house and it can do his dynasty no harm if they are eliminated. If
only for this reason, the reader is left wishing that, in verses 3 and 4,
David's repeated inquiry had been addressed to the Lord rather than to
the Gibeonites.

Scene Two (verses 7-9): David complies with the Gibeonites demand

*7 But the king spared Mephibosheth, the son of Saul's son
Jonathan, because of the oath of the Lord that was between
them, between David and Jonathan son of Saul. 8 The king
took the two sons of Rizpah daughter of Aiah, whom she
bore to Saul, Armoni and Mephibosheth; and the five sons
of Merab daughter of Saul, whom she bore to Adriel son
of Barzillai the Meholathite; 9 he gave them into the hands
of the Gibeonites, and they impaled them on the mountain
before the Lord. The seven of them perished together. They*

were put to death in the first days of harvest, at the beginning
of the barley harvest.

In accordance with his promise to Jonathan (and in keeping with
that other episode), David spares Mephibosheth. He will keep his own
oath, where Saul has broken Joshua's. But other members of Saul's
family are less fortunate. David hands over two sons of Rizpah (the
concubine of Saul's whom, in 3.7, Ishbaal had accused Abner of
going into, and who may feasibly have become David's concubine
also to judge from 12.8). One of these sons was confusingly known
as Mephibosheth, which means that Jonathan's son had an uncle by
the same name. David also delivers up five of Saul's grandsons, by
his daughter Merab. (Some manuscripts state that these were Michal's
children – but the reference to her husband makes it clear that Merab
is meant.) Of course David had a history with Merab as well as with
Michal. She had initially been promised to him by Saul only to be
withdrawn – presumably with some loss of face on David's part (see 1
Samuel 18.17-19). It is therefore possible that there was an element of
revenge for David in the action he took.

So David gave these seven into the hands of the Gibeonites, who
duly 'impaled them on the mountain before the Lord'.

The timing of the outrage further adds to the theological oddness
of this story. For the Gibeonites at least, there seems to be a pagan,
superstitious significance about the fact that the seven men are
slaughtered 'in the first days of harvest, at the beginning of the barley
harvest' (verse 9). The repetition underlines the point: the deaths are
deemed to secure, if not this year's harvest (it is too late for that), at
least the harvest of the following year.

Scene Three (verses 10-14): God finally hears supplications for the land

10 Then Rizpah the daughter of Aiah took sackcloth,
and spread it on a rock for herself, from the beginning of
harvest until rain fell on them from the heavens; she did not
allow the birds of the air to come on the bodies by day, or
the wild animals by night. 11 When David was told what
Rizpah daughter of Aiah, the concubine of Saul, had done,
12 David went and took the bones of Saul and the bones
of his son Jonathan from the people of Jabesh-gilead, who
had stolen them from the public square of Beth-shan, where

the Philistines had hung them up, on the day the Philistines killed Saul on Gilboa. 13 He brought up from there the bones of Saul and the bones of his son Jonathan; and they gathered the bones of those who had been impaled. 14 They buried the bones of Saul and of his son Jonathan in the land of Benjamin in Zela, in the tomb of his father Kish; they did all that the king commanded. After that, God heeded supplications for the land.

But the story does not end here. It is not at the end of scene two that it is said 'After that, God heeded supplications for the land'. That phrase only comes at the end of this third scene, which further subverts any simple assumption that the impaling of Saul's sons was the Lord's demand.

The spotlight switches abruptly onto Rizpah, mother of two of the victims. She took sackcloth and took up a vigil over the bodies of the dead to protect them from scavenging by birds in the daytime and animals at night. She maintained this vigil for weeks. If the start of the barley harvest in Israel is in about April, and if the rains came at around their usual time, she kept watch all summer. Rizpah is another in a lengthening list of resourceful women in this narrative, who demonstrate heroic initiative – including Michal herself (1 Samuel 18), Abigail (1 Samuel 25), the woman of Tekoa (2 Samuel 14) and the wise woman of Abel (2 Samuel 20).

Word of Rizpah's extraordinary endurance reaches David. Her example provokes him. He goes (in person apparently) to Jabesh-gilead and exhumes the bones of Saul and Jonathan, which had been buried there for decades. After Saul and Jonathan had been killed in battle, the Philistines had fixed them (impaled them?) to the wall of Beth-shan (see 1 Samuel 31.10). When the inhabitants of Jabesh-gilead had heard about this, recalling Saul's earlier valour on their behalf (1 Samuel 11.1-15), their 'valiant men' had traveled all night to rescue his corpse and those of his sons, before burying them with mourning (1 Samuel 31.11-13). At the time this was reported as an act of considerable nobility on their part and it was later commended by David (2.4b-7), so it is a little surprising to find the act pejoratively described here as a theft from Philistine territory, rather than a liberation.

Yet it is undeniably true that Jabesh-gilead was not Saul's ancestral home and therefore (while far better than Philistine Beth-shan) not his appropriate final resting place. Now at last his skeleton is repatriated by David. He gathers Saul's bones and Jonathan's and the bones of the seven who have died in Gibeon and buries them 'in the tomb of his father Kish'.

Conclusion

Thus the story, which begins with an act of dreadful atrocity towards the house of Saul, ends with an act of generosity. Of course the cynic will note that David is generous only when he has made quite certain that the house of Saul is no threat: he only brings back Saul's bones when it is absolutely safe for him to do so, because there is no possibility that the house of Saul will use these relics as a rallying point for rebellion against the house of David. But the fact is that, inspired by Rizpah, he does bring back Saul's bones. And it is undoubtedly significant to the narrative that it is only at this point – and not immediately after the deaths of the seven sons of Saul – that the narrator concludes 'God heeded the supplications for the land'. (On this phrase, used in a similarly conclusive and delayed way, see the final verse of the partner narrative in 24.25.) Theologically, it is striking that divine favour is thus directly linked not to the act of inhumanity which dominates the episode, but to the act of humanity which concludes it.

Chapter Eighteen
2 Samuel 21.15–22

David and his Servants

Introduction

This second section of the appendix to the David story relates a series of four conflicts between Israel and the Philistines. There is a further indication that this appendix falls outside the chronological framework which governs 2 Samuel 5-20 in that the last reference to the Philistines was in the opening verse of 2 Samuel 8 (see also 5.17-25), immediately after which they are supplanted as Israel's prime enemies – especially by the Ammonites (see 2 Samuel 10-12), though also by the Moabites, the Arameans and the Edomites (8.2-14).

Moreover all four conflicts involve victories by individual Israelites against a Philistine giant. In this regard, this episode is obviously closely linked to David's iconic victory against Goliath in 1 Samuel 17 (not least because in the third incident the defeated Philistine is in fact called 'Goliath the Gittite'). There are therefore grounds to suppose that the four cameos which make up this episode belong to a time early in David's reign, perhaps before the ark of God had been returned to Jerusalem.

On the other hand the fatigue which overwhelms David in the first of these cameos (together with the fact that at the end of it, in a manner very reminiscent of 18.2-3, his troops dissuade him from leading them into battle any longer) may suggest that these stories belong to a stage towards the end of his reign. Perhaps there was a recurrence of hostilities against the Philistines.

The four incidents evidently belong together. In this chapter, the first incident is taken alone in scene one. This is partly because it is the cameo with the fullest narrative content of the four (the only one to include dialogue, for example) and partly because it is the only one in which David himself appears. In the other incidents (in scene two) not only is the summary as bare as it could be, but David is simply the king for whom the other champions fight.

Scene One (verses 15-17): Abishai comes to David's rescue

15 The Philistines went to war again with Israel, and David went down together with his servants. They fought against the Philistines, and David grew weary. 16 Ishbi-benob, one of the descendants of the giants, whose spear weighed three hundred shekels of bronze, and who was fitted out with new weapons, said he would kill David. 17 But Abishai son of Zeruiah came to his aid, and attacked the Philistine and killed him. Then David's men swore to him, 'You shall not go out with us to battle any longer, so that you do not quench the lamp of Israel.'

The opening words of this scene recall 5.22. There too the Philistines were the aggressors, waging war on David. By 8.1, with his kingdom increasingly secure, it is David who attacks the Philistines and apparently inflicts on them a decisive defeat. In the tight chronological sequence of 2 Samuel 9-20, there is no further conflict between Israel and the Philistines. Indeed after 2 Samuel 12 (directly after David's adultery in other words), the focus shifts off external conflicts altogether, to focus instead on the rebellions of Absalom and Sheba.

In this summary of David's reign, the spotlight switches back onto David's struggle against the Philistines. On this occasion, in the course of the battle, David grew weary. This vulnerability is not explained. In his youth, he was occasionally discouraged (see 1 Samuel 27.1) and he occasionally needed to be strengthened (see 1 Samuel 23.16; 30.6). But even during the anxious days of his flight from Saul, the young David is never described as becoming weary. Exhaustion was in those days a condition which overwhelmed others (1 Samuel 30.10). Weariness is, however, frequently attributed to the older David (compare 16.14; 17.2, 29), a further indication that this episode may belong to the latter stages of his reign.

Seeing an opportunity, a Philistine giant called Ishbi-benob closed in. He was fitted out with new weapons, including a spear weighing three hundred shekels of bronze (compare 1 Samuel 17.7). But Abishai, one of the sons of Zeruiah and one of David's most valiant and trusted lieutenants (see 18.2, 20.6 and 23.18-19), comes to the rescue. He attacks the Philistine and kills him. There is no hint that, as in David's victory over Goliath, any sleight of hand or deception was involved. Abishai's victory was apparently won in hand-to-hand combat. David is frequently at odds with this trio of violent brothers, but repeatedly finds himself indebted to them.

The episode was a turning point; though how this story relates to 18.2-4 is unclear. The narrative sequence is less problematic if it is assumed that this story precedes that one. David's men tell him that they do not wish him to lead them into battle any more. The warrior has become a king. The individual is now an institution. When David first stepped onto a battlefield (in 1 Samuel 17.33) an attempt was made to protect him because he was too insignificant; now, he has become too significant. But if this David is greater than the one who killed Goliath, he is also lesser: in those days he was the deliverer; now he requires to be delivered.

His men employ a fascinating metaphor to dissuade him from fighting with them any longer. If he is killed in battle, they tell him, he will 'quench the lamp of Israel' (compare 1 Kings 15.4, Psalm 132.17). The king is a source of light, warmth and life to the nation. If he is killed the people will be plunged into darkness.

Scene Two (verses 18-22): David's champions fight for him

18 After this a battle took place with the Philistines, at Gob; then Sibbecai the Hushathite killed Saph, who was one of the descendants of the giants. 19 Then there was another battle with the Philistines at Gob; and Elhanan son of Jaare-oregim, the Bethlehemite, killed Goliath the Gittite, the shaft of whose spear was like a weaver's beam. 20 There was again war at Gath, where there was a man of great size, who had six fingers on each hand, and six toes on each foot, twenty-four in number; he too was descended from the giants. 21 When he taunted Israel, Jonathan son of David's brother Shimei, killed him. 22 These four were descended from the giants in Gath; they fell by the hands of David and his servants.

'After this' there follow three similar incidents. Two of these cause no great difficulty. Indeed, they put the Goliath of 1 Samuel 17 into a broader context, suggesting that there was a tribe of outsize Philistines. But the second battle in this series presents the reader with a particular puzzle, in that it too features the killing of 'Goliath the Gittite' by one Elhanan.

The first in this series of three 'head to head' battles between Israelite warriors and their Philistine opponents (in verse 18) features Sibbecai the Hushathite (who may have been one of 'the Thirty'; see 23.27 and

1 Chronicles 11.29). Little detail is added beyond the location of the battle and the name of Sibbecai's opponent. No more is known about either Gob or Saph.

The third encounter in this series (in verses 20-21) is similarly straightforward: war between Israel and the Philistines is now 'at Gath'. Another giant taunts Israel and is killed. Two details are added. The anonymous Philistine had 24 digits (six fingers on each hand and six toes on each foot); and he was killed by another of David's exceptionally combative nephews (a band which included the sons of Zeruiah and Amasa; see 1 Chronicles 2.16-17 and 17.24). On this occasion the relative in question is 'Jonathan, son of David's brother Shimei' (is this Shammah/Shimeah of 1 Samuel 16.9; 2 Samuel 13.3?).

The second conflict (in verse 19) is peculiar however. Hostilities are renewed at Gob and in the course of the battle a Philistine identified as 'Goliath the Gittite' (whose prodigious size is not stated, but can be assumed) is killed by 'Elhanan son of Jaare-oregim, the Bethlehemite'.

How does this report relate to the story in 1 Samuel 17? An obvious possibility is that this briefest of records about an otherwise unknown warrior was amplified over time and transferred to the greater glory of another altogether more famous Bethlehemite: David. An alternative is that the words 'Goliath the Gittite' constitute the name of an office rather than of an individual person, so that there was by definition more than one man so-called. There is however no evidence for such a title, and it stretches credibility to suppose that two such office-bearers were coincidentally killed by men from Bethlehem. Moreover when it says in this account that the shaft of Goliath's spear 'was like a weaver's beam', the phrase is an exact verbal parallel with 1 Samuel 17.7a – which suggests that the same Goliath is meant (although the phrase is also found in 1 Chronicles 20.5, where it is suggested that this giant is the brother of the Goliath killed by David). A third possibility is that 'Elhanan' is another name for David, and 'Jaare-oregim' another name for Jesse.

None of these explanations (including the one which assumes that the story in 1 Samuel 17 is a fiction constructed out of this brief sentence) is in itself fully satisfying. Whatever tension there might be between this verse and the fuller narrative in 1 Samuel 17, it was evidently not sufficient to prompt the editors of the David story to resolve it. It was not thought necessary, as the text was taking shape, to suppress the Elhanan tradition for David's sake. Rather, in its present position in the appendix to the narrative proper, this verse has an important literary function. Towards the end of the story of David's fall, when the reader has been made all too aware of the flaws in his character and the serious errors in his judgment, this 'Elhanan tradition' effectively sets a literary question mark even against the very episode on which the whole story of David's rise was built. The question mark has a theological value of its own. Here is an occasion when neatly resolving an apparent tension (or contradiction) in the Scriptures only impoverishes its meaning.

Conclusion

Subtly, this episode underlines David's decline: he is not all-conquering any more. Once upon a time, he was credited with the single-handed defeat of a great Philistine champion. Now even that tradition is disputed, and when he finds himself again in armed combat, he needs his servants to come to his rescue.

Chapter Nineteen
2 Samuel 22.1–51

David's Song

Introduction

If it is impossible to be certain how the material in 2 Samuel 21 relates to the chronological framework of the earlier chapters, there is no such confusion in relation to the present episode.

> *David spoke to the Lord the words of this song on the day when the Lord delivered him from the hand of all his enemies, and from the hand of Saul.*

These introductory words state not only that this song celebrates David's deliverance 'from the hand of Saul', but that David spoke these words to the Lord on that day. This song is intended to be read then against the background of David's flight from Saul in 1 Samuel 19-26 – and perhaps relates specifically to the deliverance he experienced in 1 Samuel 23.

The song recorded here is a version of Psalm 18. As such it is a rare example of an entire poem appearing both inside and outside the book of Psalms (compare Psalm 105, a version of which is also to be found in 1 Chronicles 16.8-36; again inevitably associated with David). There are many 'psalm-like' pieces outside that collection, including some which have a similar narrative function as this one. In Genesis 47 for example a 'song of Jacob' closes the story of his life, as 'a song of Moses' does for the life story of that hero in Deuteronomy 30. There are echoes also in this text of the song of Hannah in 1 Samuel 2: the two songs as it were frame the whole 'Samuel narrative'. But there is no other passage in the Bible which is a more or less word for word repetition, outside the book of Psalms, of one of the songs within it, apart from these two.

While it is true that the Hebrew phrase '*le Dawid*' (the form of attribution which occurs most often to designate 'a Psalm of David') is capable of being translated in various ways (so that it need not mean a Psalm 'by David' but perhaps 'for David', 'in the spirit of David' or 'in honour of David'), it is still extremely unlikely, given the tradition, that David wrote no psalms at all. And among the psalms attributed to him in the Psalter, its repetition here may make Psalm 18 among the most likely actually to be 'by David'.

The structure of the song is not very obvious and is clouded by the frequency, yet irregularity, with which the text alternates between the second and third persons in reference to the Lord. There is no agreed division of the psalm into stanzas among commentators. Despite the heavy use of first person pronouns (I, me, my), it is also not always very obvious how the song relates to David's experience as it is recorded elsewhere in the story. This turns out to be theologically important however: the psalm is certainly David's song, but the imprecision enables it to function as the song of every believer also.

There is nevertheless a progression to the song which this exposition seeks to draw out. It falls into four parts. In the first stanza (in verses 2 to 20), David celebrates a particular experience of deliverance. (Deliverance is in a sense the theme of the whole song, but it is especially the burden of the opening stanza. There are four references to salvation in the first seven verses and only another five references thereafter.) This stanza includes (in verses 8-16) a 'theophany' (an 'appearance' of God) reminiscent of the Lord's self-manifestation to Moses at Sinai. In the second stanza (in verses 21 to 28), David celebrates his own 'cleanness' and righteousness, in terms which (especially in the light of the narrative in 2 Samuel 11-20) require some interpretation. In the third (in verses 29 to 43), David celebrates his own achievements (recognising that these have been possible only by grace); and in the last stanza (in verses 44 to 51), David concludes by celebrating his status among the nations.

Stanza One (verses 2-20): David celebrates his salvation

2 He said: The Lord is my rock, my fortress, and my deliverer,
3 my God, my rock, in whom I take refuge, my shield and the horn of my salvation, my stronghold and my refuge, my saviour; you save me from violence.
4 I call upon the Lord, who is worthy to be praised, and I am saved from my enemies.
5 For the waves of death encompassed me, the torrents of perdition assailed me;

6 the cords of Sheol entangled me, the snares of death confronted me.
7 In my distress I called upon the Lord; to my God I called. From his temple he heard my voice, and my cry came to his ears.

8 Then the earth reeled and rocked; the foundations of the heavens trembled and quaked, because he was angry.
9 Smoke went up from his nostrils, and devouring fire from his mouth; glowing coals flamed forth from him.
10 He bowed the heavens, and came down; thick darkness was under his feet.
11 He rode on a cherub, and flew; he was seen upon the wings of the wind.
12 He made darkness around him a canopy, thick clouds, a gathering of water.
13 Out of the brightness before him coals of fire flamed forth.
14 The Lord thundered from heaven; the Most High uttered his voice.
15 He sent out arrows, and scattered them – lightning, and routed them.
16 Then the channels of the sea were seen, the foundations of the world were laid bare at the rebuke of the Lord, at the blast of the breath of his nostrils.

17 He reached from on high, he took me, he drew me out of mighty waters.
18 He delivered me from my strong enemy, from those who hated me; for they were too mighty for me.
19 They came upon me in the day of my calamity, but the Lord was my stay.
20 He brought me out into a broad place; he delivered me, because he delighted in me.

Psalm 18 begins, 'I love you, O Lord, my strength'. It is tempting to regard the omission of that clause from this version as significant and as indicative of David's fall from grace. If this section of 2 Samuel is indeed to be read as a retrospective summary of David's life, is there an implied allusion here to the loss of his first love?

In fact the substance of this opening stanza rules out that possibility, as it provides a rare glimpse of the intensity and depth of David's faith and trust in God. From his youth upwards, his relationship with God was the most fundamental of his life and the reader is given an insight into it here. The sense of personal intimacy comes over strongly in the repeated personal pronoun: the word 'my' occurs 15 times in this English translation (and in addition the word 'me' comes four times and 'I' six times). The first-person is equally prominent in the Hebrew. The Lord is 'my God' (twice), 'my saviour', 'my salvation'.

David's relationship with God was forged in the wilderness and it may well have remained instinctive to him to the end of his life to employ in prayer rugged metaphors drawn from that experience: the Lord is a rock, a fortress, a stronghold, a refuge. It is a relationship in which David calls on the Lord and is heard; he calls on the Lord and the Lord not only hears, but acts in response to deliver him.

David is celebrating here an occasion, or a period, when he felt utterly overwhelmed by his enemy. He likens his predicament to drowning and becoming fatally trapped. When all seemed lost, he called on the Lord and was saved. Yet if, as the title supposes, the reference is to the day he was saved from Saul, the reference to 'enemies' in the plural (in verses 1 and 4) is part of what 'universalises' the poem so that it can serve as Everyman's prayer. The reference to the temple at the end of the stanza has the same effect: it is an anachronism, which enables believers of later generations to enter into David's praise.

If the reference to the temple introduces imagery strictly appropriate to a time later than David's struggles against Saul, the next few verses introduce imagery strictly appropriate to a much earlier time: when the people of God were in that other wilderness at Sinai. Verses 8 to 16 are something of an aside, inserted into this stanza, couched in the language of 'theophany': the kind of appearance of God as is described in Exodus 19.16-18 and celebrated in Psalm 68 (compare Judges 5.5).

The salvation of God is earth-shattering. This is metaphorical language – it must be: God has no nostrils, mouth or feet – intended to convey a sense of the awesome power and majesty of the God on whom David has called. Not only human enemies but the earth itself reels before him. He is at once a God of brightness (verse 13; smoke, flames, glowing coals in verse 9; lightning in verse 15) and of thick darkness (verses 10, 12). This God is a God of paradox and mystery, not a tame deity or divine plaything.

The first person pronouns which occurred so frequently in verses 2-7 are entirely absent from verses 8 to 16, but they recur in verses 17 to 20. The tone and vocabulary of these final verses of the stanza are very much in keeping with the first: the God who delights in David has delivered him from his strong enemy, from those who were too powerful for him, drawing him up out of the mighty waters. The effect of the aside is therefore to root David's experience in the experience of salvation history, in the experience of his people. David sees the deliverance he himself has enjoyed as belonging to the great saving acts of God in the past, especially at the Exodus.

Stanza Two (verses 21-28): David celebrates his own righteousness

21 The Lord rewarded me according to my righteousness; according to the cleanness of my hands he recompensed me.
22 For I have kept the ways of the Lord, and have not wickedly departed from my God.
23 For all his ordinances were before me, and from his statutes I did not turn aside.
24 I was blameless before him, and I kept myself from guilt.
25 Therefore the Lord has recompensed me according to my righteousness, according to my cleanness in his sight.
26 With the loyal you show yourself loyal; with the blameless you show yourself blameless;
27 with the pure you show yourself pure, and with the crooked you show yourself perverse.
28 You deliver a humble people, but your eyes are upon the haughty to bring them down.

The second stanza strikes a discordant note. Pondering the great deliverance he has known, David attributes it to his own righteousness. What has happened to him has happened by way of reward and recompense, in accordance with David's 'cleanness' before God. David claims to have 'kept the ways of the Lord' and not to have turned aside from his statutes. He has kept himself from guilt, he says, and has been blameless.

Blameless? Perhaps there was a time when David might justifiably have made such a claim. On the assumption that David did indeed first sing this song to the Lord during the lifetime of king Saul (i.e., before he himself became king) perhaps the claim had some merit at that time. But encountering it at this point in the narrative, the reader is all too aware how far David has strayed from the straight and narrow. He has emphatically not 'kept the ways of the Lord'. In direct contradiction to his claim (verse 22), he could hardly have 'departed from [his] God' more 'wickedly'. In particular his hands (verse 21) are not clean.

Again this discrepancy was entirely evident to those who 'edited' this text throughout the process of its development. Perhaps the poem is placed here precisely to remind the reader how far David has fallen and how great the contrast between the young man and the old. The reader is faced with editorial irony here. One might wish that to the very end of his life David had remained among the loyal and pure to whom God shows himself loyal and pure. The reality however, even if David himself is too blind to see it, is that he became one of the crooked to whom God shows himself perverse. There was a time when it was appropriate for David to number himself among the humble to whom the Lord comes as deliverer. Now there is a danger that he will find himself among the haughty, whom the Lord brings down. (This poem and 'the Song of Hannah' serve as prologue and epilogue to the whole of 1 and 2 Samuel. Note the links between verse 28 and 1 Samuel 2.7, verse 14 and 1 Samuel 2.10, and verse 32 and 1 Samuel 2.2.)

Stanza Three (verses 29-43): David celebrates his achievements

29 Indeed, you are my lamp, O Lord, the Lord lightens my darkness.
30 By you I can crush a troop, and by my God I can leap over a wall.
31 This God – his way is perfect; the promise of the Lord proves true; he is a shield for all who take refuge in him.
32 For who is God, but the Lord? And who is a rock, except our God?
33 The God who has girded me with strength has opened wide my path.
34 He made my feet like the feet of deer, and set me secure on the heights.
35 He trains my hands for war, so that my arms can bend a bow of bronze.
36 You have given me the shield of your salvation, and your help has made me great.
37 You have made me stride freely, and my feet do not slip;
38 I pursued my enemies and destroyed them, and did not turn back until they were consumed.
39 I consumed them; I struck them down, so that they did not rise; they fell under my feet.

40 For you girded me with strength for the battle; you made my assailants sink under me.
41 You made my enemies turn their backs to me, those who hated me, and I destroyed them.
42 They looked, but there was no one to save them; they cried to the Lord, but he did not answer them.
43 I beat them fine like the dust of the earth, I crushed them and stamped them down like the mire of the streets.

It strikes the Christian reader, schooled in the ways of Jesus, as only marginally less discordant when in this third stanza David moves from celebrating his own righteousness to celebrating his achievements – not least because his achievements are so violent: 'I pursued my enemies and destroyed them... I consumed them, I struck them down... I beat them fine like the dust of the earth, I crushed them and stamped them down like the mire of the streets' (verses 38-39, 43). It is hard, in the light of Christ, to enter into these sentiments, which are triumphalistic and brutal.

As far as the violence is concerned, some allowance must be made for David's situation, as the opening verse defines it. He is in fact a fugitive on the run from a more powerful enemy who would take his life if he could (although in this stanza there is less sense of immediate crisis; it is as if David is looking back here over his life as a whole, rather than calling to mind a single urgent incident).

And as far as the boastfulness is concerned, David does at least acknowledge that his achievements are 'by God'. Thus the first half of this stanza (verses 29 to 37) is in praise of God, the only one who is truly perfect. The emphasis is on what God (sometimes spoken of, in the third person; sometimes spoken to, in the second) has done for David: he has girded the king with strength and opened wide his path; he has made his feet like those of a deer and set him secure on the heights; he has trained his hands for battle and made him stride freely. In short, it is God's help (verse 36) which has made David great. The same note of grateful praise recurs in verses 40 to 41: it is the Lord who girded David with strength for the battle and 'made' the kings assailants sink and his enemies turn their backs.

Stanza Four (verses 44-51): David celebrates his status among the nations

44 You delivered me from strife with the peoples; you kept me as the head of the nations; people whom I had not known served me.

45 Foreigners came cringing to me; as soon as they heard of me, they obeyed me.
46 Foreigners lost heart, and came trembling out of their strongholds.
47 The Lord lives! Blessed be my rock, and exalted be my God, the rock of my salvation,
48 the God who gave me vengeance and brought down peoples under me,
49 who brought me out from my enemies; you exalted me above my adversaries, you delivered me from the violent.
50 For this I will extol you, O Lord, among the nations, and sing praises to your name.
51 He is a tower of salvation for his king, and shows steadfast love to his anointed, to David and his descendants for ever.

If the context for the psalm identified in verse 1 fits the content of the first stanza quite well, the same cannot be said of these closing verses, which seem to belong to a much later point in David's life.

David is still celebrating deliverance and celebrating it in recognisably the same terms (compare verse 3 'you save me from violence', with verse 49 'you delivered me from the violent'). As in the opening stanza, first person pronouns abound. As in that stanza, the Lord is 'my rock', 'my God', 'my salvation', who is to be praised.

However, the deliverance which is in view in this final stanza is by no means merely from the hand of Saul. It is deliverance from 'strife with the peoples'. What David celebrates here is not a single incident in which he escaped Saul's clutches, but a series of victorious campaigns against foreigners (verses 45-46; if there is a narrative context for this, it would be 2 Samuel 8 rather than 1 Samuel 23).

David is no longer a fugitive at risk of being overwhelmed; he is 'the head of the nations' served by people he had not known (verse 44); he is the Lord's king and his anointed (verse 51), confident that the Lord will show his steadfast love to his descendants 'for ever' (an allusion, surely, to 2 Samuel 7).

Conclusion:

There is then some progression in the psalm.

If, as the title states, there is a specific occasion which gave rise to the poem, it is closest to the surface in the opening stanza, but even there the effect of verses 8-16 is to set David's experience into a larger context. The experience that David has had of the majesty and saving power of God is 'Sinaic' in character: that is to say, his experience 'fits' that of the iconic deliverance experienced by whole people of God. The effect is that all those members of the people of God who instinctively celebrate God's self-revelation at Sinai are drawn into David's celebration of his own salvation and are able to identify with it.

In stanza 2, the reader is painfully aware of the gap which has opened up between the integrity of the David who first sang this song, and the king he became by the end of his reign. In the final two stanzas that original context, in Saul's lifetime, is forgotten. David is king himself, triumphant over all his enemies, assured of his position as the Lord's anointed. The sense of transition from David's own song to a song about David is complete in the final clause, where reference is made to him in the third person.

In fact of course the title-verse says that this song is about the deliverance David experienced not just 'from the hand of Saul', but from the hand of 'all his enemies'. Perhaps a song he first sang early in his life, he gradually developed and built upon as the years went by, overlaying the original with the celebration of later deliverances too.

David's Last Words

Introduction

Even in the context of this 'appendix' to the main narrative (i.e., 2 Samuel 21-24), the 'last words of David' come upon the reader abruptly. The only hints of his ebbing vitality have been the rescue of David by Abishai and the decision of his troops not to permit him to lead them into battle any longer. But the whole appendix sits outside the overarching chronological framework of the narrative, and the placement of this 'oracle' here owes more to formal literary concerns than to chronological ones. It is therefore no particular surprise when David speaks again in 1 and 2 Kings.

From a literary point of view, the placement of this oracle is entirely appropriate. In terms of the 'chiasmus' in the appendix, a turning point has now been reached: after a narrative, a list and a poem, there follows a poem, a list and a narrative. Insofar as the whole appendix offers a summary overview of David's life, here at its heart the end of his life is anticipated and the fullest retrospective is offered.

There are other passages in the Hebrew Scriptures in which 'last words' are recorded in poetic form, such as those of Jacob (in Genesis 49.2-27) and Moses (in Deuteronomy 33.2-29 – where they follow 'the song of Moses' just as this oracle follows 'the song of David'). However the differences between this passage and those ones are as significant as the similarities. Those are (or at least claim to be) 'blessings'; this is not. Those are addressed to the tribes of Israel; this refers only to the house of David.

Since the 'last words of David' are in the form of verse, they are treated here (as was the psalm in the previous chapter) in 'stanzas' rather than, as in the prose sections of the biblical text, in 'scenes'.

Poetry seldom translates easily and this oracle is a case in point. In Hebrew the structure is easy to follow even if the language is a little condensed. In translation the structure is much less obvious. The oracle is made up of six four-line units. One unit forms the introductory first stanza. Three more make up the second stanza, in which David recalls what God has said to him and goes on to ponder prophetically the implications for the future of his dynasty; this stanza is thoroughly positive in tone. The last two units make up the third stanza, in which David ponders the implications of God's words for the wicked; this stanza is correspondingly negative in tone.

Stanza One (verse 1): the last words of David

> *Now these are the last words of David: The oracle of David, son of Jesse, the oracle of the man whom God exalted, the anointed of the God of Jacob, the favourite of the Strong One of Israel:*

This first unit of the poem is an introduction. David is not the speaker, but the one spoken of. In Numbers 24 the pronouncement of the prophet is introduced as follows: 'the oracle of Balaam son of Beor, the oracle of the man whose eye is clear'. The parallel to the introduction of David's last words is obvious, down to the repetition of the word 'oracle' (*ne'um*).

Presumably some conventional form is being followed, which also accounts for the use of such extremely august titles. David is God's messiah, the chosen one ('the anointed', *meshiach*). Verse 1 also makes explicit what has been implicit in the narrative from the moment David was anointed by Samuel, particularly in any comparison of David's experience with Saul's: that he is the favourite of the God of Israel. The God who shows no partiality (Deuteronomy 10.17; 2 Chronicles 19.7) nevertheless favours some over others. But 'election' in the Bible is always an exclusive means to an inclusive end, as the call of Abraham in Genesis 12 already makes crystal clear and as St Paul argues at length in his letter to the Romans chapters 9-11.

The stress on David's high calling in this introduction to his 'last words' invites the reader to reflect on the extent to which his life was and was not a worthy response to it.

Stanza Two (verses 2-5): A just ruler is like the sun rising

> *2 The spirit of the Lord speaks through me, his word is upon my tongue.*

*3 The God of Israel has spoken, the Rock of Israel has said
to me: One who rules over people justly, ruling in the fear
of God,
4 is like the light of morning, like the sun rising on a cloudless
morning, gleaming from the rain on the grassy land.
5 Is not my house like this with God? For he has made with
me an everlasting covenant, ordered in all things and secure.
Will he not cause to prosper all my help and my desire?*

The second stanza involves a triple transition. First, at its outset, David (having been the one spoken of) becomes the speaker. To begin with however he speaks only indirectly of what the spirit of God has spoken. Then (from the mid-point of verse 3), he quotes directly what God has said to him. Finally (in verse 5), he reflects on what God's words mean for his 'house'.

The effect of verses 2-3a is to heighten the expectation of the reader: the oracle, when it comes, will warrant careful attention. It is no merely human message. The God of Israel has placed his word immediately on David's tongue, so that the Spirit of the Living God is as it were speaking through him. Here if anywhere David is surely talking the talk.

The content of the oracle, when eventually (in verse 3b) it comes, is perhaps surprising. It is not in any obvious sense a promise to David and his descendants. It is a profound and gracious statement of the effect of good leadership. One who rules justly is like the light of morning, like a sun-rise, like the renewing impact of rain on grassy land. These are hugely positive similes. The impact of a just ruler on his people is like the impact of the sun and the rain on the land: it promotes life and growth. Leadership is all too often exploitative and suffocating of others. But a ruler in any sphere who reflects the rule of God (this is not only true of the rule of a king over a state), will be a source of life and renewal to those over whom authority is exercised. The mark of such rulers is this: they know themselves to be accountable. They rule in the fear of God (verse 3b). Life-giving rulers know themselves ruled.

This then is the biblical pattern of election. The chosen one is chosen precisely to be the means by which the blessing of God is poured out upon others. The favourite is to be the agent through whom the favour of God is made known to all. For this reason, much is expected of those to whom much has been given (Luke 12.48). Judgment begins with the household of God (1 Peter 4.17). To be chosen by God, to be God's favourite, is not all sweetness and light. It is to be severely accountable. It is to live in the fear of God.

This, David claims, is true to his own experience because God has made an everlasting covenant with him. This *berit olam* is something of a technical term in the Old Testament (compare Genesis 9.16, 17.7; Psalm 105.10; Isaiah 55.3 and elsewhere).

The train of thought is a little confusing in the Hebrew. The sense seems to be that God's dealings with David illustrate definitively the effect of 'just rule': because God himself rules justly, David's house is ordered and secure. God will be David's help. David's every desire will flourish. The sense seems also to be that these things are true, because David himself also rules justly, as Israel's help, so that the nation is ordered and secure and the people can flourish. And perhaps there was a time, earlier rather than later in David's reign, when these sentiments were borne out in practice. But as David's last words they barely ring true: his house, following the rebellion of Absalom and immediately before the uprising of Adonijah, is anything but ordered and secure. It has become something disordered and insecure. By the same token, the people of Israel are hardly flourishing. The reason for it is simply that instead of fearing the Lord, David has despised him (12.10). Once again the reader is confronted with the gap between David's calling and his actions, his aspirations and his experience.

Stanza Four (verses 6-7): The godless are like thorns

> 6 But the godless are all like thorns that are thrown away;
> for they cannot be picked up with the hand;
> 7 to touch them one uses an iron bar or the shaft of a spear.
> And they are entirely consumed in fire on the spot.

In the final stanza a different tone is struck. If for the most part the effect of godly rulers is to cause the grass of the field to blossom and flourish, this is not their only function. They also weed out the thorns and throw them away to be consumed in the fire (compare Genesis 3.18; Hebrews 6.8). The difficulty of this aspect of the ruler's task is not minimised: thorns (middle eastern thorns) are not easily 'picked up with the hand'. Yet the task has to be tackled, if the grass is to flourish as it should.

It has also to be said that while the primary goal of election in the Bible is blessing, this end is not universally achieved. There is also (to quote the words of Jesus' parable in Matthew 13.41), a rooting out of 'all causes of sin and all evildoers'. God himself comes in judgment and the godly ruler will find an echo of this role impossible to evade.

David does not only note the destruction of the worthless, however. He also emphasises their intrinsic destructiveness and intractability. It is not possible to handle them easily.

In verse 6, the Hebrew for 'godless' is '*belial*' ('worthless' in 1 Samuel 25.17 and 2 Samuel 20.1; but compare 2 Corinthians 6.15). David presumably had in mind opponents to his rule and to his dynasty; but the verse is capable of being understood in a much wider context.

Conclusion:

The last words of David introduce some theologically profound themes. Those who are called by God are blessed by him. But this is in order that they might be a blessing to others. It is not for their own sake alone. Conversely those who are chosen by God are required to be instruments of his judgment as well as of his blessing. As such they are subject to his judgment as well as to his blessing.

What is most sobering about the last words of David is that he seems oblivious to the flip side of his election. There is no hint that, looking back over his life, he perceives that he himself is subject to God's judgment on account of having failed to live up to the job description set out here of the godly ruler.

The note of contrition is so conspicuously absent from these 'last words', that the reader is relieved that they are not actually his last words at all.

Chapter Twenty-One
2 Samuel 23.8–39

David and his Warriors

Introduction

One of the marks of good leadership is the way that it nurtures and develops the gifts of others. Good leaders (or to use the language of the previous episode, 'godly rulers') empower those they lead, enabling them to flourish and realise their potential – just as the warmth of the rising sun and the moisture of the falling rain causes the grass to grow (verse 4).

David was a good leader. He was a fine warrior not only in the sense that he was himself brave and skilful (though he was this from his youth; see 1 Samuel 16.18), but also in the sense that under him a great company of other warriors emerged, whose gifts and achievements were celebrated. Like Saul before him, David presumably recruited valiant men whenever he found them (see 1 Samuel 14.52). But these men were then honoured. The penultimate section of this appendix to the main narrative is an inventory of these men. It corresponds, in the chiasmus which makes up chapters 21-24, to the list of warriors who fought against the Philistines and their exploits, recorded in 21.15-22. The Philistines are again easily the most prominent of Israel's enemies in this episode. It is above all against them that David's warriors demonstrate their prowess. David himself appears only fleetingly in this episode in an incident (in verses 13-17) which provides a glimpse of how David inspired the men he led.

This episode falls into three 'scenes'. There is a manifest tailing off in narrative content through the three scenes. In the first, an elite triumvirate is named (Josheb-basshebeth, Eleazar son of Dodo, and Shammah son of Agee) and its deeds are reported. For each man, an individual act of valour is recorded in story form; and the scene concludes with an incident in which all three were involved. Four stories are thus required to do justice to 'the Three'. In the second scene, almost as an aside, mention is made of two warriors who excelled in bravery and yet 'did not attain to the Three'. Two stories suffice here for two warriors. Intriguingly these are both men about whom much else is known (much more in fact than is known about any of the Three): Abishai son of Zeruiah, and Benaiah son of Jehoida. There follows in the third scene a list of the other warriors who were numbered among 'the Thirty'. In this scene however, there is no narrative content at all: the summary is a bare list.

There is an explicit hierarchy in the ordering of the three scenes: the Three are the most exalted; the two 'did not attain to the Three', but excelled among the Thirty. So it is odd to find 'the chief of the Thirty' (Abishai, in verse 18) relegated below the Three. It is even odder to find his older brother Joab included only obliquely in verses 18, 24 and 37.

Scene One (verses 8-17): The Three Warriors

8 These are the names of the warriors whom David had: Josheb-basshebeth a Tahchemonite; he was chief of the Three; he wielded his spear against eight hundred whom he killed at one time.

9 Next to him among the three warriors was Eleazar son of Dodo son of Ahohi. He was with David when they defied the Philistines who were gathered there for battle. The Israelites withdrew, 10 but he stood his ground. He struck down the Philistines until his arm grew weary, though his hand clung to the sword. The Lord brought about a great victory that day. Then the people came back to him – but only to strip the dead.

11 Next to him was Shammah son of Agee, the Hararite. The Philistines gathered together at Lehi, where there was a plot of ground full of lentils; and the army fled from the Philistines. 12 But he took his stand in the middle of the plot, defended it, and killed the Philistines; and the Lord brought about a great victory.

13 Towards the beginning of harvest three of the thirty chiefs went down to join David at the cave of Adullam, while a band of Philistines was encamped in the valley of Rephaim.

14 David was then in the stronghold; and the garrison of the Philistines was then at Bethlehem. 15 David said longingly, 'O that someone would give me water to drink from the well of Bethlehem that is by the gate!' 16 Then the three warriors broke through the camp of the Philistines, drew water from the well of Bethlehem that was by the gate, and brought it to David. But he would not drink of it; he poured it out to the Lord, 17 for he said, 'The Lord forbid that I should do this. Can I drink the blood of the men who went at the risk of their lives?' Therefore he would not drink it. The three warriors did these things.

There is a further little oddity in the fact that the 'chief of the Three', Josheb-basshebeth, occupies far less text than his two colleagues Eleazar and Shammah. There is no narrative embellishment of the incident in which he made his name. It is simply stated that he once killed eight hundred with his spear, single-handed and at one time.

The 'vignettes' about Eleazar and Shammah share some significant features. In both cases the heroes were involved in battles against the Philistines, the Israelite army fled, the hero stood his ground and slew the Philistines. Perhaps most significant of all, in both cases it is concluded that 'the Lord brought about a great victory'.

The two references to 'the Lord' in the final vignette (in verses 13-17) are worth noting. The story seems to belong to a time early in David's career, perhaps even before he became king. The cave of Adullam is the place where, on the run from Saul, David had first become the 'captain' of a band of men (1 Samuel 22.1-2). It was his stronghold (1 Samuel 22.5), close enough to his family home in Bethlehem for 'all his father's house' to go down to him there. Even at that time, while evading Saul, David was leading raids on the Philistines. It was a time when he called easily on the Lord and often (1 Samuel 23.1-5).

It makes sound psychological sense if the story presupposes this 'wilderness' period of David's life. His movement at that time was restricted not only by the garrison of the Philistines but by his need to remain hidden from Saul. Under those circumstances he might well express a homesick longing for water from the well at Bethlehem – it suggests the experience of living in that city was still a relatively recent one for David. Alternatively the incident may date from a time shortly after David had become king of all Israel, when the Philistines were certainly 'spread out in the valley of Rephaim' (5.22; this is where 'the Chronicler' places it: compare 1 Chronicles 11.15-19).

The response of the three warriors to their leader's desire indicates what loyalty he inspired in his men. His response to them may indicate why. When he utters his wish for water, the three warriors take up the challenge. They break through the Philistine ranks at Bethlehem, draw from the well and then race back to David. When they present him with the dripping bucket, he refuses to drink it. Presumably watched by his entire band (a group of up to six hundred, if this story does relate to the wilderness years), David pours out the water on the ground as an offering to the Lord. The last clause is crucial. It confirms the high value David is placing on what the three warriors have done. The sacrifice involved in obtaining it renders the water too precious to drink. To drink it would be to drink the blood of the men who risked their lives to get it. In Jewish tradition, blood is not for drinking; it is only to be offered to the Lord and to be poured out on the ground like water (compare Deuteronomy 12.16, 23-24; Leviticus 17.10-14).

Scene Two (verses 18-23): Those who did not attain to the Three

18 Now Abishai son of Zeruiah, the brother of Joab, was chief of the Thirty. With his spear he fought against three hundred men and killed them, and won a name beside the Three. 19 He was the most renowned of the Thirty, and became their commander; but he did not attain to the Three.

20 Benaiah son of Jehoiada was a valiant warrior from Kabzeel, a doer of great deeds; he struck down two sons of Ariel of Moab. He also went down and killed a lion in a pit on a day when snow had fallen. 21 And he killed an Egyptian, a handsome man. The Egyptian had a spear in his hand; but Benaiah went against him with a staff, snatched the spear out of the Egyptian's hand, and killed him with his own spear. 22 Such were the things Benaiah son of Jehoiada did, and won a name beside the three warriors. 23 He was renowned among the Thirty, but he did not attain to the Three. And David put him in charge of his bodyguard.

There seems to be some sensitivity around the introduction of Abishai. There is definite emphasis on his status as well as his achievement. He was chief of the Thirty. He was the most renowned of the Thirty and became their commander. By fighting against three hundred men and killing them 'he won himself a name beside the Three'; but ultimately (and this is the last word on the matter) 'he did not attain to the Three'.

Abishai's secondary status is further underlined by the reference to his brother. He is defined not just as his mother's son, but as 'the brother of Joab'. This is the first of three occasions when Joab's name is used in this way to identify others, which makes it all the odder that he does not appear in these lists in his own right. It is as if Joab has been airbrushed out of the picture.

Benaiah son of Jehoiada is distinguished by the fact that three of his acts of heroism are recorded – but curiously none of them involved the Philistines. There is mystery surrounding the first exploit. The Hebrew text is unclear. Did he kill two lion-like men, two lions, or two sons of a man whose name (Ariel) meant something like 'lion of God'? There is an obvious link to the second (and entirely unambiguous) exploit: on a snowy day, he went down into a pit to fight a lion and killed it. It's easy to imagine the traces of the combat in the snow. For good measure, he later fought an Egyptian of startling (rather than handsome) appearance and killed him with his own spear. It is not clear in what context this last fight took place. It may be that the man was fighting as a mercenary for the Philistines.

Like Abishai, Benaiah was renowned among the Thirty, and won himself a name 'beside the Three'; but like Abishai, 'he did not attain to the Three'. Also like Abishai, Benaiah plays a leading role in the narrative outside these lists. Indeed in a rare link to the narrative as a whole, it is noted in verse 23 that he became David's bodyguard. This fact is presumably implied by the note in 8.18 and elsewhere that he was 'in command of the Cherethites and the Pelethites'. He remained a man of great influence in the palace into the reign of Solomon (1 Kings 2.34-35).

Scene Three (verses 24-39): The Thirty

24 Among the Thirty were Asahel brother of Joab; Elhanan son of Dodo of Bethlehem; 25 Shammah of Harod; Elika of Harod; 26 Helez the Paltite; Ira son of Ikkesh of Tekoa; 27 Abiezer of Anathoth; Mebunnai the Hushathite; 28 Zalmon the Ahohite; Maharai of Netophah; 29 Heleb son of Baanah of Netophah; Ittai son of Ribai of Gibeah of the Benjaminites; 30 Benaiah of Pirathon; Hiddai of the torrents of Gaash; 31 Abi-albon the Arbathite; Azmaveth of Bahurim;

32 Eliahba of Shaalbon; the sons of Jashen: Jonathan 33 son of Shammah the Hararite; Ahiam son of Sharar the Hararite; 34 Eliphelet son of Ahasbai of Maacah; Eliam son of Ahithophel the Gilonite; 35 Hezro of Carmel; Paarai the Arbite; 36 Igal son of Nathan of Zobah; Bani the Gadite; 37 Zelek the Ammonite; Naharai of Beeroth, the armour-bearer of Joab son of Zeruiah; 38 Ira the Ithrite; Gareb the Ithrite; 39 Uriah the Hittite – thirty-seven in all.

This final section lists others who were 'among the Thirty', beginning with Asahel brother of Joab, ending with Uriah the Hittite and including another thirty individuals (assuming that there were two 'sons of Jashen' in verse 32). The 'thirty-seven [men] in all' (verse 39) is therefore made up of the Three (in verses 8 to 17), the two who did not attain to the Three (in verses 8 to 23), and the thirty-two individuals listed here. Presumably 'the Thirty' was a standing body, to which new members were admitted as established ones were killed or became unable to fight – hence there are more than thirty men listed 'among the Thirty'.

Textual 'archaeology' suggests that this list is derived from a particularly ancient and historically credible source. It may even be that the sequence of the names constitutes some sort of chronological record. Certainly Asahel is an obvious example of a warrior who was active early in David's career and not later (see 2.18-23). There is a concentration early in the list of names which derive from territories in the kingdom of Judah (from Bethlehem, Hebron and Jerusalem for example) and which may indicate those who were recruited to David's cause before he became king over all Israel. Alternatively it may be that the list is organised geographically rather than chronologically. This, as well as a chronological basis, would account for the occasions when two men from the same place of origin are listed one after another (Harod in verse 25, Netophah in verses 28-29, the Hararites in verse 33 and the Ithrites in verse 38). The presence of so many foreigners (including not just a Hittite, but an Ammonite), may reflect the custom of using outsiders as mercenaries and bodyguards (to which David's use of the Cherethites and Pelethites bears witness).

Only a very small number of the names listed here belong to individuals who feature elsewhere in the narrative. Elhanan son of Dodo of Bethlehem is perhaps not to be identified with Elhanan son of Jaare-oregim the Bethlehemite in 21.19. Presumably in verses 32-33, Jonathan is the son of the same Shammah who is listed in verse 11 as one of the Three.

Conclusion

About two individuals however there is more to be said: Joab and Uriah. In different ways these two men were problematic for David.

The one place in this episode in which David is named redounds to his credit. He is depicted as a leader who inspired his men; and the reader is given a glimpse of why that might be. He is a hero who motivated a band of heroes. But there were two men in his entourage above all who would not bend to his will. One was Joab. His absence from this list is remarkable, particularly given the presence in it of his two brothers and even (in verse 37) his armour-bearer. He was the commander of David's army, but his name is not included in a list of the king's thirty most valiant warriors. A member of his own staff is included, but he is not. His two younger brothers are included, but the most senior of the three 'sons of Zeruiah' is not. Yet while he himself is not listed here, he casts a long shadow over those who are and over David too perhaps. His relationship with the king was increasingly strained as time went on. He will eventually side with Adonijah against David and Solomon and will be the first to be condemned to death by the dying king (1 Kings 2.5-6). It seems likely that his absence from these lists amounts to a retrospective judgment on Joab.

By contrast, the presence of Uriah's name (and in particular the placement of it) serves as a tacit judgment on David. There is a definite emphasis on his name, simply because it comes right at the end of the list of the Thirty. His name is not last in the equivalent though very different list in 1 Chronicles 11, which makes the placement here suggestive. If verse 34 also refers to Uriah's father in law (that is, if Eliam son of Ahitophel the Gilonite is to be identified as Bathsheba's father, compare 11.3), then the impression is reinforced that an allusion is being made to David's wrongdoing here.

In different ways then the occurrence of these two names, Joab and Uriah, constitutes a reminder that David's leadership of this warrior band was not something uniformly easy and uncomplicated. Their loyalty to him was not consistent, and nor was his to them.

Chapter Twenty-Two
2 Samuel 24.1–25

David and the Census

Introduction

The final episode in this chiastic appendix to the narrative proper is full of theological riddles. The first verse alone raises a host of questions: why was the Lord angry with Israel? How and why did he incite David? Why was the census David conducted sinful? How and why did this sequence of events resolve the anger which the Lord had at the outset?

The reader of the biblical text has a double obligation in these circumstances. The first is to ask the obvious questions even when they are the difficult ones. Such questions are not only entirely legitimate for the faithful bible reader; they are essential. To suppress or evade them is to risk the suppression or evasion of the truth. On the other hand it is always necessary for the faithful bible reader to attempt to read the text from the inside. This often means getting past the questions which preoccupy the modern reader in an attempt to identify the question which preoccupied the author of the text. It is thoroughly appropriate for the faithful reader to interrogate the text; but eventually such a reader will want to ask, 'what question is it that the text is attempting to answer?' or even, 'in what ways does the text interrogate me?'.

There are close parallels between this episode and its 'chiastic' partner in 2 Samuel 21: in both cases, an offence is committed unwittingly against God; a national disaster follows, which it requires a royal act at a holy place to put right; so God is propitiated and his blessing of Israel is renewed.

The episode falls into three scenes. The first (in which the Lord's anger is kindled against Israel) features David and Joab – whose name was so notably absent from the list of the Thirty in the previous episode. The second (in which the Lord sends a pestilence against Israel) features David and his prophet Gad. Gad's only previous involvement in the narrative was to deliver a brief prophetic message to David in 1 Samuel 22.5, which may strengthen the argument that this episode and its precursor belong chronologically to the period of David's wilderness years (see 23.13 and 1 Samuel 22.1-2; 23.14 and 1 Samuel 22.5). The third scene (in which the Lord answers David's supplication for the land) features David and Araunah.

Scene One (verses 1-9): The Lord's anger is kindled against Israel

Again the anger of the Lord was kindled against Israel, and he incited David against them, saying, 'Go, count the people of Israel and Judah.' 2 So the king said to Joab and the commanders of the army, who were with him, 'Go through all the tribes of Israel, from Dan to Beer-sheba, and take a census of the people, so that I may know how many there are.' 3 But Joab said to the king, 'May the Lord your God increase the number of the people a hundredfold, while the eyes of my lord the king can still see it! But why does my lord the king want to do this?' 4 But the king's word prevailed against Joab and the commanders of the army. So Joab and the commanders of the army went out from the presence of the king to take a census of the people of Israel. 5 They crossed the Jordan, and began from Aroer and from the city that is in the middle of the valley, towards Gad and on to Jazer. 6 Then they came to Gilead, and to Kadesh in the land of the Hittites; and they came to Dan, and from Dan they went round to Sidon, 7 and came to the fortress of Tyre and to all the cities of the Hivites and Canaanites; and they went out to the Negeb of Judah at Beer-sheba. 8 So when they had gone through all the land, they came back to Jerusalem at the end of nine months and twenty days. 9 Joab reported to the king the number of those who had been recorded: in Israel there were eight hundred thousand soldiers able to draw the sword, and those of Judah were five hundred thousand.

As in its partner episode in 2 Samuel 21, this whole episode seems to sit theologically as well as chronologically outside the framework of the narrative proper. Both the theological vocabulary and the conceptual paradigm are distinctive. There is for example a greater degree of divine intervention in this episode and that partner than elsewhere in 1 and 2 Samuel: God speaks and acts directly, as a character in the drama. There is a greater tolerance of divine inscrutability and sovereign freedom: thus, the opening sentence raises the question why the Lord's anger was kindled against Israel. Likewise, for God to incite David to do something which incurs divine disapproval is an entirely new development. (Interestingly, in 1 Chronicles 21.1 it is Satan who incites David. Both here and there the biblical writer is grappling with the mystery of evil. In the theology of the Chronicler, there is an increasing tendency to associate good with God and evil with Satan. But in this text, the emphasis is on God as the source of all that is, good and evil. Yet the divine initiative does not relieve human beings of responsibility for the decisions they make. However much David is incited by God in this episode, he remains culpable for his actions.) This is not to say that this material is any less theologically instructive for the careful reader; it does mean that the text has to be read carefully.

For some unstated reason then the Lord is angry with Israel, and for some unstated reason he incites David to do something about which he will be angry: he prompts or provokes David to count the people of Israel and Judah.

David does not question the idea. He simply instructs his military leaders to execute it. The fact that he turned to the commanders of his army may suggest that the proposal had a military motivation: perhaps David was attempting to establish the potential for a new conscription. The way in which the outcome of the census is eventually reported at the end of this episode (in verse 9) supports this reading.

But if David is unquestioning, Joab is not. Joab is an ambiguous character in this narrative; he is to some extent David's opposite. David is essentially godly, but is given to moments of weakness and folly. Joab by contrast is essentially ungodly, but is given to moments of insight and wisdom. This is a case in point. When he hears David's order to take a census of all the tribes of Israel, he recoils. He sees the spiritual implications immediately and prays that 'the Lord your God' might increase the number of the people a hundredfold. He even dares to confront the king with a direct question: 'Why do you want to do this?'. The text may not state explicitly that David's proposal is sinful or why; but Joab senses that it is so.

Despite the support of his fellow officers, Joab is overruled by the king. The census is undertaken. It takes over nine months to complete. Joab and his colleagues travel to the corners of David's kingdom, from Tyre and Sidon in the north to Beersheba in the south.

Ominously, Joab reports two figures at the end of the census and not one: he has recorded 800,000 fighting men in Israel and 500,000 in Judah. Though it is quite likely that the 'thousands' are battalions or military units, rather than exact numbers, the separation in the census hints at David's fundamental failure to unite the northern and southern parts of his kingdom.

In any case, why might this information matter to David? It is hard to suppose a noble reason. If he wanted to establish a basis for taxation, this implies a degree of greed on his part. If he meant rather to establish the size of his fighting force, any increased confidence in the resources at his disposal implies a corresponding loss of trust in the Lord. On any reading, there is evidence here of the kind of centralisation and appropriation of which Samuel warned when the elders of Israel first asked for a king. It is in the nature of monarchy to take (compare 1 Samuel 8.11-18). King David has come a long way since he stepped onto the battlefield against Goliath; and not all his progress has been in the ways of God.

Scene Two (verses 10-19): The Lord sends a pestilence on Israel

10 But afterwards, David was stricken to the heart because he had numbered the people. David said to the Lord, 'I have sinned greatly in what I have done. But now, O Lord, I pray you, take away the guilt of your servant; for I have done very foolishly.' 11 When David rose in the morning, the word of the Lord came to the prophet Gad, David's seer, saying, 12 'Go and say to David: Thus says the Lord: Three things I offer you; choose one of them, and I will do it to you.' 13 So Gad came to David and told him; he asked him, 'Shall three years of famine come to you on your land? Or will you flee for three months before your foes while they pursue you? Or shall there be three days' pestilence in your land? Now consider, and decide what answer I shall return to the one who sent me.' 14 Then David said to Gad, 'I am in great distress; let us fall into the hand of the Lord, for his mercy is great; but let me not fall into human hands.'

15 So the Lord sent a pestilence on Israel from that morning until the appointed time; and seventy thousand of the people died, from Dan to Beer-sheba. 16 But when the angel stretched out his hand towards Jerusalem to destroy it, the Lord relented concerning the evil, and said to the angel who was bringing destruction among the people, 'It is enough;

now stay your hand.' The angel of the Lord was then by the threshing-floor of Araunah the Jebusite. 17 When David saw the angel who was destroying the people, he said to the Lord, 'I alone have sinned, and I alone have done wickedly; but these sheep, what have they done? Let your hand, I pray, be against me and against my father's house.'

18 That day Gad came to David and said to him, 'Go up and erect an altar to the Lord on the threshing-floor of Araunah the Jebusite.' 19 Following Gad's instructions, David went up, as the Lord had commanded.

Joab, having completed the count, drops out of the action. The spotlight in the second scene falls on David and his 'seer', Gad.

The text passes over some of the things the reader is curious to know. How long after Joab had submitted his census return was David conscience-stricken? The numbering of the people had taken so long, David had certainly had ample time to reflect on his decision to carry out the exercise. In the end, what pricked David's conscience? How did he become convinced he had done wrong and what exactly was the wrongdoing he regretted?

Instead the text focuses on the whole-hearted nature of David's penitence. This is the defining characteristic of David in the story of his fall. It is a characteristic which distinguishes him from both his predecessor, Saul, and his successor, Solomon: unlike them, he is quick to acknowledge his fault when he has done wrong and his re-pentance is heartfelt. This is the mark of someone who, despite all his weakness and folly remains 'a man after God's own heart' (1 Samuel 13.14; Acts of the Apostles 13.22). He turns at once to the Lord and pours out his confession: 'I have sinned greatly in what I have done... I have done very foolishly'.

The following morning, the Word of the Lord comes to Gad. The prophet approaches David with a terrible dilemma. He is required to choose his punishment – except that the punishment is not his alone. It will fall on the people he has numbered. They are to suffer either three years of famine, or three months of slaughter at the hands of an enemy, or three days of plague; and David is to choose. It is striking to find a circumlocution on the lips of the prophet in verse 13 ('the one who sent me'), when the Lord is named in every single other verse of the whole scene (that is, in each of verses 10-12, and again in each of verses 14-19). Gad can hardly bring himself to attribute the dreadful judgment to God.

David is not so coy. He understands that it is God with whom he is dealing. That is both his distress and his relief. In his distress the one thing he knows is that he wishes to be in the hand of God. He understands full well that 'it is a terrible thing to fall into the hands of the living God' (Hebrews 10.31). But he also understands that it is a still more terrible thing not to. He fears the Lord, but trusts him too. He knows the Lord to be both Judge and Saviour and he senses that if in the face of God's wrath, mercy is to be found anywhere, it will be found in God himself.

David opts for three days of plague. He does so not because it is the swiftest punishment of the three and he wishes to get it over with as quickly as possible, but because it is the punishment he is able to attribute most directly to God. He does not want to fall into human hands: for this reason obviously he rejects the option of being at the mercy of some enemy for three months. But somehow even famine offers David a less immediate sense of being in the hand of the Lord. Plague in the Bible is peculiarly God's work, whether (as in Numbers 14.12, 21.6 or Amos 4.10) it afflicts the people of Israel or (as in Exodus 9.14, 11.1 or 1 Samuel 5.6) it afflicts their enemies.

So the Lord sends a pestilence on the people that very morning. There is an echo of the census in verse 15: the dead (70,000) are counted as carefully as the living had been 'from Dan to Beersheba'. But just as the destroying angel stretched out his hand towards Jerusalem, the Lord called a temporary halt to the killing 'at the threshing floor of Araunah the Jebusite'. (Before it became the city of David, Jerusalem was a Jebusite stronghold; see 5.6-10.)

There follows in verse 17 one of the most noble and godly speeches of David's life. When he sees the destroying Angel (there is no attempt to explain what this might mean or even what David was doing at Araunah's threshing floor), David cries out to the Lord. He not only repeats his confession ('I have sinned, I have done wickedly'), he intensifies it by taking full personal responsibility: 'I alone have sinned, I alone have done wickedly', he says. 'These sheep', he continues in an obvious allusion to his own shepherd origins, 'what have they done?'. They are innocent of any wrongdoing, he protests: why should they be punished at all, let alone so severely? (In fact however the whole episode presupposes from verse 1 that God's wrath had justly been kindled against Israel for some undisclosed wrongdoing, well before David had commissioned the census; but David is ignorant of this.) 'Punish me', he concludes, 'me and my house'.

David epitomises the godly ruler here (compare 23.3-4), governing not for himself but for his people and putting their interests before his own.

The king begins the first scene giving instructions to Joab ('Go, count'). He ends the second scene accepting them from Gad ('Go up'). The prophet tells David to erect an altar to the Lord on the threshing-floor of Araunah, and the king does as he is told.

Scene Three (verses 20-25): The Lord answers David's supplication for the land

20 When Araunah looked down, he saw the king and his servants coming towards him; and Araunah went out and prostrated himself before the king with his face to the ground. 21 Araunah said, 'Why has my lord the king come to his servant?' David said, 'To buy the threshing-floor from you in order to build an altar to the Lord, so that the plague may be averted from the people.' 22 Then Araunah said to David, 'Let my lord the king take and offer up what seems good to him; here are the oxen for the burnt-offering, and the threshing-sledges and the yokes of the oxen for the wood. 23 All this, O king, Araunah gives to the king.' And Araunah said to the king, 'May the Lord your God respond favourably to you.'

24 But the king said to Araunah, 'No, but I will buy them from you for a price; I will not offer burnt-offerings to the Lord my God that cost me nothing.' So David bought the threshing-floor and the oxen for fifty shekels of silver. 25 David built there an altar to the Lord, and offered burnt-offerings and offerings of well-being. So the Lord answered his supplication for the land, and the plague was averted from Israel.

Just as Joab dropped out of the narrative at the end of the first scene, having completed the census, so Gad does so at the end of the second, having delivered his instruction to David. The cast of the third scene is David and Araunah.

Seeing the king and his entourage approaching, Araunah comes to meet them and prostrates himself before David apparently unaware of the occasion for the visit. 'Why has my lord the king come to his servant?', he enquires. David's reply shows that he regards as potentially temporary any respite there has been in the destruction. He has come to buy the threshing-floor in order to build an altar to the Lord, in order finally to avert the plague. Araunah, as convention demanded, offers the king not only the threshing-floor as a gift, but the means for a burnt offering: oxen to sacrifice and even the wood to burn them on. 'All this, O king, Araunah gives to the king'. Araunah adds his hope that David's God will respond favourably to him.

But David here resists the tendency of kings to appropriate what does not belong to them. Offered the opportunity to 'take' (verse 22) what seems good to him as kings are wont to do (compare 1 Samuel 8.13-17), David refuses. 'No', he says. 'I will not offer burnt offerings to the Lord my God that cost me nothing'.

David's answer underlines the whole-hearted sincerity of the repentance he expressed in scene two. He is determined that the burnt-offerings offered on the altar he has been commanded to build will be as fully his, and his alone, as the sin of the census had been. A sacrifice which costs the sacrificer nothing is no sacrifice at all. So he buys the threshing-floor from Araunah for fifty shekels of silver. (It is worth noting that according to the Chronicler, this became the site of Solomon's temple; 1 Chronicles 22.1; 2 Chronicles 3.1.)

Sure enough, when the altar is built and the burnt offerings are made with offerings of well-being, the plague is finally averted as the Lord hears David's supplication for the land (a phrase which ties this narrative closely to that in 2 Samuel 21 – see verse 14).

Conclusion

This final episode in the appendix to the narrative proper amounts to a digest of the whole story of David's fall: in his self interest, he brings trouble on others; yet once his conscience is pricked, he is quick to repent; he takes full responsibility for his wrongdoing and sincerely attempts to make amends, demonstrating in the process a genuine concern both for the welfare of his people and for the worship of God. He twice cries out in prayer to the Lord and twice responds obediently to the word of the Lord; and in the process he expresses to God's prophet his desire to fall into the hand of the Lord.

As such this final episode completes the 'narrative arc' of the appendix itself. The chiasmus of 2 Samuel 21-24 presents its own portrait of David, as the reader moves from story to list to poem, to poem to list to story. It has been suggested that if there is a slightly fragmentary feel to this sequence of material, it perhaps symbolises the fragmentation of David's family and kingdom, and perhaps of his own sense of self, in 2 Samuel 9 to 20. Certainly the appendix, like the

Succession Narrative, subverts the image of an all-conquering David presented in 2 Samuel 5-10. In 2 Samuel 21 the story of David's acquiescence in the deaths of seven members of Saul's household is disturbing. The lists of David's mighty men subtly emphasise his own declining powers and the dark forces of violence in the story of his fall. The poems serve to stress the gap which developed between the man David was called to be and the man he ultimately became. Yet this last narrative, without at all glossing over his weaknesses and folly, shows that for all this, the one thing that did not fragment was his sense of himself in relation to God and his awareness of himself as a sinner.

ACT FOUR

The Rule of David Ended

1 Kings 1.1–2.11

Chapter Twenty-Three
1 Kings 1.1–53

David and Adonijah

Introduction

The first chapter and a half of the book of 1 Kings complete the story of David's life. They resume the narrative of 2 Samuel 8-20 in the same literary style, but after an indeterminate interval. One of the features of this is the way that the Lord is once more at work 'behind the scenes': there is no more direct intervention of the kind which characterises the narrative portions of the 'appendix' in Act Three. As the story of David moves towards its conclusion, there is no doubt that God is working out his good will and purpose for his people; yet the Lord, though often spoken of, no longer speaks or acts directly.

It is clear from the opening words that the final act in the drama is underway. David is old and advanced in years and has become bed-ridden. He is king in name only, too weak even to sit on his own throne. The crucial question is who will sit on his throne after him (see verses 13, 17, 20, 24, 27, 30, 35, 46, 47 and 48). This is an open question both in the sense that it is asked openly and in the sense that the answer is not clear.

This lengthy episode is made up of seven scenes, revolving around a protracted central scene in which alone David speaks and acts. In the three scenes either side of that one, David is either entirely absent or (in the case of the first one) entirely passive. The initial scene introduces David in his dotage; the second introduces Adonijah and his rebellion; the third re-introduces Bathsheba and Nathan (both of whom have been surprisingly absent from the story since the end of 2 Samuel 12). After David acts in scene four to confirm Solomon as his successor, the final three short scenes relate first how Solomon is anointed as king, then how Adonijah and his circle heard this news and reacted to it, and finally how Solomon then dealt with Adonijah.

By the end of the episode, Solomon's position is secure and David can 'go the way of all the earth'.

Scene One (verses 1-4): David and Abishag

> *King David was old and advanced in years; and although*
> *they covered him with clothes, he could not get warm. 2*
> *So his servants said to him, 'Let a young virgin be sought*
> *for my lord the king, and let her wait on the king, and be*
> *his attendant; let her lie in your bosom, so that my lord the*
> *king may be warm.' 3 So they searched for a beautiful girl*
> *throughout all the territory of Israel, and found Abishag the*
> *Shunammite, and brought her to the king. 4 The girl was*
> *very beautiful. She became the king's attendant and served*
> *him, but the king did not know her sexually.*

David is not just 'old and advanced in years'. He is confined to bed.
Moreover, his circulation has ceased to function properly and he can't
get warm. His servants have tried heaping up layers of bedclothes, but
to no avail. So they attempt an alternative strategy: they procure a young
woman to act as a human 'hot-water bottle' for the king: she can lie in
his bosom and keep him warm. But they don't just seize the nearest,
most readily available woman. They search for a national beauty and
eventually bring to the king the most lovely young virgin in all the
territory of Israel: Abishag the Shunammite. She was, it is emphasised,
exceptionally beautiful and she became the king's attendant. But, the
scene concludes, 'the king did not know her sexually'.

The last clause is shocking. Christian readers often take it to be a
good thing that David did not sleep with this maidservant, since she
was not his wife. How inappropriate it would have been for him to
form a sexual relationship with someone who was only enlisted to
keep him warm and who was generations younger than himself.

But that is not the perspective of the narrator. There is an inescapable
sexual undertone to these opening verses which makes the last clause
startling. The king is in bed with the most beautiful young virgin in
all Israel. But the man who was once so inflamed with lust by the
sight of a beautiful woman bathing that he could not restrain himself
from adultery now cannot know her sexually. The king is impotent,
and his sexual impotence is the most dramatic possible symbol of the
political impotence on which this whole episode turns. The girl's name
(Abishag) means 'My father strays'. The irony is that though David
does not stray sexually, politically he has lost his way.

The sexual undertone is confirmed by the sequel. In the following chapter, after David has died, Adonijah requests Solomon (via
Bathsheba) that he be given Abishag as a wife. Bathsheba apparently

sees nothing sinister in the request, but Solomon is clear (verse 22) that it is tantamount to a request for the kingdom. Just as David inherited Saul's wives (12.8) and Ishbaal took such exception at the thought that Abner was sleeping with one of Saul's concubines (3.7), and just as Ahithophel advised Absalom to sleep with David's concubines (16.21), so the destiny of David's bedmate becomes a crucial political symbol. Adonijah's request is met by Solomon with a severe response: he orders him killed (2 Kings 2.25) by Benaiah son of Jehoiada.

The rest of 2 Kings 2 records the assassinations of Joab and Shimei by Benaiah. When it then concludes, 'So the kingdom was established in the hand of Solomon', the reader supposes that Abishag was established in his hands too.

Scene Two (verses 5 -10): Adonijah exalts himself as king

5 Now Adonijah son of Haggith exalted himself, saying, 'I will be king'; he prepared for himself chariots and horsemen, and fifty men to run before him. 6 His father had never at any time displeased him by asking, 'Why have you done that?' He was also a very handsome man, and he was born next after Absalom. 7 He conferred with Joab son of Zeruiah and with the priest Abiathar, and they supported Adonijah. 8 But the priest Zadok, and Benaiah son of Jehoiada, and the prophet Nathan, and Shimei, and Rei, and David's own warriors did not side with Adonijah.

9 Adonijah sacrificed sheep, oxen, and fatted cattle by the stone Zoheleth, which is beside En-rogel, and he invited all his brothers, the king's sons, and all the royal officials of Judah, 10 but he did not invite the prophet Nathan or Benaiah or the warriors or his brother Solomon.

David's political impotence has created a vacuum at the centre of government. Who is to rule in his stead? One of his sons, surely? This has been the assumption ever since Nathan had uttered his great oracle in 2 Samuel 12. But which one? Amnon the first-born is dead, as is Absalom. Of Chileab, the second-born son of 3.3, nothing has ever been heard. In all likelihood he is dead too.

Adonijah (whose name is propitious: it means 'Yhwh is the Lord') is David's fourth son (see 3.4), born to his father in Hebron, the son of David's fourth wife Haggith. Like his father (see 1 Samuel 16.12) and his brother Absalom (2 Samuel 14.25), Adonijah is a handsome man. Like Amnon (13.21) and Absalom (13.39), Adonijah has never been disciplined by his father, only indulged. David's parenting skills, even in his younger and more energetic years, left something to be desired. So like Absalom before him (15.1), Adonijah secures chariots and men to run ahead of him, and sets out his stall to be king. He confers with some of David's most longstanding officials, one from the army (Joab) and one from the priesthood (Abiathar), and gains their support. Presumably they can see that David's reign has run its course and are anxious to avoid any destabilising period of uncertainty in the kingdom. Verse 8 may hint at the fact that Adonijah's pretensions became a matter of open knowledge: it does not say that he did not confer with Zadok, Benaiah, Nathan and the rest (including David's warriors), but that they did not side with him.

Then, adhering to his brother Absalom's template for rebellion against their father David, Adonijah arranges a sacrifice at En-rogel (just a mile or two from Jerusalem) to which he invites a crowd of officials – specifically those from Judah. The only surprise is that the feast is not held in Hebron (see 15.7). He did not however invite the officials who had not sided with him. And although verse 9 states that he invited 'all his brothers, the king's sons', verse 10 clarifies that this means all except Solomon. Presumably David's preference for Solomon was likewise a matter of public knowledge.

Scene Three (verses 11-14): Nathan conspires with Bathsheba

> *11 Then Nathan said to Bathsheba, Solomon's mother, 'Have you not heard that Adonijah son of Haggith has become king and our lord David does not know it? 12 Now therefore come, let me give you advice, so that you may save your own life and the life of your son Solomon. 13 Go in at once to King David, and say to him, "Did you not, my lord the king, swear to your servant, saying: Your son Solomon shall succeed me as king, and he shall sit on my throne? Why then is Adonijah king?" 14 Then while you are still there speaking with the king, I will come in after you and confirm your words.'*

Nathan, Bathsheba and Solomon form an axis of power in this episode. All three feature in the narrative for the first time in this episode since the announcement of Solomon's birth in 12.24-25.

It is Nathan who takes the initiative in response to Adonijah's move. He seeks out Bathsheba to inform her that 'Adonijah son of Haggith has become king'. When he adds 'and our lord David does not know', David's political and his sexual impotence are again linked: just as he did not 'know' Abishag, so he does not know about Adonijah. Nathan (realising that Bathsheba's life is at risk together with Solomon's) urges her to act at once. He directs her to speak to David and tells her what to say. She is to challenge the king with a double question: 'Did you not swear to me that Solomon would be your successor? Why then is Adonijah king?'.

If David had indeed made such a commitment to Bathsheba, the narrative does not record it. The narrative gives the impression that Solomon is the Lord's favoured candidate to succeed David – but 2 Samuel 7 and 2 Samuel 12 contain no promise by David to Bathsheba to that effect. It is quite possible of course that the narrative assumes the promise was given at some point in the intervening years when Solomon was growing up, and the fact that Solomon is singled out by Adonijah as a rival may suggest that this promise had indeed been made. But it is also possible that Nathan's instruction to Bathsheba is a ploy intended to trick a confused and bewildered king David. There is certainly an element of ploy in verse 14, when Nathan tells Bathsheba that he will time his own entry into David's presence to coincide with her words so that he is able to confirm them. Nathan is at the least astute enough to combat the intrigue of Adonijah with intrigue of his own.

Scene Four (verses 15 -37): David is roused to action

15 So Bathsheba went to the king in his room. The king was very old; Abishag the Shunammite was attending the king. 16 Bathsheba bowed and did obeisance to the king, and the king said, 'What do you wish?' 17 She said to him, 'My lord, you swore to your servant by the Lord your God, saying: Your son Solomon shall succeed me as king, and he shall sit on my throne. 18 But now suddenly Adonijah has become king, though you, my lord the king, do not know it. 19 He has sacrificed oxen, fatted cattle, and sheep in abundance, and has invited all the children of the king, the priest Abiathar, and Joab the commander of the army; but your servant Solomon he has not invited. 20 But you, my lord the king – the eyes of all Israel are on you to tell them who shall sit on the throne of my lord the king after him. 21 Otherwise it will come to pass, when my lord the king sleeps with his ancestors, that my son Solomon and I will be counted offenders.'

22 While she was still speaking with the king, the prophet Nathan came in. 23 The king was told, 'Here is the prophet Nathan.' When he came in before the king, he did obeisance to the king, with his face to the ground. 24 Nathan said, 'My lord the king, have you said, "Adonijah shall succeed me as king, and he shall sit on my throne"? 25 For today he has gone down and has sacrificed oxen, fatted cattle, and sheep in abundance, and has invited all the king's children, Joab the commander of the army, and the priest Abiathar, who are now eating and drinking before him, and saying, "Long live King Adonijah!" 26 But he did not invite me, your servant, and the priest Zadok, and Benaiah son of Jehoiada, and your servant Solomon. 27 Has this thing been brought about by my lord the king and you have not let your servants know who should sit on the throne of my lord the king after him?'

28 King David answered, 'Summon Bathsheba to me.' So she came into the king's presence, and stood before the king. 29 The king swore, saying, 'As the Lord lives, who has saved my life from every adversity, 30 as I swore to you by the Lord, the God of Israel, "Your son Solomon shall succeed me as king, and he shall sit on my throne in my place", so will I do this day.' 31 Then Bathsheba bowed with her face to the ground, and did obeisance to the king, and said, 'May my lord King David live for ever!'

32 King David said, 'Summon to me the priest Zadok, the prophet Nathan, and Benaiah son of Jehoiada.' When they came before the king, 33 the king said to them, 'Take with you the servants of your lord, and have my son Solomon ride on my own mule, and bring him down to Gihon. 34 There let the priest Zadok and the prophet Nathan anoint him king over Israel; then blow the trumpet, and say, "Long live King Solomon!" 35 You shall go up following him. Let him enter and sit on my throne; he shall be king in my place; for I have appointed him to be ruler over Israel and over Judah.' 36 Benaiah son of Jehoiada answered the king, 'Amen! May the

> *Lord, the God of my lord the king, so ordain. 37 As the Lord has been with my lord the king, so may he be with Solomon, and make his throne greater than the throne of my lord King David.'*

The opening lines of this central fourth scene link to the first: Bathsheba visits the king not in the throne room of the palace, but in his bedroom. The reader is reminded that he is very old; and that the young Abishag is attending to him. His impotence is underlined by the arrival of the woman who once so inflamed him.

This drawn out middle scene is neatly structured: two speeches are made to king David to rouse him from his lethargy, the first by Bathsheba and the second by Nathan; then two speeches are made by king David, duly roused, the first to Bathsheba and the second to Nathan (and colleagues).

Bathsheba carefully observes the proper formalities and does obeisance to the king. He asks her what she wants. In Hebrew his question is just two syllables ('What you?') – as if he is too weak to muster a fuller greeting. Bathsheba replies by improvising forthrightly on Nathan's advice. Where he had advised her to pose two questions ('Did you not swear? Why then?', verse 13), Bathsheba makes two direct assertions ('You swore! But now suddenly!' verses 17-18). She is as galvanised in David's old age as Abigail had been in his youth (compare 1 Samuel 25). She emphasises David's ignorance, and the fact that all Israel waits to see what he will do. She pours out a full report of what Adonijah has done and whose support he has secured, stressing Solomon's exclusion from the sacrifice-feast he has arranged and the threat this poses to her life and that of her son, when David sleeps with his ancestors. Hers is a long speech, occupying verses 17 to 21.

Before David can make any response, Nathan arrives. As planned, he makes his entrance just as Bathsheba finishes speaking. He too observes the formalities and does obeisance to the king, before launching on a lengthy speech of his own (verses 24-27). He covers much the same ground as Bathsheba had done (confirming her words, as he had said he would), though he begins more deferentially with a question. At points his speech mirrors Bathsheba's word for word (reflecting the collusion there has been between them): Adonijah 'has sacrificed oxen, fatted cattle and sheep in abundance and has invited all the children of the king' (verses 19, 25). But there are subtle differences too: Bathsheba stresses Solomon's exclusion from the feast (verse 19); Nathan stresses his own and that of Zadok and Benaiah. Nathan adds a little flourish to the bare facts supplied by Bathsheba, warning David that Joab and Abiathar are right now 'eating and drinking before him and saying, 'Long live King Adonijah'. It is a detail calculated to fire David's indignation. And where Bathsheba states clearly that David is ignorant of Adonijah's plot (as Nathan had informed her in verse 11), the prophet himself (ending, as he had begun, with a question) feigns uncertainty about this, asking if it is possible that Adonijah is acting with David's full support and that David has failed to tell his servants?

The two speeches together are enough to rouse king David. His languor gives way to new energy and for the penultimate time in his life he exercises leadership.

It transpires that Bathsheba has left the room during Nathan's speech and has now to be summoned. (This is typical of Hebrew dialogue, which doesn't often permit three-sided conversation. Nathan likewise has to be summoned again in verse 32.) When Bathsheba returns, David swears at once by the Lord 'who has saved my life from every adversity' (he had used almost exactly this same expression in 4.9; compare also 1 Sam 26.24), promising that 'this day' he will implement his promise that Solomon would succeed him as king. In other words, he goes beyond anything imagined by Nathan (in verse 13) or demanded by Bathsheba (in verse 17) by elevating Solomon to his throne *in his own place* (verse 30, that is during his own lifetime).

David then summons the three officials snubbed by Adonijah: Zadok the priest, Nathan the prophet and Benaiah, son of Jehoiada. His second speech is longer and more detailed than the first as if his sap is still rising. Where he had simply told Bathsheba that Solomon would be made king, here he tells his officials how that is to happen. They are to take Solomon, mounted on the king's own mule, to Gihon, where priest and prophet are to anoint him. (It is not clear why this site should be chosen for the ceremony; Gihon has played no part in the narrative before this.) They are to blow the trumpet and announce, 'Long live king Solomon!'. They are then to process back up into the city, into the palace, where Solomon is to take his place on David's throne, as 'ruler over Israel and ruler over Judah'. (The last clause tacitly acknowledges the danger that the kingdom might at any point descend into civil war, as indeed it did after Solomon's death.)

It is left to Benaiah son of Jehoiada to acclaim David's instructions. He cries aloud a triple prayer: 'May the Lord so ordain [what David has proposed]. May the Lord be with Solomon as he has been with David; and may Solomon's throne be even greater than David's'.

Scene Five (verses 38-40): Solomon is anointed as king

*38 So the priest Zadok, the prophet Nathan, and Benaiah
son of Jehoiada, and the Cherethites and the Pelethites, went
down and had Solomon ride on King David's mule, and led
him to Gihon. 39 There the priest Zadok took the horn of
oil from the tent and anointed Solomon. Then they blew the
trumpet, and all the people said, 'Long live King Solomon!'
40 And all the people went up following him, playing on
pipes and rejoicing with great joy, so that the earth quaked
at their noise.*

At once the three officials (priest, prophet and, inevitably where
David is concerned, soldier) lead Solomon, mounted on the king's own
mule, to Gihon – with the Cherethites and the Pelethites providing
an escort just in case (see 8.18). At Gihon Solomon is anointed king.
The anointing is apparently undertaken by Zadok alone (rather than by
Zadok and Nathan as David had instructed), using oil 'from the tent'
(presumably the sacred tent referred to in 6.17, 7.2). There is a double
departure from precedent here. For one thing this is the first time a
king of Israel has been anointed by a priest. Saul and David had been
anointed by the prophet Samuel (see 1 Samuel 10.1, 16. 13). Saul and
David had secondly been anointed in pledge of a future kingship. There
was a delay in both cases between the anointing and the 'coronation'.
Solomon is made king by his anointing.

Sure enough the trumpet is blown and all the people acclaimed
Solomon as king. There had presumably been some recruitment of the
crowd who celebrated so robustly as the new king returned to the city
that 'the earth quaked at their noise'.

**Scene Six (verses 41-49): Adonijah and his guests hear that Solomon
is king**

*41 Adonijah and all the guests who were with him heard it
as they finished feasting. When Joab heard the sound of the
trumpet, he said, 'Why is the city in an uproar?' 42 While
he was still speaking, Jonathan son of the priest Abiathar
arrived. Adonijah said, 'Come in, for you are a worthy man
and surely you bring good news.' 43 Jonathan answered
Adonijah, 'No, for our lord King David has made Solomon
king; 44 the king has sent with him the priest Zadok, the*

prophet Nathan, and Benaiah son of Jehoiada, and the
Cherethites and the Pelethites; and they had him ride on
the king's mule; 45 the priest Zadok and the prophet Nathan
have anointed him king at Gihon; and they have gone up
from there rejoicing, so that the city is in an uproar. This is
the noise that you heard. 46 Solomon now sits on the royal
throne. 47 Moreover, the king's servants came to congratulate
our lord King David, saying, "May God make the name
of Solomon more famous than yours, and make his throne
greater than your throne." The king bowed in worship on the
bed 48 and went on to pray thus, "Blessed be the Lord, the
God of Israel, who today has granted one of my offspring to
sit on my throne and permitted me to witness it." '

49 Then all the guests of Adonijah got up trembling and went
their own ways.

The noise was so great that Adonijah and his guests heard it while
they were still feasting. But the military man, Joab, had ears only for
the trumpet. He himself had given the signal sufficiently often to know
that the sound meant the city was for some reason in uproar (see 2.28,
18.16, 20.22).

While he was still speaking (compare verse 22; there is a frenetic
feel to the action right through this episode) a messenger arrived. It
was Jonathan, son of Abiathar – the priest who had defected with
Adonijah. He had been a courier of political secrets for years and
had previously been among David's most loyal followers (see 15.36,
17.17-21). Adonijah makes the same mistake as David himself had
made following the battle in which Absalom was killed: he assumes
that a good and loyal messenger is surely bringing good and propitious
tidings (see 18.27).

Jonathan contradicts his new master; he has not come with good
tidings at all. On the contrary. He pours out a summary of all that
has happened, accurately reporting David's intentions. He tells how
Solomon has been taken on the king's mule, with the support of Zadok,
Nathan and Benaiah (with the Cherethites and the Pelethites) to Gihon
where he has been anointed as king. Barely pausing to draw breath,
Jonathan continues: the city is now in uproar because Solomon has
returned there with rejoicing and now sits on David's throne.

Jonathan's speech might easily have ended there. But his torrent
of news goes on. Jonathan is not only privy to Benaiah's prayer that
Solomon's throne might be still greater than David's – he is also able

to report what had not previously found its way into the narrative: that David had himself prayed in thanksgiving that he had lived to see one of his sons (not Adonijah) sit upon his throne.

Adonijah's guests don't even wait for his reaction. They know a fait accompli when they see one. They get up trembling and flee in their separate ways.

Scene Seven (verses 50-53): Solomon sends Adonijah home

50 Adonijah, fearing Solomon, got up and went to grasp the horns of the altar. 51 Solomon was informed, 'Adonijah is afraid of King Solomon; see, he has laid hold of the horns of the altar, saying, "Let King Solomon swear to me first that he will not kill his servant with the sword." ' 52 So Solomon responded, 'If he proves to be a worthy man, not one of his hairs shall fall to the ground; but if wickedness is found in him, he shall die.' 53 Then King Solomon sent to have him brought down from the altar. He came to do obeisance to King Solomon; and Solomon said to him, 'Go home.'

Adonijah also knows that the game is up. Afraid for his life, he goes at once 'to grasp the horns of the altar'. Later in Israel's history a fugitive would obviously have taken refuge in the temple. At this point it is not clear which altar is meant.

The tactic is at least temporarily effective. The news is conveyed to Solomon that his brother has sought sanctuary at a sacred place and is refusing to leave without an assurance that Solomon will not put him to death by the sword. It speaks volumes for the efficacy of his anointing that it is Solomon who now acts as king and not David. There is no hint that Adonijah was afraid of reprisals from his father.

The new king's response is carefully guarded. It is merciful but not naïve. These are the first words spoken by Solomon in the narrative and they bear the marks of the wisdom for which he would become renowned: 'If he proves to be a worthy man', he says, 'he'll not come to any harm. But at the first sign of any further wickedness, he will die'.

Adonijah is then brought before the new king. He becomes the first person recorded as doing obeisance before him. Afterwards he is dismissed with contempt. Solomon sends him home.

Conclusion

This episode is as full of scheming and plotting as any in the
narrative. Adonijah has an agenda and all that the reader has learned
about Joab would suggest that the rebel's chief supporter has one of
his own. Nathan certainly has an agenda, which he perhaps shares with
Bathsheba and Solomon; and king David also has one, at least in the
central scene.

Yet in and through these various competing purposes, it is clear
that the good purpose of God is fulfilled. Not all the characters in this
episode show any awareness of the fact. Bathsheba does, though verse
17 gives the impression that she is seeking to align God's purpose with
her own, rather than vice versa. But other characters are apparently
seeking in all sincerity to align their own purpose with God's. Among
them are, particularly, Benaiah son of Jehoiada (in verses 36-37), and
of course David himself (in verses 29-30, and if Jonathan's words can
be taken as a reliable quotation, in verse 48).

This is often as much as a faithful believer can do: in the midst of
competing human schemes, to endeavour to align one's own will and
purpose with that of the Lord God in trust that hidden and indirect as it
might be, the Lord's good will and purpose is indeed being fulfilled.

Chapter Twenty-Four
1 Kings 2.1–11

The Death of David

Introduction

One of the remarkable and moving legacies of the terrorist atrocity of '9/11' is the record of 'last words' spoken by those who knew they were about to die. Message after message left on voice-mail and answer machines was full of love. Mostly calmly and with great dignity, sometimes using a borrowed cell phone, the victims (particularly those on Flight 93 which ultimately crashed in a field in Pennsylvania) chose in their final minutes to call someone dear to them and simply say, 'I love you'.

If 23.1-7 constitutes 'David's Last Words' in some formal, official sense, this final episode in his life presents a more private, intimate version. This final episode in David's life consists of a single scene, followed by a brief epilogue. In the main scene, where the dying king addresses his favourite son, the reader instinctively looks for an expression of love and tenderness. It is easily overlooked in the midst of so much less inspiring material – but it is there.

David's exhortation to Solomon falls into two parts. These reflect the two sides of his character which have been evident and in tension since his youth: his deep devotion to the Lord his God and his preoccupation with his own reputation; his sincere efforts to walk in God's ways and his inclination to violence. His exhortation to his son thus begins positively as a summons to 'be strong and courageous' and to 'keep the charge of the Lord your God'. But from verse 5 it degenerates into a appeal to avenge David for the wrongs he has endured. Yet the passage is gloriously relieved by David's recollection of Barzillai, to whom Solomon is to show *hesed:* covenant loyalty and steadfast love.

Scene One (verses 1-9): David exhorts Solomon

When David's time to die drew near, he charged his son Solomon, saying: 2 'I am about to go the way of all the earth.

*Be strong, be courageous, 3 and keep the charge of the Lord
your God, walking in his ways and keeping his statutes, his
commandments, his ordinances, and his testimonies, as it is
written in the law of Moses, so that you may prosper in all
that you do and wherever you turn. 4 Then the Lord will
establish his word that he spoke concerning me: "If your
heirs take heed to their way, to walk before me in faithfulness
with all their heart and with all their soul, there shall not fail
you a successor on the throne of Israel."*

*5 'Moreover, you know also what Joab son of Zeruiah did
to me, how he dealt with the two commanders of the armies
of Israel, Abner son of Ner, and Amasa son of Jether, whom
he murdered, retaliating in time of peace for blood that
had been shed in war, and putting the blood of war on the
belt around his waist, and on the sandals on his feet. 6 Act
therefore according to your wisdom, but do not let his grey
head go down to Sheol in peace. 7 Deal loyally, however,
with the sons of Barzillai the Gileadite, and let them be
among those who eat at your table; for with such loyalty
they met me when I fled from your brother Absalom. 8 There
is also with you Shimei son of Gera, the Benjaminite from
Bahurim, who cursed me with a terrible curse on the day
when I went to Mahanaim; but when he came down to meet
me at the Jordan, I swore to him by the Lord, "I will not put
you to death with the sword." 9 Therefore do not hold him
guiltless, for you are a wise man; you will know what you
ought to do to him, and you must bring his grey head down
with blood to Sheol.'*

Sensing that his death is imminent, David calls for Solomon. First
he charges the new king to remain faithful to 'the Lord your God'.

The vocabulary of the charge in verses 2 to 4 is distinctive. It is often
called 'Deuteronomic': that is to say, like many other passages in 1 and
2 Kings, it reflects the theological interests of the book of Deuteronomy.
These verses are full of key phrases from that book: thus for example,
'keep the charge of the Lord your God' reflects Deuteronomy 11.1;
'walking in his ways' recalls Deuteronomy 8.6, 11.22, 19.9 etc; 'all
their heart and with all their soul' echoes Deuteronomy 4.29, 6.5,
10.12 etc; and lists of such words as 'his statutes, his commandments,
his ordinances, and his testimonies' occur frequently. In fact verses
2-3 as a whole are reminiscent of the Lord's words to Joshua after the

death of Moses. In Joshua 1.1-9 (the passage which comes directly after the end of the book of Deuteronomy), at a crucial moment of transition, Joshua is summoned to 'be strong and courageous' and is assured that if he only keeps the law of Moses, he will prosper. At this equally crucial moment of transition, Solomon is summoned to be Joshua to David's Moses.

In this 'Deuteronomic' context the absence from the exhortation of any reference by David to love is all the more surprising, since the word features strongly in Deuteronomy. In particular, the phrase 'all [your] heart and all [your] soul' (verse 4) is famously linked to the summons to love God in Deuteronomy 6.5.

It is then specifically the law of Moses as set out in the Book of Deuteronomy that David urges Solomon to keep and like later kings of Israel it is in terms of his faithfulness to this inheritance that he is to be judged. If Solomon keeps this law, then, says David, the Lord will establish his promise. The form of the promise quoted by David in verse 4 is subtly different from the form in which it first comes in 2 Samuel 7: there is somewhat more emphasis now on the need for obedience on the part of David's heirs if the promise is to be fulfilled, and somewhat less emphasis on the sheer unmerited favour of God – and crucially on the eternal assurance of his steadfast love (7.15). Mindful perhaps of his own disobedience to the Lord's ways since he received that promise, David has apparently lost sight of its basis in grace.

In verses 5 to 9 David turns from looking ahead into Solomon's reign, to looking back over his own. Most of the material in the five remaining verses of David's speech is ugly. It makes a grim end to his life story. There are scores to settle in relation to Joab (verses 5 and 6) and Shimei (verses 8 and 9). But sandwiched in between these two exhortations to vengeance, the middle verse (verse 7) shines like a bright light in the darkness: Solomon is urged to show *hesed* (loyalty, or steadfast love) to old Barzillai. It is worth noting that all three men were intimately involved in their different ways in the events surrounding Absalom's rebellion (that is, 2 Samuel 15-19).

The sections which refer to Joab and Shimei are full of parallels: in both cases Solomon is urged by his father to act wisely or in accordance with his wisdom; both refer to blood, to the grey head of the enemy in question and to Sheol. David's recall of the detail of how each of the two men wronged him is astonishing in one who early in the previous episode was so frail he could not even get warm.

First, in verses 5 and 6, David urges Solomon to have Joab executed. Ostensibly this act will avenge what Joab did by murdering both Abner and Amasa 'at a time of peace' for what they had done in a time of war. The narrative bears out David's memory: in 2 Samuel 3 one of the striking features of the story is the three-fold repetition in verses 21, 22 and 23 that David had dismissed Abner in peace; similarly, in 20.9, Joab had approached Amasa with a traditional greeting of peace ('Is it well – shalom – with you, my brother?'). That murder was effected with a subterfuge involving the belt around Joab's waist to which David specifically refers. But David has other motives for wishing Joab dead. Quite apart from the fact that Joab knew what might be regarded as David's worst secret, having received the letter instructing him to kill Uriah, there is the matter of Joab's support for Adonijah (1 Kings 1.7).

Then, in verses 8 and 9, David urges Solomon to have Shimei executed also. The terrible curse Shimei uttered against David evidently still rankles. Ironically, the king is about to furnish evidence that there was at least a grain of truth in Shimei's words: he called David a 'murderer', a 'scoundrel' and 'a man of blood'. There is something especially scurrilous about this final instruction, as it involves David in a feeble attempt to escape the obligations of his promise (which he now recalls and which is recorded in 19.23) not to kill Shimei. 'I swore to him by the Lord, "I will not put you to death by the sword". But that doesn't mean you can't do it'.

The sequel is swift and dreadful. In the remainder of 1 Kings 2, the deaths of Joab (verses 28-35) and Shimei (verses 36-46) are related. Both are killed by Benaiah son of Jehoiada on Solomon's orders.

Yet in between, David remembers a loose end of an altogether happier kind. He recalls the kindness he had received from Barzillai the Gileadite when he was fleeing from Absalom (in 17.27-29) and how he had later promised to provide for Barzillai's son Chimham (19.31-40). This oath is one David intends to keep even beyond his own lifetime. So he urges Solomon to show covenant loyalty and steadfast love to the sons of Barzillai. The plural 'sons' may even represent a widening of generosity.

Scene Two (verses 10-11): An Epilogue

10 Then David slept with his ancestors, and was buried in the city of David. 11 The time that David reigned over Israel was forty years; he reigned for seven years in Hebron, and thirty-three years in Jerusalem

Verse 10 notes David's death and burial; verse 11 records the length of his reign. Verse 11 thus corresponds to the similar summary which is to be found at 5.4-5. Its placement there marks not only the start of his reign (this is, in the history of Israel's kings the conventional place for such details), but also the end of the story of David's rise. Here the recurrence marks the end of the story of his fall.

Similar notices occur frequently in 1 and 2 Kings. Mostly they occur at the beginning of a king's reign (though for example in Jeroboam's case, it comes at the end: 1 Kings 14.20). It speaks volumes for the peerless status accorded to David among the kings of Israel that he alone is furnished with two such notices.

Concluding Reflections

How a person responds in the face of accusation is a matter of real spiritual significance. Most of us, charged with wrongdoing, find an urgent defensiveness surging up inside. We tend to justify ourselves. Even when it is impossible for us to protest innocence, we want to offer excuses or plead mitigating circumstances. David models another way: he repents. The argument of this book is that in the years after he has become king this capacity for repentance is as much what it means for him to be 'a man after God's own heart' (1 Samuel 13.14; Acts of the Apostles 13.22) as was his capacity for restraint in the years beforehand.

Our 'never apologise, never explain' culture does not find it easy to understand contrition or to value it. It is especially rare to hear a politician repent. Guarded expressions of regret, carefully worded to avoid any admission of actual fault, are much more common among community leaders even in the church. In this context, the story of David's fall confronts us powerfully with the Word of the Lord.

It is able to do so, because its depiction of its 'hero' is so counter-cultural. In the church as well as in wider society, leaders are required to be above reproach: but this narrative makes no effort to hide David's shortcomings. Again, as much in the church as in the wider world, leaders are seldom open to effective challenge: but this narrative depicts David as responsive to criticism. Thirdly, in an increasingly litigatious society in which legal advisors counsel against anything that may be taken as an acceptance of liability, leaders are inhibited about acknowledging culpability: but this narrative depicts David as simply contrite.

1. David is flawed

In fact all the major characters of the Bible (apart from Jesus) are flawed. It is one of the features of Scripture that it presents faith heroes in all their weakness and vulnerability, 'warts and all': from Abraham's misguided attempt to pass off his wife as his sister to Moses' lethal fury, from Peter's impetuousness and fickleness to Paul's impatience with others, from Sarah's mirth at God's promise to Rachel's theft of her father's goods – all are flawed.

The flawed nature of all God's servants, as they are portrayed in the Bible, is part of its message of grace. It is ordinary, earth-bound sinners that God chooses and uses. This is partly what encourages us to see that we may have a part to play in the same story of God's salvation. It also encourages us to hope that ultimately the salvation of God depends not on human merit or achievement, but on the work of God himself – such that no amount of human sinfulness can prevent the coming of God's kingdom.

But for all this, it is remarkable just how freely the biblical text depicts the flaws of David in particular. In Act One, when his power is at its height, he is ruthless in his oppression of those he has conquered in battle; in Act Four, when his power is all but gone, he is petty and mean-spirited in his pursuit of those who have wronged him. In between, in Acts Two and Three, it is a major task to list his misdemeanours. So unfavourable is the light in which it casts him that it must have been sorely tempting for an editor somewhere along the line to erase from the record the story of David's adultery and his subsequent murder of Uriah (as indeed it appears that the compiler of 1 and 2 Chronicles has done). There is a lingering sense both within this part of the biblical text and beyond it that David has just too much blood on his hands.

2. David is confronted

The ministry of the prophet in Israel truly came into its own in relation to the king. True, there were prophets in the period before Israel became a monarchy. It was in the wilderness (Numbers 11.29) that Moses expressed the desire that all God's people might be prophets. But the great named prophets of Scripture (from Samuel to Zechariah) all exercised their office in relation to a king. This is the case both in regard to the prophets whose stories are found in the narrative books of the Bible (notably Elijah and Elisha), and in regard to those whose oracles are recorded elsewhere (such as Isaiah, Jeremiah, and Amos). Prophecy in Scripture is above all the way that God speaks his word to the powerful. It is because they are called to confront kings that prophets in the Bible live so dangerously and are so often killed 'in Jerusalem' (the king's city) up to the time of John the Baptist and arguably Jesus of Nazareth too.

In the story of David's rise, prophecy is essentially spoken by Samuel and addressed to Saul. In fact Saul's role as king is so defined by Samuel's role as prophet that when his final crisis approached, he actually went in search of a word from the dead prophet. He would be more of a king addressed by a dead Samuel than not addressed by a prophet at all. Named prophets (Nathan and Gad) thus address setpiece speeches more fully to David in the second half of his lifestory than in the first, precisely because he is by then the king.

A crucial test of a monarch in Scripture is his capacity to respond to the Word of the Lord as spoken by the prophet. The good king in the Bible is open to challenge; the wicked king is not. The prophet is the conscience of the king and the crucial question is how the king will respond to prophetic rebuke. Saul failed this test. When he was challenged by Samuel (in 1 Samuel 13 and 15), his response is precisely the one which comes most naturally to us all: he prevaricates and equivocates and justifies himself.

It is against this background that the significance of David's response to both Nathan and Gad becomes clear. He is open to challenge. When Nathan tells him a parable to hold up a mirror in which David might behold his wrongdoing, he says simply, 'I have sinned against the Lord' (12.13). There is no bluster, no rage, no evasion of responsibility. In 2 Samuel 24, although the double repetition of those same words in verses 10 and 17 comes each time before the king hears the Word of the Lord as spoken by Gad, David's obedience to the prophetic word on both occasions underlines the point: powerful people need prophets around them. Wise leaders will seek out the prophetic voice and will endeavour to be open to prophetic rebuke.

Further to his credit, it may indicate a degree of success on David's part in the integration of his private and public roles, that he responds in the same way in these two very different circumstances. In the first case, while David's sin was emphatically not just a matter of private morality (his use of royal power to assassinate his rival was an abuse of his office), it did involve what in modern times tends to be regarded as the archetypal politician's 'indiscretion': an affair. In the second case, David's sin (whatever its precise nature) was evidently more political.

3. David is contrite

Alongside these two setpiece stories in which David is confronted by Nathan and Gad and proves responsive to a prophetic Word of the Lord, there is a third incident in the narrative which illustrates his capacity for contrition. If those two well-known episodes are essential to the portrait of David which emerges in the story of his fall, the less celebrated account of Shimei's cursing is not to be overlooked.

In 2 Samuel 16, David is vulnerable. Absalom has claimed the kingdom and taken possession of Jerusalem, 'the city of David'. David has been forced to flee and is heading for the relative sanctuary of the lands beyond the Jordan. As he goes, Shimei comes out to curse him. David recovers the restraint which had characterised his behaviour in his younger days and rejects the offer of Abishai to cut off the head of 'this dead dog'. Shimei is not a dead dog to David. He is potentially a prophet. This is the implication of his response to the bloodthirsty son of Zeruiah: 'Let him alone and let him curse, for the Lord has bidden him. It may be that the Lord will look on my distress, and the Lord will repay me with good for this cursing of me today'. David is not saying that he deserves to be cursed. But he is able to accept that this cursing is within the good will and pleasure of the Lord and that the agent of it may have been sent by God. It illustrates David's capacity not simply to bear rebuke when it is merited, but even when it is not, or might not be. This is the response of a man who does not find it necessary to justify himself at every turn or to receive public vindication.

This humility in David may relate to another prominent aspect of the story: his grief in the face of bereavement. Even in the story of his rise David was no stranger to sorrow. Towards the end of that time, he mourns the loss of Jonathan and Saul (1.17-27) as well as of Abner (3.31-35). In the story of his fall, his anguish at the terminal illness of the infant born to Bathsheba is intense (12.16-23) and his lamentation over Absalom is extreme (18.33-19.4). Grief over lost love is the near cousin perhaps of grief over wrongdoing. A broken heart is not far from a contrite one (compare Psalm 51.17; the Psalm is of course introduced as one David wrote 'when the prophet Nathan came to him, after he had gone in to Bathsheba').

The two sequels to the Shimei incident are also instructive however. The first comes in 19.18-23, when Absalom is dead and David is making the return journey to resume his reign in Jerusalem. Again, Shimei appears, this time with words of repentance. He is the one now who says, 'I have sinned'. The king is magnanimous, again rejecting Abishai's offer to execute David's tormentor. His mercy to another penitent sinner is as impressive as, elsewhere, is his own contrition. How sad then that in the second sequel, in 1 Kings 2.8-9, his dying wish should be for Shimei's blood. Absolutely his last recorded act is to urge Solomon to do what he has twice restrained Abishai from doing. If the experience of bereavement seems somehow to have quickened his capacity for contrition, it seems the prospect of his own death quenched it.

By the end of his life then David's 'fall' is complete. He has apparently fallen even from the one virtue which most characterises his life from the day he becomes king. And yet it would be wrong to regard the second half of David's life as a fall 'from grace'. David himself understood that to fall as a child of God is not to fall from God, but to God – not from grace but to grace. His greatest wish in the midst of his severe trials following the misjudgment he made over the census was 'to fall into the hand of the Lord'.

If this story promotes a view of contrition which our culture finds it hard to understand, it also holds out a vision of grace and forgiveness to which our culture is by and large equally a stranger. The narrative leaves no doubt that it is possible to be a thoroughly flawed individual and yet to remain the chosen one of God, and 'a man after God's own heart', if only there is an open acknowledgment of fault on the part of the sinner and a readiness to respond to the judgment of God.

Index

Lightning Source UK Ltd.
Milton Keynes UK

171567UK00002B/2/P